Swingers' Little Helper

Uncover the curious swinging lifestyle
of consensual non-monogamy

By
Dr. Georgia Fuchs & Will Fuchs

NOTITIA PUBLISHING

First Printing, 2017

ISBN-13: 978-0981883892

ISBN-10: 0981883893

This book is written for curious people & anyone interested in exploring consensual non-monogamy. We often refer to new swingers in this book as couples because couples make up the majority of this welcoming sex-positive community. This doesn't mean singles aren't welcomed. We are an inclusive community that welcomes everyone who is respectful of others regardless if you are single, dating, married or whatever.

We use the term "lifestyle" in the book because swinging often becomes a lifestyle. There are many other lifestyles that don't involve consensual non-monogamy, so please don't think swingers have a monopoly on that term. We are honored to share the lifestyle term with many other sex-positive people. Thankfully there are no sex police (except at sexy Halloween parties) who go around enforcing rules.

Our community is just like the regular world and often you will find there are many shades of gray instead of clear black & white. We hope this book helps you to better understand & navigate through these sexy shades of gray on your way to a life that is just right for you. Enjoy!

Table of Contents

Welcome to the Swinging World!   1

Who Swings?   11

Why Swing?   17

Jealousy vs. Compersion   22

Risks of Swinging   28

Swinging Won't Fix Cheating   35

Rookie Questions & Misconceptions   41

Types of Swingers   48

Avoiding Landmines   65

Understanding Romance vs. Lust   74

Balancing Religion With Swinging   79

Sharing Your Swinging Interest   85

Swinging Rulebook   94

Relationship Toolbox   104

Handling Feelings   111

Managing Time   120

Looking Your Best   125

Online Swinging Sites   142

Wanna Go Swinging? 156

Your Lifestyle Travel Agent 168

Packing Your Swinging Party Bag 174

Safer Sex is Smarter Sex 180

Fakers and Ghost Stories 193

Conversing and Cliques 201

Etiquette AKA Polite Phucking 207

Safeguarding Privacy 214

Coming Out 222

Rural Swinging 228

ED Issues & Performance Pills 235

Ladies & Mother Nature's Calendar 246

Ice Breaker Games 250

Hosting House Parties 257

Younger & Senior Swingers 264

Swingles 270

Breaking Up 280

Swinging Glossary 284

Are You Ready for Swinging? Quiz 297

Visit SwingersHelp.com for links & bonus materials.

Welcome to the swinging world!

It probably sounds crazy but there are healthy & happy people in loving, committed relationships who are having sex with other people besides the love of their life. Welcome to the Swinging Lifestyle. We aren't claiming this is a good idea for everyone but we are happy to explain how this has helped us and many other couples grow closer to our special someone and enjoy life to the fullest!

Maybe you think your sex life is too vanilla and are interested in what other flavors are available. Maybe you are fearful of swinging and want to understand it better. We're still happy you are here and can't wait to share the concept of the swinging lifestyle with you!

No matter why you're approaching this, the first thing to do is to go over some basics of what is swinging and how it all works.

Ask yourself, is sex fun & awesome? Have you ever found other people attractive? Are you able to respectfully follow rules and limits? If you kept answering yes, then it's your lucky day & you have the basic requirements it takes to be a swinger.

Swinging is consensual non-monogamy. It is when you engage in sexual fun with anyone other than your special someone but with the happy consent of your special someone. You and your partner should view sex as being healthy, fun, pleasurable, and natural. You should see sex between informed and consenting adults as a wonderful thing. Not everyone shares this point of view. We aren't saying they are wrong but we respectfully have a different opinion and prefer to see the world with a more sex-positive perspective.

Another important thing to mention is that swinging is not just about sexual pleasure. While Hollywood often portrays the lifestyle as purely sex-based, the reality of swinging is a bit more complex. Swinging is more about communication, community, and consent. Communication is extremely important, both with your partner and with the other swingers you encounter. This communication helps the swinging community be a safe space, where personal needs and preferences are respected. In your everyday life you probably encounter judgment, cruelty, disrespect, and pressure. That negativity is unwelcome in the swinging community. All happy people are invited to the lifestyle! The swinging community is very low-pressure, where you can involve yourself as much or as little as you want. Life is short! Swingers want to enjoy life as much as possible & that starts by being nice and respecting each other.

Swinging might sound nice for other people but maybe you still have reservations when it comes to your own relationship? Society has strongly engrained the concept of strict monogamy and it can be hard to consider an alternative. You have probably been told "people that enjoy sex are sluts and they should be ashamed" or a similar sentiment. Does that sound familiar? Take a deep breath and relax. More and more people understand that sex is fun and we shouldn't be ashamed that we enjoy it and definitely shouldn't be ashamed if we have sexy talents.

2

Polyamory, open relationships, and swinging are slowly gaining respect and more attention. We'll explain how it is possible to safeguard and even enhance your loving relationship while adding some sexy spice to your life. In the swinging lifestyle, happiness can be achieved in many ways, including sometimes breaking out of manufactured boundaries imposed by society.

Society likes to lump sex and romance together but they are most definitely two unique things. Yes, sometimes we can use sex to show our romantic love to our special someone but they are not the same thing. Won't you still romantically love your special someone when you are a 100 years old and past your sexy time? Since romance and sex are two distinct concepts, let's imagine going to a concert with friends. If your friends asked you to join them dancing at the concert, would you be upset? Doubtful, you would probably say yes, because dancing is fun. The more people dancing together is just more fun for everyone. At the end of the night, everyone is going to head home with the love of their life because it was just dancing and you were only having fun. We are going to make a jump here, so take a deep breath and exhale. Now what if it wasn't a dance but a sexy fun time? What if you temporarily had physical fun with your friends before going home with your loved one? That jump was probably too big for you right now and that is ok since we haven't even finished reading the first chapter.

Swingers understand that sexy fun is just that … physical fun. It is not romantic and definitely not a replacement for the sexiest person they know … that special someone who they love above all others.

For those having trouble understanding swinging, it might help to imagine it in terms of food. Your partner is an amazing cook. The food he or she makes is your absolute favorite. You'd be happy to eat their food every night for the rest of your life. No one can make their recipes quite the same way. But, sometimes, you like to go out to eat, or eat at a friend's house. It's not because you're tired of your partner's cooking, or don't like it anymore, but because you're curious about what the new café in town is serving. It's fun to break out of your routine and try something new. Your love for your partner's home cooked meals doesn't diminish even if you discover you like the appetizers at a restaurant. You might even discover a new way to spice up a favorite home-cooked dish that makes it even better. Some recipes are perfect on their own, but there's always the possibility to improve others. Swinging allows you to sample some new sexual flavors, and enhance your sexual relationship with your own partner, without diminishing your love, desire, or affection for your special partner.

Another way to look at swinging is by comparing it to a library. A very sexy lending library. You have your favorite book. You love this book! This book gets you, it knows you, it connects with you like no other book has or ever will. This book seems like it was written just for you, and you're amazed every time you read it. You could spend the rest of your life stuck on a deserted island with this book. But sometimes, you still look at other books. You're interested in their attractive covers. You're curious about what's inside. This curiosity is perfectly natural. Opening a new book is fun and exciting. You can really enjoy a new book. It doesn't mean the new book is better than your favorite book. It's just different, and those differences make it fun to read new books. You might learn something from the new book that makes your favorite book even more special, or helps you understand your favorite book better.

For swingers, the lifestyle provides a huge lending library of sexy books you can briefly check out. Your favorite book can be read by others, too – sharing your favorite book with another person doesn't make it any less special. In fact, having someone else read your favorite book for the first time might remind you why it's your favorite book, and reinforce your appreciation for it. You can return home from this sexy lending library with a new, deeper enjoyment of your favorite book, and maybe some new plot twists you can introduce to the narrative.

In these situations, you can acknowledge that as much as you love your partner and find them attractive and sexy, it's natural to be curious about other people. Sex with people outside your relationship can help you enhance the sexy fun time in your romantic relationship. You may both learn new things to bring home and try out on each other, and find renewed passion for things that have grown a little stale.

Before we go too far, let's restate that swinging is not for everyone.

While the benefits of swinging are great, there are risks involved. Every relationship has its weak points, and the swinging lifestyle can test those weak points. Making friends in the swinging lifestyle is fun but the primary goal is to enhance the relationship with your forever partner. The best way to avoid damaging your relationship is to be honest and open about your boundaries, your expectations, and your fears. Success comes from trust and communication, not taking shortcuts. The last thing you want is for your relationship to suffer instead of flourish.

This means that if you're already experiencing issues in your relationship, you should hit the brakes right now. Swinging will not fix serious problems in your relationship, and can make them worse. If there are trust issues, doubts, or inequalities in your relationship, swinging can expose them in a very painful way. Please make sure you and your partner are on steady ground before engaging in the lifestyle.

This is especially relevant if you're currently in a situation where one partner wants sex and the other is not interested – known colloquially as a "dead bedroom". Swinging will not likely solve this issue. It has about the same chance of turning a heterosexual into a homosexual as turning a low-libido partner into a high-libido partner. If you're in a dead bedroom situation, you should first seek to work on the problem privately with a trained counselor. Not only will forcing a swinging lifestyle be upsetting and uncomfortable for your low-libido partner, it will also turn off potential swinger friends who sense the reluctance or issues within your relationship. If you're in a dead bedroom situation, there are many resources online to help you begin working on the problem within your own home.

If your relationship has a serious issue, it is time to put down this book and seek a professional relationship therapist. You might even be able to solve your issue faster with the sexy appeal of swinging waiting as a reward. Only after you address whatever situation is causing your relationship trouble, should you revisit the idea of becoming swingers.

Let's also mention swinging can change things ...for better or worse

Swinging is a major step in any relationship, so let's not rush it. You can't unsee the things that your partner does at a swinging event, and they can't unsee what you do. It is wise to proceed very slowly and talk privately before swinging so you both agree to some ground rules. You both should be honest about your comfort level. Don't say you're comfortable if you aren't – unless, of course, you love drama and want to increase the odds of breaking up.

Your partner is super sexy and they are going to be doing super sexy things with other people. Are you the type of person that is proud to have such a sexy partner show-off their sexy talents, or do you tend to be jealous & insecure? Talk, think, talk some more, think some more. Make sure that you are both comfortable with what might happen.

Honestly, many of the changes from swinging are usually positive. Communication with your partner will likely grow more open and honest. Avoiding drama in the lifestyle depends on frequent communication, which normal day-to-day life doesn't necessarily require. This new & exciting secret will be a great fresh topic to keep talking about with each other.

You'll likely find that swinging empowers you to trust your partner even more. Rarely is anyone completely, absolutely, 100% jealousy-free, even in the lifestyle. You will probably encounter a moment where jealousy and insecurity rear their ugly heads. This is where communication comes in: making those feelings known and talking them out with your partner can help you deal and defuse those feelings and result in more trust in your partner as you work together to find your comfort zone. Knowing you are working together as a solid team to jointly develop rules & boundaries is a great way to reinforce your trust with each other.

Another positive change? You are likely going to become even more attractive to your partner. You'll probably want to take better care of your body so you can attract more swinging play dates and last longer during those sexy play dates. You'll probably upgrade your wardrobe to better represent in the swinging lifestyle. Swingers love looking good for their partners. We might not be airbrushed supermodels but we want to do our best to look as good as possible.

Even if you never end up swinging, simply taking the steps to improve your appearance to attract other couples can help reignite the sexy spark in your relationship. An awesome way to enhance a relationship is when partners help and support each other to remember how super sexy they can really be. The work and family stress in the vanilla world (aka the non-swinging community) can make it hard for a couple to keep their sex appeal flying high. Swinging is a good catalyst for couples to remind themselves how important it is to maintain a healthy sex appeal for their partner and their own ego.

Another change many people don't anticipate involves their vanilla friends. You might not be comfortable sharing your new swinging stories with them and want to keep your vanilla world separate from your swinging world. So it might be hard to juggle your existing vanilla friends with your new swinging friends. Having too many friends is a great problem to face.

If you both feel that your relationship is healthy and are open to trying something new then swinging can be a wonderful way to enjoy life. You can relive the giddiness that you first felt when you started dating. You can discover new & exciting things. Swinging is generally a team event, so together you can research it, experiment, and maybe even play with another couple. As you work together, the closer you'll be as a couple. Even if you never get to the level of engaging sexually in the lifestyle, you can still gain a new circle of friends with positive attitudes and warm, open hearts. There's plenty of room for vanilla fun before you take the leap into sexually playing!

Remember that swinging is about adding not subtracting. It is about finding new friends & sexy connections for some hot adult fun. At the end of every swinger event, we all want to go home with the best person – our own special someone. This is a big reason why veteran swingers tend not to worry about losing their own partner. Swingers have spent a very long time growing a great & vibrant connection with their special someone. We love our own partners and they love us. Spending a few hours showing off our sexy side just can't compete with true love. Temporarily having hot adult fun can definitely take the passion in a true love relationship to another level!

Take your time and relax.

Swinging has been going on before you were born and will go on long after you. Based on our experience and research, husbands and boyfriends are often too eager at first. Dear Men, please don't pressure your ladies. Many ladies who are enjoying the lifestyle took a very long time to slowly become comfortable or at least less nervous enough to try swinging and that is ok. Trust us, it is worth waiting for your special lady. Now ladies, we also need to chat with you. Ladies usually take longer to become comfortable with the idea of swinging but once they are comfortable ladies can often go full speed without a gradual ramping up. Many men (especially the ones talking in extremely confident tones) will need some adjusting to the sexy lifestyle that is unlike anything you have enjoyed before. So to be safe, please ease into swinging once you feel comfortable and regularly check with your special man because even men have feelings.

Our Swinging Journal: Sprinkles are for winners...

Our lifestyle friends found an outdoor music festival & invited us along. See, not all lifestyle events are late at night or sex filled orgies. We had a great time with our friends that afternoon. So why are we sharing this mundane story? We think this outing is a great explanation of how we perceive winning in the lifestyle.

To us winning is about making good connections with good people. Imagine getting together with friends that honestly enjoy & value you. Being able to freely communicate your honest opinions and do what you enjoy without being judged. We felt like

---

dancing, so we danced even though Mr. is a bad dancer. There were no jokes just supportive cheers from our friends. Doesn't that sound nice? We all work hard, so it is nice to surround ourselves with fun, interesting people who know how to enjoy life.

After the festival, we headed back to their place for dinner & dessert. The taxi driver was worried we wouldn't be willing to sit so closely with each other. Little did he know! We had a blast driving back as the ladies kept teasing the guys with playful touches and whispering naughty things in the men's ears. As things were beginning to arise, we arrived back at their place.

As we are relaxing over dessert and enjoying more caresses, clothes start to drop away. We are just lounging around, when the lady takes a swipe of the decadent cake frosting covered in sprinkles and then sensually places it on certain male anatomy as she whispers "sprinkles are for winners" and we most definitely agree.

We are lucky to be such big winners. Having supportive friends is a win. Enjoying vanilla times is a win. Having thoughtful friends that provide the best dessert course is a win. Oh yeah, a four hour sex orgy is also nice. Curious vanilla people will only focus on the sex but for us, swinging is less about great sex, and more about winning at enjoying life to the fullest. Enjoy your sprinkles!

PS Yes it really was a four hour sexcapade. That included several water & snack breaks because you need to keep your energy up. We all took some rest breaks to just admire the sexy scene. XOXXOOXO

Who Swings?

Swingers are normal, everyday people like you. They live in your town. You walk past them every day. The only thing that makes a swinger a swinger is a desire to have consensual, sexy fun with other sexy people!

Swingers are part of the "lifestyle". The lifestyle is a generic term that includes many groups of different sexy flavors, including swingers, voyeurs, and fetish fans. Even monogamous people who enjoy spending time in a sexy, open-minded setting can be part of the lifestyle. It's safe to assume that all swingers are part of the lifestyle, but not all people in the lifestyle may want a non-monogamous relationship.

A study in 2014 found about 5% of adults in relationships were in a consensual, non-monogamous relationship. [1] Of course, any scientific data about swingers or sex should be taken with a grain of salt or a whole bag of salt. Research about sex and swinging can have accuracy issues due to social stigma & fear. That being said, it's nice to know that at least 5% of couples in the study were brave enough to admit to being part of the swinging lifestyle!

---

[1] Rubin, J. D., (2014). On the margins: Considering diversity among consensually non-monogamous relationships. Journal für Psychologie, 22(1).

You might want to know how to "spot a swinger". What does a swinger look like? Imagine your local supermarket on an average day. That is what you will find in the lifestyle. Some people will be young, from the 20's to their 30's but not a large percentage. Younger people tend to still be single and are busy dating other single young people. More commonly, you will find couples in their late 30's or older. These people are usually done raising their children, or have teenagers that don't need a babysitter while mom & dad go out and have sexy fun.

Looking beyond age groups, you'll find skinny swingers and overweight swingers and plenty of swingers in between. You'll find swingers of all races and ethnicities, coming from all over the world. Swingers are nurses, cops, lawyers, plumbers, teachers, office workers, and everything else. Many have college degrees and earn a comfortable enough income that they have some extra money to enjoy a sexy time.

The thing most people in the lifestyle have in common is their relationship status. Only a small portion of swingers are single. The majority are couples. Those couples might have been dating for a few months or married for years, but most swingers are in committed relationships.

This doesn't mean that there aren't single people in the lifestyle. There are a good amount of single people but they are just outnumbered by the couples in the lifestyle.

Single women in the lifestyle are known as "unicorns", because they can be hard to find like the mythical equine and tend to be in high demand from many couples. Single men in the lifestyle are known as … actually they don't have a special nickname because they are a bit underappreciated. The single men in the lifestyle tend to be very respectful and fun guys. Later in the Swingles chapter we'll cover more tips for singles and couples interested in swinging with them. For now let's get back to who swings.

Yes, there are already swingers in your town.

You probably never realized it but there are swingers in your town. There's no special tattoo or secret pin that distinguishes a swinger from vanilla people so it is easy to live a discreet life and still enjoy a sexy swinging life. All you need to join the lifestyle is a sex-positive attitude, respect for others, and the desire to have a good time!

Remember, that being a swinger is about having a fun. Weird as it sounds, there is no expectation of sex in the swinging lifestyle. We aren't nymphomaniacs. Swingers have sex only when they want to have sex and only with people they want to have sex with. Yes, there is a lot of sex going on, but only when everyone involved has agreed to it wholeheartedly. If a swinger doesn't feel like having sex, they don't. It is just that simple. You can attend a party and have fun without getting physical at all. It is very common to attend a swinger event and keep your clothes on the entire time you are having a fun time.

Swingers do need to respect other swingers and honor their personal boundaries. If you don't like how someone looks or acts, you can always politely decline to play and swingers will respect that. Swingers will keep their hands to themselves. They ask before doing anything and everyone knows that NO means NO. It is a no-pressure event amongst respectful people.

It's important that you don't enter the lifestyle thinking that it's going to be a sexy free-for-all. If you think it was hard to hook-up with someone when you were single, you'll probably find that it's harder when you're swinging as a couple. Instead of making a connection with a single person, you are now building a four-way connection between you, your partner and the other couple.

Of course, there are the occasional bad apples. Nothing in life is perfect, including the lifestyle. Overall, respect and honoring personal boundaries is very important to the swinging community and swingers will stand up for each other. Swingers want to maintain a sexy, fun, non-threatening atmosphere, and will try to make sure everyone is comfortable – newbies included!

By now, you might be wondering if you could fit in at a swinger event. As long as you're not rude or disrespectful, the answer is probably yes! The lifestyle accepts adults of all shapes, ages, and experience levels. Just have an open mind, find consent and communication sexy, and you can fit right in with the lifestyle.

If you're worried about not fitting in due to your weight, know that many people entering the lifestyle find themselves motivated to improve their appearance. The promise of sexy times and encouraging compliments from new friends is super inspiration to get into the best shape of your life! You'll find that even more than looking good, getting in shape will help you feel good, and give you the stamina and strength to enjoy long, intense play sessions. As unbelievable as it sounds, play sessions can last for hours and be action-packed, if the chemistry is right.

This is not an exaggeration; many couples find that they must fit their sexy time into a few minutes when they're at home, but the lifestyle lets them set aside extended periods of time to focus on enjoying sex! With no distractions and no time constraints, couples can let go of their stresses and forget about going to the post office before it closes or getting to the grocery store in time to make dinner. There's no pressure to climax quickly so you can get on with your day. Swinging events allow you to relax and enjoy your body and your partner's body, with some new bodies thrown in for fun.

Later in this book, we'll discuss fitness and appearances in greater detail. For now, rest assured that you can be a welcome addition to a swinger event if you're respectful of those around you.

Our Swinging Journal: Vanilla people sure are curious about swingers...

Journalists seem to be fascinated with the juicy topic of finding swingers. They keep writing stories about what signs to use for spotting swingers in your local town. They have said stuff a bunch of different stuff like garden gnomes, pink flamingos, pineapples and certain types of plants in the front yard are the tell-tale signs of a swinger's house. Yeah, because us swingers totally want complete strangers walking up to our front door uninvited at any time of day or night, dropping their pants and saying we are here for sex. How could anyone think that is reality? We just don't understand what journalist or editor approved those stories but we understand the demand of their audience for being deliciously curious about the lifestyle.

We have been approached by curious vanilla people several times while we are out on dates with other swingers. The last time was at a great music concert with some of our swinger friends.

Our group of swinging ladies were sexily dancing together at the concert and even made a few friends with some vanilla ladies who joined their dancing circle. Mr. F came back with beers for the swinging ladies and starting dancing with Dr. G. Then one after another, our swinging lady friends started grinding on Mr. F with Dr. G just smiling on. The vanilla ladies started freaking out, not understanding what was going on.

They eventually asked Dr. G if that was cool and Dr. G responded "of course, why not". They were so confused, they could only stutter out "but... but... the other women...it's wrong" Dr. G just smiled back and said "who says it's wrong if I'm ok with it? ". Well that lit a lightbulb over their heads and a flood of questions on how it works and if they might possibly have a similar arrangement with their men.

If we had stayed longer, we might have inadvertently converted those vanilla ladies right there & then but things were getting too steamy. Our swinging group of friends decided it was best to head back to privacy. Being sexy in public is fun but getting arrested for indecent exposure isn't as much fun.

As we were enjoying some sexy moments with our swinger friends in private, we all had fun interrupting the sexy time and shouting out "but...but... the other women...it's wrong" as the sexy pile of bodies would climax over & over again.

Why Swing?

It's easy to focus on the wild sex of the swinging world. Many people incorrectly assume swingers are crazy nymphomaniacs. We won't lie, the sex is awesome but there's a lot more to the lifestyle than just sex. In fact, many swingers find sex comes second to being part of a welcoming and inclusive community. The lifestyle is much more about enjoying life by sharing new experiences with your loved one and making awesome new friends.

Some people who have been in the lifestyle for years never take the step of having sex with other people. They participate in the lifestyle just for the fun friendships at sexy parties where they can let loose and not be judged. Some are nudists and others just appreciate an environment where people can show a bit of skin without being judged. The flirting and foreplay is enough excitement for them.

It just isn't easy to find good friends when you become an adult.

Most of the people you meet as an adult are friendly acquaintances rather than close friends. You might be friendly with the parents at your school, or friendly towards your coworkers. These people rarely become real friends. In the swinging community, you can make great new friends and share a real connection. Many swingers prefer to do fun vanilla things together and build a four-way connection before having any sexy play time. Swinging has given us a great collection of friends that we can meet for dinner dates, concerts, pool parties and much more. We have gained many trusted friends that we would never have discovered without swinging.

Of course, there are people in the lifestyle that definitely enjoy swapping sex partners (like us). You might be thinking that these people are swingers just for the sex. Think again.

Let's forget about swinging for a little bit and imagine you and your partner have planned a white water rafting trip through the Grand Canyon. It's easy to see how such an exciting shared experience can make your relationship stronger and bring you closer.

It starts with the two of you looking forward to the trip, and the shared anticipation uniting you together. Then, the teamwork involved to successfully navigate through the flowing river would pull you even closer together. Finally, the excitement of the stupendous view of the Grand Canyon as you share this experience would give you memories to keep you close for a long time moving forward. This is actually very much like swinging. You'll prepare for each swinging event together. You'll use teamwork to optimally navigate the sexy lifestyle in the way you both want. Finally, you'll both have an amazing, shared, sexy experience with new friends.

As we said, amazing sex is a huge benefit of being a swinger. You can live out your sexiest fantasies; who doesn't want that? Foreplay for swingers can be sexier than the actual event for vanilla couples! Play partners can teach you new tricks to use at home, so your private sexy time is even hotter. Communication about what you like and don't like comes naturally for swingers, so your partner will grow very in tune with your wants and desires. Better sex can really help you enjoy a stronger bond in your more important relationship.

It's hard to explain how making a physical connection with other people outside our marriage has forged a stronger emotional bond between us, but it's true: our relationship is stronger than ever since we started swinging. We share and open up more than we did in our vanilla only life. We were already pretty good at reading each other's body language, but since we started swinging we can just about read each other's minds (most of the time). We know that swinging is a risky venture for any relationship, so there is motivation to work even harder to boost our trust and communication. It is an amazing feeling to see your loved one become even more sexy, help each other have earth-shattering moments, and then go home to relive those sexy memories in private.

Swinging can also provide a huge ego boost. Compliments from your loved one can grow stale or lack conviction because you've heard it all before. When new people compliment you, and show desire for you, you can't help but feel good about yourself. Hearing about how sexy you look in an outfit or being complimented on a special skill you have can boost your ego for days, and self-confidence is a huge part of a happy, healthy life – in the vanilla world, in your relationship, and in the lifestyle.

So, why do people swing? The simplest answer is because it's fun. There are more complicated answers that tend to bring up the debate about whether monogamy is natural. Only 9% of mammal species are monogamous, and 84% of indigenous societies were polygamous before Western civilization got involved. But you don't have to know those facts or debate monogamy to be a swinger. You just have to love and trust your partner, know that you can communicate with each other, and consensually agree about how to have your fun. Swingers know that consenting adults can make decisions about what is right for your relationship, regardless of societal norms.

Swinging is a wild ride! You can have some truly memorable and exciting moments in the lifestyle. That three-way make out session your vanilla friend had in college might not seem so thrilling once you've had a six-way sexcapade that left you simultaneously exhausted and eager for more!

The reasons for swinging are as varied as the people in the lifestyle. Obviously, there is great sex but there is also friendship, community, understanding and so many other benefits available from this welcoming community. So let's continue reading to see if this might be a good fit for you and your special someone.

Our Swinging Journal: Life is short and some people enjoy it more

You never know who you will meet in the swinging world. Seriously you can really be surprised by the many different types of people and backgrounds you will come across.

Friends of ours invited us to a winery tour with a few other couples. We knew most of the others on the tour including a school teacher, CEO, construction worker, and architect... like we said you can meet many different people in the lifestyle. There was a new couple that we hadn't met. Over the course of the day we had a great time tasting wines, enjoying a picnic lunch in a pretty setting and getting to know each other a bit more. Turns out the new couple runs an awesome charity. It also turns out the "new" couple isn't new at all - they are returning to swinging after a long break they took for medical reasons. Hmmmm? What medical reasons? Turns out the husband had an organ transplant. Wow! We did not expect that answer.

It was a great reminder that life is short and we should seize the day! Make sure we live each and every day to the fullest. We should make sure that family craziness and work stress does not take over our lives. It is important to enjoy the more pleasurable moments of life with the person you love and with the people you love to share some naked fun.

We did end up playing with our new friends, although it did take a longer than normal warm-up session since he was very sensitive about getting naked and revealing his scar. Not gonna lie, it was a massive scar. None of us are supermodels, we all have flaws. Some are just bigger than others. But you can't see flaws if you are busy making out!

Now his doctor did say regular exercise is a good way to stay fit and healthy. So the ladies wanted to ensure he got a good sexy workout... purely for medicinal purposes of course. We aren't sure if the doctor would have been happy with our three hour sexy play session so we did take rest breaks to let the guys recover in between each sexy round as we all lived that day to the fullest.

Jealousy vs. Compersion

Entering the lifestyle can bring up a lot of feelings that should be addressed if you don't want a really bad experience. One of the more common and frightening feelings associated with starting a lifestyle journey is jealousy. Jealousy has an interesting place in society; it's encouraged in some situations, vilified in others. Society often encourages jealousy in relationships. Think about all those rom-com movies where the guy has no idea how much he cares until he sees the object of his desire being swept off her feet by a new suitor. Society practically demands some level of jealousy in committed relationships: heaven forbid that you are "too" secure because if you're not jealous "enough" you could be judged for being an inattentive or unfeeling partner. We personally find this idea pretty crazy. Why on earth should such an unpleasant emotion be the hallmark sign that you sufficiently love your partner? Wouldn't it make more sense to demonstrate love by focusing on positivity and support?

Life is too short to spend feeling jealous; we feel that our time is better spent loving and supporting each other as we travel together on an honest and open path. Jealousy might be natural, but we should strive to overcome it in the same way we would strive to overcome resentment, frustration, and other natural negative emotions.

Still, striving to overcome jealousy doesn't mean that it will magically disappear overnight. You're going to experience it at some point in your relationship - everyone does. That is not a bad thing, and it's important to recognize these feelings instead of trying to ignore or repress them. Jealousy is subjective and can be different for each person and each situation. Some people feel jealous when someone else uses a special nickname for their partner, while other people have no problem with that. Maybe you don't feel jealous of your partner holding someone else's hand or even touching them sexually, but the thought of them kissing someone else drives you crazy. There is no right or wrong when it comes to feelings. What is important is that we identify, understand, communicate and evolve to better address our feelings, jealousy included.

At various times in our lives we might feel insecure or confused, and that can flame the feelings of jealousy. The first step to positively handling unpleasant feelings like jealousy is to acknowledge them. By acknowledging our feelings, we remind ourselves that we are all humans and this is real life, not a scripted sitcom. Not everything is going to be perfect. We may feel lonely, insecure, or jealous, and that is 100% natural. We are doing nothing wrong by having perfectly natural human emotions. There's no point in beating ourselves up for having these feelings. Most swingers and other people in the lifestyle have experienced these unpleasant feelings. Participating in this sexy lifestyle does not mean that you flip a switch and become some shiny little sex machine devoid of any unpleasant human emotions. The good news is that there are ways to handle and address these unpleasant emotions so we can move forward towards a more positive future.

Once you realize you are having unpleasant feelings like jealousy or insecurity, you should take a moment to reflect on why it is happening. We want to understand the underlying contributors to our unpleasant feelings. That is easier said than done, since these unpleasant feelings can be quite powerful and be confused with other strong feelings. You may need to take several days to relax so you can more clearly reflect on what has triggered your emotions. Is there something specific that has caused you to feel jealous? Is it a new feeling, or have you been feeling jealous for a while? Can you think of anything you or your partner can do to help soothe the jealous feelings and boost your confidence?

Taking a step back from the situation is a great tool for gaining perspective. Once you have had a chance to reflect on what triggered your feelings of jealousy, you can use this valuable information to learn more about yourself and what you value in your relationship. Did you get jealous seeing how excitedly your partner got ready for a date with someone else? Perhaps you miss experiencing that level of excitement yourself and need to plan a special adventurous night out (with your partner or someone else) to do something brand new or something you love but haven't been able to do in a long time. Did hearing your partner talk about how great another person's eyes looked the other night feel like a blow right to the gut? Perhaps you haven't felt very noticed lately and need your partner to really see you (and your eyes!) too.

One helpful step to dealing with jealousy and maximizing your happiness is to cut out the negative and judgmental people in your life. Negative people who teach us that we need to be jealous to prove our love should be ignored and avoided. If they aren't complaining about one thing, they will be complaining about another thing. We want to surround ourselves with positive people who encourage us to make the best decisions for ourselves and our partners based on love and support instead of fear or jealousy.

What about Compersion?

Jealousy is one of the first emotions that comes to mind when people think about swinging. But there's another emotion that very few people will think of when they consider swinging: it's called compersion, and it's the opposite of jealousy. It's a very positive feeling you experience when your loved one is enjoying something. It's a form of empathy, where your partner's good time becomes your good time, even if you're not directly involved. Basically, compersion boils down to "whatever gives my partner pleasure gives me great pleasure."

Imagine you are eating a great new snack that you just discovered. Let's share this snack with your loved one, because even though this snack is amazing, you really love your partner and want to share it with them. If you enjoy that snack more after sharing it with your loved one, you are feeling compersion. You are not jealous that your loved one is also enjoying your new favorite snack. You don't resent having less of the snack for yourself. There is excitement and happiness that your partner is having a great experience. Vicariously, you are enjoying your partner's happy taste buds. You are experiencing compersion.

To go a step further, imagine that you're at your local spa for a couple's massage. You're both getting massaged in the same room, sharing a wonderfully romantic moment together. Do you feel a little happier than you would during a normal, solo massage because your partner is also enjoying a great massage? This is another example of compersion.

Many people join the swinging lifestyle without even knowing about the joys of compersion but soon come to experience it deeply. Swinging doesn't cause them to have jealous fears over losing their partner. Instead, they experience an exciting, warm and positive feeling by seeing and/or hearing about their partner's additional sexual pleasure. Bringing that excitement back to their private bedroom, to fuel their intimate enjoyment of one another, only helps that feeling grow!

Compersion is a feeling, and like all feelings it can't really be manufactured. You can't force yourself to feel compersion, just like you can't force yourself to feel happy when something good happens to your worst enemy. If you are someone who generally experiences a lot of jealousy, it is less likely you will experience compersion without a great deal of emotional work. Not reaching compersion doesn't mean you're a bad person or that swinging is not for you, but compersion can help you and your partner share even more happy, sexy, fun experiences in the lifestyle.

Our Swinging Journal: Not Playing Can Still Be A Successful Playdate...

We noticed there was an upcoming hotel takeover arranged near us. Over 200 couples were already signed up and these people were looking pretty attractive so we started to get very excited. We bought our party tickets and reserved a room at the hotel which thankfully still had space. Our sexy hotel weekend is approaching so we arrange our schedules to keep the weekend free for our fun. We pack our luggage so we can have a few options depending on how we feel and the party vibe. Then we pack our travelling bar because life is more fun being able to invite people back to your room for drinks. Then we pack our play bag because hey all of this planning & work is because we want some sexy play time!

We arrive at the hotel and walk-in expecting to see a bunch of sexy swingers but instead find a bridal party including some little flower girls in the lobby. Yikes! Time to pretend we aren't deviant sex fiends ready to party hard. The event organizers are profusely apologizing and swear the bridal party will be leaving very soon because their limo was late. Ok no worries, we can pretend we are normal people checking into the hotel till they leave.

So we get into our reserved hotel room and it is on the main party floor but discover the lock isn't working properly. The front desk is nice enough to offer us another room which is also on the main party floor. Hey, that's weird that they still have space left on the main party floor with over 200 couples attending this hotel takeover. Whatever we are lucky, so let's go grab some dinner.

Just a handful of couples are downstairs having dinner. Guess most of the attendees went to other restaurants. Time to head back upstairs and get ready for the party. As we are crossing the lobby, the convoy pulls up. It is a convoy of buses loaded with elderly tourists. Woah! This is supposed to be a full hotel takeover where we can party hard and feel comfortable in our sexy outfits without any vanilla people around. Elderly tourists are about as vanilla as you can get. Ok, we are party veterans and can deal with this unwelcome curveball.

Let's head to the swinger party and ... what did you say? I can't hear you. Wow the music is crazy loud. It's fun to dance hard but seriously I can't hear a word of what you are saying and there is no way we can talk with other couples not that there are many couples that are exciting us. Ok let's go in the hallway and talk. Uh, yeah so this isn't what we wanted. Do you want to go home? You read my mind!

So we pack up and leave our hotel takeover to spend a sexy night together in our nice big comfy bed. You might think this was a frustrating failure. It definitely was not what we were promised or expecting. Getting to enjoy a sexy night together is still a win even when if it might not have been the type of win we may have been expecting.

PS We also learned not to trust first time hotel party organizers. Stick with party organizers with a long & proven track record.

Risks of Swinging

As exciting and awesome the rewards of swinging can be, the lifestyle does come with some real worries & risk. You should talk with your partner to see if you are both comfortable with the risks and share your worries with each other. You want to work together when deciding if the risks are worth the potential rewards of swinging.

To help explain the risks you may encounter in swinging, let's think of your relationship as a car. Right now, you are driving around in your car on the local roads doing the local speed limit. Your car might have a few dings in it from small things, like a shopping cart bumping into it. Those are your standard vanilla fights. Most relationships can handle driving on the local roads with ease. You are moving at a manageable speed with few road hazards and the occasional pothole that can be handled easily at these low speeds.

The swinging lifestyle is like taking your car onto the highway and hitting the gas pedal. A small pothole can become a big problem when you are doing 70mph sandwiched and dealing with an 18-wheel tractor trailer weaving into your lane. It is very helpful to spot and avoid these potholes. What potholes might you encounter in the lifestyle?

Health Risks

Having the condom break with your loved one can be a nerve-wracking moment. Now imagine having the condom break when you are having sex with someone you just met that night.

Even if you always use condoms, you can still catch some STI's. Herpes, HPV, crabs, and syphilis can all be exchanged from simply rubbing thighs together. Many swingers don't use condoms for oral sex, so you should talk with your partner about your risk comfort level.

You might be surprised to find out that swingers don't have higher STI rates than the general population. It makes sense when you stop and think about it. Swinging is not like those random, late-night, drunken hookups that are common among single people. Let's be honest, drunk people make bad decisions. Swingers know that alcohol is a nice social lubricant, but it is also a boner-killer – so most swingers avoid drinking too much. Going easy on the booze also helps protect couples from doing something stupid that could hurt their relationship.

Swingers also operate as a couple, so you have two sets of minds and eyes to help minimize bad decisions. The swinging community is a strong network of couples that talk with each other. So when a health scare pops up it, it can be identified and addressed quickly. Even though swingers tend to have more sex and with more partners, we are doing it with eyes open and help from others to minimize bad situations. This does not mean swinging is 100% safe because nothing in life is ever 100%

safe. Being informed and avoiding drunk mistakes helps to protect you and your partner.

Emotional Risks

If your relationship isn't very strong right now, the stress from swinging can ruin it. You probably wouldn't drive a car with a busted windshield and missing the car doors on a high-speed highway, so why would you take a damaged relationship into the stresses of swinging?

If you have any trust or communication issues, they can become worse when your partner is sexting or flirting with new play partners. Your partner may not even do anything wrong, but if you are uncomfortable you can become defensive or accusatory, turning a slight miscommunication into a horrible fight. To minimize the emotional risks, you want to have great communication skills.

The lifestyle has helped us to greatly improve our communication skills. Before we entered the lifestyle, we used the swinging fantasy as a conversation starter between us. We watched and read many things about the lifestyle and then communicated with each other about what scared us, what entertained us, and, most enjoyably, what turned us on. Researching the lifestyle and roleplaying was driving us closer together. We found ourselves freakishly thinking the same exact thoughts throughout the day. We were fortunate to be close with each other at the start of our journey and to move even closer as we progressed.

Some people are not so fortunate. They are fearful that their partner is going to cheat or leave them for someone more attractive, so they reluctantly agree to enter the lifestyle to keep their relationship together. This is a bad idea. Most people don't leave relationships because of sex.

They leave relationships due to lack of communication and shared principles. Not being truthful with your partner about your desires or fears is a good way to sabotage your swinging experience - and your long-term relationship.

What about falling in love? Don't worry. Swingers love good sex and they love their spouses, but in general we tend to only like our play partners. Admittedly, some play partners we really, really like because sex is fun and who doesn't really like fun friends? Swingers tend to operate as couples, so they aren't looking to fall in love.

You have been spending a long time developing a great relationship with your true love. You both know each other better than anyone else. Spending a few hours with a fun swinger friend just can't compete with that type of deep romantic connection. Let's plat devil's advocate and say still somehow find yourself growing romantic feelings for a play partner (which is very unlikely), it is probably safest to find a new play partner. Once you accidentally – or purposely – voice those feelings, your play partner and their spouse will likely choose to avoid you and that potential drama because they love each other. Swinging is about having fun sex with fun friends. Swingers aren't looking to replace their special partner because swingers know they already have found the best person to be their special someone.

Being Exposed as Swingers

This is a big fear of many potential swingers. We will talk later about ways to protect yourself from having your regular vanilla world and swinging lifestyle collide. People have been outed as swingers in the past, and unfortunately more will be outed in the future. Your private life should be your own, in which to do whatever you want, but there are negative people in the world who love to gossip and judge others.

One of our friends has a very colorful past - to put it mildly. He has done crazy things, like snorting coke off a hooker's body (we presume not a dead hooker's body, but he never said and we never asked). He has a regular appointment for a dominatrix to peg his bum, and gave us these infamous words of wisdom: "never ask a dominatrix to 'really surprise you this time'". Oh, and did we mention he is married and cheating on his wife? You would think that if anyone could be trusted and able to deal with our swinging lifestyle it would be this guy. Nope. He knows all about it, and this swinging thing blows his mind. He is super worried for us and keeps telling us how terrible it is (that is when he isn't doing drugs, visiting his dominatrix, or cheating on his wife).

You should be careful entering the swinging lifestyle. You may think friends will be accepting but you just can't predict who will or won't understand.

If you are lucky enough to have supportive friends, you still need to worry about family, co-workers, employers, neighbors, your kids' friends and their parents, and so many more. We have heard too many stories about family members shunning swinging relatives. You may think it is illegal or impossible to be fired as a swinger. Unfortunately there are creative ways an employer or co-worker can make your life hellish until you quit or get fired over some manufactured reason.

Neighbors that were friendly may start to worry that you are secretly trying to seduce and sleep with them. We know swingers are picky about who they sleep with, but they don't. Some people may start seeing you as a sex-obsessed freak. It just takes one neighbor to say something in front of their kids, who will then spread the gossip around school. Suddenly, your kids are being harassed and bullied over your private sex life.

It's not fair, but it's a real risk, and you should talk it over before charging forward and enjoying the sexy swinging lifestyle. To help minimize this risk, we will talk about privacy safeguards later in this book.

Eyes Wide Open...

Swinging is dangerous like alcohol. Having a few drinks is unlikely to ruin your relationship ... unless your relationship already has problems. Maybe there are money troubles, or maybe you are having a disagreement, or maybe your schedule is too filled. If you don't have a strong & stable relationship then getting drunk at your local bar is more likely to cause big problems instead of solving anything. Swinging is very similar to alcohol. If you don't already have a strong relationship filled with trust then swinging will just make things worse. When you work on your relationship and are ready to party & celebrate then the alcohol & swinging will be waiting but until then you should probably hold off.

Our Swinging Journal: More drama than a Shakespeare play

The allure of swinging can be strong for some people but trust us it is not all smiles and sunshine. We've learned to be especially leery of people that constantly say they are drama free. They tend to be the most drama filled people. One couple takes the grand prize of drama for us.

We had some sexy fun at the start but things soon became bumpy with

---

this couple. The other lady insisted that three of us follow special rules. Three of us? That's right - she felt that her ridiculous rules didn't apply to her. Yeah that wasn't going to happen. They kept having mini meltdowns before, during, and especially after play sessions. It all came to a head with an epic meltdown at a party when she felt like she wasn't getting enough attention. Nevermind that the four of us weren't even on a date that night! Call us picky people but meltdowns are not sexy to us, and we're doing this lifestyle thing for fun not for drama. So we decided it would be best to not play with them anymore. We tried our best to nicely explain we'd rather be happy friends with them than risk being drama inducing play partners. These decisions and communications are not fun for anyone. Emily Post never covered this in her etiquette book.

They kept insisting on emergency group conference calls to "get closure". After the third conference call (honestly we have no idea why we even agreed to a single one of these) we finally said there wasn't anything more to discuss. They finally relented and stopped hounding us. To avoid the big pile of drama, we started avoiding parties near them just so we wouldn't accidentally bump into them. We hoped everything (ahem, they) would calm down.

We thought it had worked and it was in our rearview mirror until six months later they both started texting and emailing us. They said they were now cool with just being good friends and agreed with everything we had said six months ago. After a few days they restarted pressuring us to play with them again.

On one hand, let's admit it is a huge compliment that a couple is so smitten with our sexual prowess that they hounded us to play again. On the other hand, WTF can't they respect our wishes to avoid drama and not play with them?!?!?? Unfortunately some couples don't have the best social skills and will bring drama into your life. Thankfully that has been a minority experience for us. Sorry this isn't sexy but the swinging lifestyle isn't always just lace and lingerie. XOXOXO

Swinging Won't Fix Cheating

Thankfully most you of you have not had to deal with cheating. Regardless if you have been touched by infidelity or just want to safeguard your relationship, we are going to talk about why the swinging lifestyle is usually a bad idea for relationships touched by infidelity and better ways to address troubled relationships.

An important and highly valued cornerstone of swinging is trust. Being able to trust and be honest with each other is a big difference between swinging and cheating. Yes, swingers and cheaters both have sex with people other than their partners, but they are not the same thing.

Swingers are open and honest with their partners and have come to a mutually agreed-upon decision to enjoy a lending library of sexy people. There is no deception or deceit with swinging, just a mature conversation in which they agree how to explore more sexual experiences while still protecting their emotional fidelity and connection.

Cheaters are liars who do not have permission from their partners. These liars are breaking the trust and faith in their relationships. Without strong trust in your relationship, you are unlikely to have a good time in the lifestyle or improve your relationship. Swinging is usually not the best option to fix wounded relationships. It's a way for healthy relationships to grow and evolve along with the people within the relationship.

If you insist on swinging with a very wounded relationship, you are likely going to have a bad time. Swingers don't like drama and are pretty good on reading body language. You may not realize how much your problems and issues can be read in your posture and facial expressions.

Some people in cheating relationships think they are the exception to the rule and that swinging can save the relationship. Here are some excuses that cheaters use to justify their actions, and better ways to address it.

Liars

Cheaters are liars. Liars don't stop lying just because they are having sex. In fact, swinging can just give them more opportunities to lie. They can lie about using condoms, playing outside agreed sexual boundaries, or secretly communicating with others. If a partner wasn't trustworthy when they were outside the candy store, why would they become trustworthy inside the candy store? Be smart and honest. Do not expect that swinging will magically make them trustworthy. Swinging can give them more opportunities and temptations to be an even bigger liar. Trust issues can extend to financial matters, child-rearing, and day-to-day life. It is better to work with a trained professional to repair broken trust instead of entering the lifestyle.

Bad Sex

If a partner is not sexually satisfied, swinging is often not the answer. It is often wiser to first work together to improve intimacy at home. Bad sex is caused by both people in a relationship. One person is not doing the things that their partner desires. The other person is also guilty for not doing a good enough job communicating their desire and needs to help their partner connect with them. More open and frank conversations about your unique sexual desires can help a couple grow closer. It is possible you might not currently be sexually compatible.

You would be better off seeking out a sex therapist to help you learn to better communicate and connect. If you enter the lifestyle, you likely won't have much fun. Swingers are likely to avoid couples who are not communicating and playing well with each other. Consider a sex therapist or a sexual workshop to help you unleash the great intimacy potential of your own relationship. It is often smarter to learn to walk before we try to run.

Insecurity

Some people cheat because they are chasing insecurity issues. They worry they aren't desirable enough or good enough, or don't meet whatever made-up requirement they judge themselves against. Maybe they feel like they aren't getting enough attention in the relationship and seek it from others. Cheating and seeking validation from other partners made them feel secure and confident for a short period of time, but they likely returned to feeling insecure. The lifestyle is not going to make them feel secure in the long-term, either. It will just present more opportunities for that insecurity to flourish and cause even bigger problems in a relationship. It is better to resolve that insecurity before adding the pressures of sex with other people. Protect your relationship and make it bulletproof before jumping into the lifestyle.

Immature

Some cheaters are just immature. They have never fully accepted the responsibilities of being an adult. They do not see how their actions impact other people. This is an unwelcome mindset in the lifestyle. Immature people quickly end up getting blacklisted and shunned by other swingers that don't want to deal with drama.

Addiction

Cheating can also be a problem that directly or indirectly involves addiction. This isn't limited to sex addiction; drug or alcohol addiction is just as likely to lead partners astray. People that have addiction problems have problems with proper decision making and impulse control. They act compulsively, which eventually lands them in bad situations. If your partner has an addiction problem you should get them help instead of complicating matters even more. Their health may be in jeopardy, and their health should take priority over anything else.

Breaking Up

As sad as it is to say, cheaters might not be happy in their relationship and want out. Not all cheaters are unhappy with their partners, but some cheaters are. Sometimes, people cheat because they don't know how to end a long-term relationship. If you believe that you're in this kind of situation, you should speak with a relationship counselor – or break up. Once your relationship gets to the point where one or both of you are considering ending it, you are well past the point where swinging can help you. Introducing your unhappy partner to new sex partners will only alienate you, as happily connected swingers will pick up on the troubles and blacklist you. If you're getting into swinging as a desperate attempt to save a relationship, you may not be in the right mindset to enjoy the lifestyle and find it only makes you feel worse.

Boredom

Boredom can happen naturally in any relationship. Swinging can be a great distraction. But eventually your shiny new toy, AKA your swinging lifes, will start to lose some of its luster and your partner will go right back to cheating. It's possible that they are drawn to cheating because it's illicit and dangerous, so they'll always return to it to get their kicks. The lifestyle is a wonderful way to add spice to your life, but it is usually not a good idea for it to become the biggest part of your life. If you can't have fun in the bedroom without other people involved, you're not getting the most out of the lifestyle. You should talk together to figure out how to stay connected and interested in the same things.

Our Swinging Journal: Why we don't believe in cheating...

We wish we could share some uplifting & inspirational reason why we don't believe in cheating. Instead we are gonna be honest and share one of our stories that has helped keep cheating at bay for us.

Dr. G has had some sleepless nights. One really bad time she just couldn't fall asleep for almost two nights. Needless to say, she was not feeling her best and acting a bit unlike her normal self. So on the second night, she turns on the TV and starts watching a TV series about "black widow" wives. Each episode was about a different wife that snapped and killed her cheating husband. Oh what luck for her, it was an all night marathon of "black widow" wives.

Mr. F. wakes up and asks what she is watching. She says not to worry and that he should go back to sleep. Mr. F. wakes up later and same exchange happens. A bit more time passes and

Mr. F. wakes up again. Ok now Mr. F. is not feeling comfortable at all with the TV sounds.

Finding out your sleep deprived wife is watching a marathon on how wives kill their husbands is not the most calming thing. Mr. F jokingly says "Is this something I should be worried about you watching". Dr. G just looks at him and says with her sleep deprived emotionless face "oh honey, you don't have anything to worry about, I already knew how to kill you and dispose of your body". Yeah that was not the reassurance Mr. F. wanted to hear.

Then it gets worse. She says "besides you know your family likes me better than you" Ouch the truth hurts the worst.

That is our funny & true story. You might be thinking that the lesson here is being afraid of your partner will prevent cheating. Fear can be a deterrent but honestly the bigger deterrent is teamwork. When Dr. G has sleeping issues, Mr. F has sleeping issues. We try to fix it together because we are there for each other. It is a team effort. Using a team effort point of view, then logically speaking it is kinda silly to cheat because you are just cheating on yourself.

Life is much easier to conquer when you work together as a team.If you can't work together solving the problems that life throws at you, then seek out a professional counselor to help you learn how to be a better team. This will help you both sleep better and avoid your spouse from watching an all night marathon on how to kill cheating spouses.

Rookie Questions & Misconceptions

If you're like most new people, you're probably very nervous and excited to get answers to your questions immediately. Before you read on, we are going to briefly cover some of the more common questions, so you can relax and take it slow as you read the rest of this book.

What if I am not good looking enough?

You are more than good looking enough. End of story. Seriously. The lifestyle is a very inclusive community for all kinds of people, all of whom have their own special look. We all have personal preferences when it comes to what we find attractive. Think of your body as a gem: some people prefer rubies or sapphires or diamonds or opals. But you know what? All of those stones are freaking gorgeous! You will be gorgeous, too, as long as you spend a little bit of time to present yourself well. Most swingers agree that confidence is incredibly sexy, and a bright smile is the best way to draw positive attention from a potential play partner. If you feel good about yourself, that will come through and be way more appealing than a pretty face covering a rotten attitude.

41

Do I need to be equipped like a porn star?

Nope. Porn-quality packages are not required for happy swinging. The community is very inclusive and happily welcomes people with all different sizes of equipment. You will see big boobs and small boobs, big male equipment and small male equipment. And you will see people eager to experience them all. There are no height, weight, girth or cup size requirements for successful swinging. From our own experience and the many swingers we've interviewed, good technique is often a much better predictor of sexual fun than the size of any body part. One of the best aspects of the lifestyle is exposure to many different pleasure-inducing techniques!

What if I get stuck alone?

Masturbation is a solo act. Swinging is not. At its core, the lifestyle is a team sport. At parties, you will mostly see couples walking around together, meeting other couples together, and having fun together. There are some single people in the lifestyle but they are the exceptions. Many couples have rules about always playing together, so even if you wanted to ditch your partner you wouldn't have that much opportunity. Some couples do allow one another to play separately during one-on-one dates with external partners. It's much less common for couples to split up to play separately at clubs or swinger events. If you and your partner decide that separate play is within your comfort zone and your partner finds a playmate before you do, it's not a big deal. Just relax at the bar with a drink or hit the dance floor with a smile and you'll soon have company, too! The lifestyle is about having fun and enjoying life so you already have something in common with everyone else at the party!

Will people try to seduce my partner?

Yes. Can you blame them? Heck, you weren't able to resist your
partner's charms were you? What's so great about the lifestyle is that
most couples aren't interested in seducing just one half of a couple – they
more likely want to seduce both of you for a sexy foursome.

Flirting and being sexy doesn't mean your marriage is at risk. Swingers
are really good about not confusing sexual attraction with romantic
interest. Swinging is generally a team event and mostly done by couples
with other couples. Yes, there can be some hot and sexy flirting, but
swinging is still basically a lending library. As incredible as you & your
partner are, after sexy time the other couple just wants to go home with
their special someone, and not yours. Afterwards, there might be some
flirty texts or emails so the other couple can play with you again, which
is a huge ego boost. But at the end of the day, it really is just a sexy
lending library. If you begin to feel threatened by one person's special
attention on your partner, be honest about your feelings and work with
your partner to resolve them before it becomes an issue.

How can I trick/convince my partner to join the lifestyle?

You can't. (And it would be a very bad idea even if you could.) You can
have an honest discussion with them to see if they share the same
feelings and want to try the lifestyle together to improve your
relationship. The lifestyle is for couples that are in sync with each other.
If you try to force it, you will have a really bad time, upset your partner,
and scare away potential lifestyle friends who want nothing to do with
your drama. The good news is that couples usually share the same
feelings even if they haven't discussed the lifestyle in the past. So keep
reading and we will talk about how to carefully bring up this topic,
without scaring your awesome partner, so you can be honest with each
other and resolve your concerns and anxieties.

What about those masked parties to protect my identity?

A masked party is something you see in Hollywood films. They are rarely a reality, because swingers want to see your sexy face. Relax, the swinging community understands discretion - oh boy, do we understand, value and protect discretion! The community is very protective of our shared secrets. Later in the book we will talk much, much more about protecting your privacy, because it is really important. You'll find out that many public figures like police officers, teachers and politicians are in the lifestyle; more importantly, you'll find out how they protect their privacy.

Are swingers nymphomaniacs?

Sorry to clear up this naughty misconception but swingers are regular, healthy people who occasionally like to have sexy times with other regular, healthy people they find attractive. Swingers don't try to have sex with every random person they meet because of some deep seated need for tons of sex. Just because we have a sex-positive attitude and a non-judgmental stance does not mean we don't have standards. Swingers can be very picky. They tend to be very inconclusive during party time, but picky when it comes to sexy time. Many people attending swinger parties just enjoy the sexy vibe and don't actively participate because there isn't a mutual attraction at that party.

What about key parties?

Sadly, key parties are mostly Hollywood myth. You are not going to have sexy time with another person unless you all voluntarily agree. Remember that swingers have standards and we all have our own personal preference, which is why this is another Hollywood myth ... well, usually. Every now & then you may hear about a key party but it is usually organized by a new swinger couple that thinks that is how you host a swinger party. These tend to be less successful parties than when swingers pick their own play partners. Some small groups of close friends who have all been intimate in various foursome or moresome scenarios for a long time occasionally do key parties as a lark and can enjoy it but blindly being paired up isn't common in the lifestyle.

Can I say No?

Absolutely YES! NO means NO is a golden rule in the swinging community. You can always say no to any situation at any time with any person in the lifestyle. You do not have to explain yourself to anyone. If you're not interested, you're not interested. Period. The swinging community is much more fun when everyone is happy, comfortable & drama free. Never assume consent is given. Always make sure to ask before doing things.

Are swingers creepy?

Creepy people get ostracized from the swinging community because creepy aint sexy at all! Yes, Hollywood likes to make stereotyped jokes about swingers, but in reality, we're just a friendly group of people who like to embrace our sexier side and have a good time with each other.

Is the swinging lifestyle perfect?

Nope. Just like everything else in real life, nothing is perfect. Our community is overall very awesome, but there are a few bad apples. Make sure to use your common sense and read the rest of this book to prepare yourself for some wild situations you probably never even dreamed about. Let's be honest, swinger rookies make a bunch of mistakes because they don't know better - but hey, we were all rookies at one point!

Another weekend and another swinger club to visit. We get our "sexy" on & head out. The party is in full swing, with great music & ladies taking turns showing off on the swinger pole. We are enjoying cocktails, the good looking crowd & a very sexy party vibe.

We are having fun dancing, drinking, chatting & enjoying life, before you know it, it is already 1am.. So we ask the couple we've been chatting, if they want to play. Next thing you know we are all driving back together to the hotel & find out this is their first full swap. What an honor to be this couple's first!

So we head up to their hotel room and the guys prepare some drinks while the ladies get more comfortable. Everyone is complimenting everyone else about their sexy body parts till we casually ask if it would be ok to become more familiar with those body parts. Now the clothes are slowly falling off as the heat builds up.

The guy is ecstatic and just can't believe his luck with this super sexy scene unfolding in front of his eyes. He is just so overeager for this to progress. The lady is happy but very nervous and unsure. The guy is too excited & trying to increase the pace to start the main event. We both notice this and slow down the pace to make sure everyone stays comfortable and happy. It works like a charm, everyone is happy & ready to take the plunge with our different partners.

The lady isn't used to being with someone different, so we take the big plunge slowly. She quickly relaxes and starts to lose herself in passion. Now our overeager guy just got a reality check witnessing his wife take the plunge with another guy. It is turning into a mental hurdle for him and his sexy time is deflating. To salvage the situation we switch back to same partners and a happy ending was enjoyed by everyone. The next day, the other couple sent us a happy email and looking forward to the next time. So yay for us, we didn't scare away full swap newbies!

It did remind us that newbies may talk a good game, but it is hard to predict how people will react during their first time. If you are newbies, go slow and you might want to play with veterans your first time to avoid rookie mistakes.

Types of Swingers

Everyone is a little bit different, and good sex is going to be a little bit different for every person. As with any type of community, swingers come in many different shapes and forms. We are going to cover the distinct types of swingers and nomenclature you will likely encounter as you explore the swinging lifestyle.

This is more about learning the many different shades of gray in the swinging lifestyle than it is about applying labels to stereotype people or box them in. People can be a little bit of two things, a little bit of three things, or even a little bit of everything. There are no swinging police that are checking paperwork to make sure you stay in your lane - unless you are attending a swinging costume party and like to be frisked by sexy people! This list will show you the many options available to you and your loved one to find your own sexy path in the swinging lifestyle. Every path has different curves, and whichever path works for your relationship is the right path to follow.

The main types of swingers are Soft Swap, Full Swap, and Swayers. Those groups are further broken down by "same room play" or "separate room play". The rest of the non-swinging world is referred to as Vanilla. Vanilla are the "plain" or "standard" people who are not involved with any of the different "spicy" swinging lifestyle options. Vanilla people can be loads of fun but if you want risqué fun then seek out the swingers & other groups of sex-positive people.

Voyeur/Exhibitionist

As we've said before, just because you attend a swinger party doesn't mean you have to play with anyone. You can attend as a sexy voyeur or exhibitionist. You can relax, enjoy a drink, participate in sexy conversation, and be yourself without fear of being judged. Many different types of sexual fantasies are more common than you'd think, and sex-positive people are willing to share those fantasies aloud. Even if no one else shares your fantasies, swingers are unlikely to judge you for sharing them.

Besides just sharing your sexy fantasies, feelings, and ideas, you can share your sexy body without physically engaging. Hot, skin-baring outfits are common – so are no outfits at all! You may see two ladies take their tops off to compare breasts – you're allowed to enjoy this, because boobs are fun and sexy. As more people go topless and people grow more comfortable, you might see other couples going fully nude or even having sex. While you should try not to gawk or ogle, you can certainly appreciate and enjoy the sexy atmosphere around you. Things will probably get even hotter, and you may have to control your instinct to stare as the party ramps up beyond your expectations. Try to keep your jaw off the ground! If you and your partner are feeling really excited, you can do your own public display of affection. The hotter your performance, the more likely you will be asked by others if they can join. If you don't want to swap, just say no thanks. Swingers are very respectful and will understand you just want to have a hot and sexy time with your own partner.

Many newbies find that being a voyeur or exhibitionist just isn't satisfying enough when they are at a swinger party, so check in with your partner and see if you both want to take it to the next level.

Soft Swapping Swingers

Soft swapping swingers are people that like to engage in foreplay and other sexy acts with other people, but reserve full penetrative sex for just their partner. Soft swapping could include kissing, caressing, playing with breasts, oral sex or anything else except for penetration below the waist. Many soft swap couples prefer this style so they can have fun without crossing boundaries they have set for themselves. Some couples find full sex with someone other than their partner too intimate, but they enjoy the excitement of soft swap.

When you soft swap, you can switch back to your own partner for full sex so you can relish the sexy atmosphere with your loved one, or you can head back home to finish the sexy night in private. Another benefit to soft swap is that it can limit your health risks but keep in mind that some STIs don't require penetration to be spread.

Another reason for soft swapping is to help with erection issues. Some guys don't feel comfortable performing for another lady or they have a hard time maintaining an erection with condoms, so soft swap brings the fun & excitement without any pressure-induced ED issues. People that soft swap tend to feel less performance pressure. This lack of pressure can actually lead to an even hotter performance.

If you are inexperienced, you might think that there is no way soft swap can be hotter than full swap, but with the right people it can be very much hotter. Many couples even feel that soft swapping is more intimate than full swap. When you are having a full swap, the focus can end up being more physical. When you are having a soft swap, you are kissing, caressing and saying some sexy things – all of which can feel much, much more intimate and sexy.

Soft swap sessions can also last much longer than full swap sessions. You are enjoying the moment and savoring the sexy fun. You aren't in a rush to orgasm. Soft swap sessions also tend to be more inclusive since you can have many people kissing and caressing in a sexy pile. You can be kissing someone while touching another person's body as a third person is touching you, and that is pretty freaking hot.

Soft swap empowers you to have more variety in your sexy life without the headaches that full swap swinging can introduce. Communicating early and often is a good way to have a sexy and happy play session. You shouldn't think that soft swap is just for beginners. Full swap swinging veterans can and have changed their preferred play style to soft swap from full swap. Each couple has their own unique definition of soft swap, so you should ask new soft swap play friends about what is or is not on the menu and feel comfortable telling them your own rules.

Full Swap Swinging

By now, you've probably figured out what full swap swinging means – full, penetrative sex. Seeing your loved one having full-on sex with another people can be emotionally intense, especially if you've been together a long time. Heck, it can be emotionally intense if you've only been together a short time! When you full swap, it's more likely that you'll pair off and focus only on your play partner. Full swap play sessions often begin like a soft swap but tend to ramp up quickly as couples pair off.

If you are having a full swap experience on the same bed with others, you should realize that you might get close to naked body parts that you weren't expecting to deal with. Most likely this is an accidental foot to your face or someone reaching out and grabbing the wrong body part. Some inexperienced guys might have a hard time feeling comfortable being naked next to other men. You should think about it beforehand so you can accept it calmly in the moment.

Taking the step into full swapping can greatly increase the chance of ED issues for men because it increases the performance pressure. If this sounds likely for you, try not to worry. It isn't a competition and no one is judging you. Full swap is about everyone having a sexy time in their own way.

There are also some bigger potential headaches that come with full swap swinging, specifically safer sex and pregnancy concerns. Make sure you talk with your partner and agree on the rules beforehand when you are calm and sober. Communicating with each other when there is no pressure is a good step towards a happy and sexy experience, no matter what type of swinging you choose to engage in. Often full swap couples insist on condoms for sex but not for oral play.

You should also make sure to talk with your partner and your potential play partners about where and how the men should finish in a full swap. Don't assume anything and always ask first.

Speaking about asking first: just because full swap is full-on sex, that does not mean there is a greenlight for anal play. Backdoor fun is not usually on the play menu. Remember to ask early and often so everyone is clear about their personal boundaries. Communicating well helps your body relax so you can savor the moment. You can end up starring in a sex scene hotter than anything you have ever seen in any porno … seriously, this isn't an exaggeration.

Full swap swinging can truly be amazing. It isn't better than sex with your partner. It is a different type of sexy and shouldn't be compared. Again, think about diamonds, emeralds, rubies and sapphires. They are different, but all are sparkling beauties to be enjoyed. Just like you have a preference amongst these beautiful gems, you will probably have a preference in your play style and it won't compete with the sparkling sex you have privately with your loved one.

Swayers

Swayers is a less commonly used term but it describes a good amount of people. Newbies especially will want to learn about swayers. Swayers are typically vanilla, and enjoy being vanilla, but sometimes dabble in swinging. Often this dabbling occurs on vacation or when there's a special opportunity or occasion. Swayers will "sway" across their vanilla boundary to engage in the swinging lifestyle for a short period of time. They reap the benefits of the sex-positive community without engaging in any of the complications that can come from committing to the lifestyle. Swaying couples are like students who give themselves a hall pass to have some extra-curricular fun.

Being a swayer can be a safe way to test drive the lifestyle to see if it is a good match for you and your partner. Some people are permanent swayers. They might not have much free time or maybe they don't like regularly sharing their partner and just want some intermittent sexy fun.

The downside with swayers is that they are often ill prepared and can lack the strong communication skills needed for a 100% mistake-free night of fun sex. If you are thinking of being sawyers, you should still talk about what each of you likes and dislikes, confirm your boundaries, and check in with each other during the night. You don't want one night of dabbling in the lifestyle to result in six months of fighting and marriage counseling because of an accidental misunderstanding.

Your spouse might be smiling as you flirt with another person, but they might only be pretending in order to avoid a public fight. When in doubt, err on the side of caution and communicate. There will be another chance to have sexy fun, assuming you don't rush too much, too soon. Protect your partner and their trust in you. Swinging and the lifestyle is just a bonus to your already great life.

Ok, so you've chatted with your partner and decided on being soft or full swap, or just a sexy swayer the next time you go on vacation. The next big decision is to decide between same room play or separate room play. Many swingers go with same room play, but this is your sexy time so you should decide what works best for you.

Same vs Separate Room Play

Same room is, predictably, when you all play in the same room. It can be a threesome, foursome, or moresome in the same room. It is up to you to decide if you want a big king-size bed or separate beds.

Playing in the same room makes it easier to check in with each other throughout the play session. You can reach out and touch or kiss each other while playing with your new friends. Same room swinging makes it easy to exchange a thumbs up to let each other know you are having some crazy, awesome fun. It can be oh-so-sexy to hear your partner moan in delight as you also enjoy yourself. After you have fun with your sexy play friend, you can switch back to your partner or have some girl-on-girl fun while the guys recharge for another sexy round. You can form all sorts of combinations of sexy fun when everyone is in the same room.

If you are going to try same room play, you should also agree on what to do if you finish first. Some people like to talk after sex or do things that can be distracting to others who are still working towards their own happy, sexy finish. Being in the same room keeps everyone on the same page, since they will be able to see and hear everything you do. You won't be wondering where your partner is and if they are having a good time because you are all together.

Same room play is pretty awesome - but it is not for everyone. It can also be a bit nerve racking and weird for some couples to hear or see their partners having sexy time with someone else. Some swingers prefer separate room play so they can focus on their new sexy play friend without being distracted or rushed. When you are in your own separate room for play time, you can go at your own pace and not feel like there is a competition to moan louder or last longer. It is just about you and your sexy friend having a fun time enjoying each other's body. This can be very beneficial for men and women alike.

Ladies do not want to feel rushed. Men can have performance issues if it is too sexy, noisy or distracting in the same room. We all live crazy stressful lives juggling work, family and everything else. Being placed in the spotlight of a crowded room and expected to perform on demand can be too much stress, resulting in less than stellar performance.

On the other side are some men who find same room sex just too sexy and they become overexcited and finish too soon. You can't really blame them; it's super hot to see your sexy wife showing off her hottest bedroom moves while your gorgeous, new play friend is ravaging your body! So yeah, it can be too distracting in the same room. When you are in a separate room, you can go at your own pace without any pressure or spotlight from other people. That helps many men to perform at a higher & harder level. Being able to just focus on your new play friend helps simplify the equation.

Plus, when you are having separate room fun, you can let yourself go without worrying about being too loud. Some people hold back in same room situations because they don't want others to hear how much they truly enjoy their new play friend for fear of making another person distracted or jealous. Separate room play can be a really fun time and give you an opportunity to reconnect with your partner later to exchange new sexy stories or techniques you might have learned.

Cuckolding Confusion

In case you aren't familiar with the cuckold concept, here is a very oversimplified explanation … a cuckold takes pleasure from having his wife cheat on him. There are many different permutations and styles of cuckolding. Some cuckolds like to be embarrassed, others like to have their sperm compete with other men, some cuckolds want to watch and others don't. Cuckolding is part of the BDSM lifestyle and tends to focus more on the power dynamic and less on the actual sex. BDSM and the swinging lifestyles often brush shoulders with each other. They are both part of the overall sex-positive world. Cuckolding is not swinging.

You might encounter cuckolding in the swinging world just like you might encounter some swingers wanting to be spanked. We all have different fetishes and some BDSM fetishes can occasionally cross over into the swinging lifestyle. This is not typical but it happens. Typically swingers aren't looking to play power games. Usually the swingers' goal is to have hot sex. We are not intentionally trying to mentally embarrass or humiliate another guy.

If you are worried about cuckolding, don't be. It isn't typical for sexy swinging playtime. There is nothing wrong with cuckolding but it usually is not a good fit with many swingers. More often swingers are swapping partners and if there is a cuckold in a swap, then there is probably going to be an upset lady who is not having sex. When a lady is upset, the sexy fun is quick to end. This is why cuckolding is not common in swinging.

If you want to have cuckolding fun in the swinging world, it is easier to setup a MMF or MFM swinger threesome (2 guys & 1 lady). There are many single men in the swinging world and you can find one willing to be your bull (the dominant man having sex). You can debate if this threesome is swinging or a BDSM play session. We choose not to worry about definitions and enjoy the many different opportunities in the wide world of being sex positive.

Biased Bisexuality

While we are covering the different types of swingers let's clear up a few things about exploring sexuality; specifically, the biased bisexuality in the lifestyle. The lifestyle technically welcomes people of all types of sexuality. Realistically, guys are often expected to be straight heterosexuals and women are expected to have a bit of flexibility, and they are actively encouraged to be bisexual or at least bi-curious. Thankfully, the newer generation of swingers (20 & 30 year olds) tend to be more accepting of guys who may or may not be curious about bisexuality.

To be honest, we are all a little gay.

For example, many men like watching hot porn where a sexy woman is getting drilled by a well-hung guy. Well, getting turned on by watching a well-hung man is a little bit gay. What if a guy is watching a really hot lesbian porno? That isn't gay at all, unless you realize that you're watching two homosexuals have sex. When it's phrased that way, it does sound a bit gay.

These examples are a little silly, but they're also true. There has been real sex research done by people with fancy PhDs for over 50 years and they have found that most people (men and women alike) have at least a little gray area in their sexuality. If you don't believe us, just look up Kinsey Scale on Google. There are over 200 different scales for measuring the varying degrees of sexuality!

So how does sexuality fit into the swinging lifestyle? It's different for guys and girls. Let's explore both sides so you can see where you might fit in.

Guys Sexuality

Don't kill the messenger. We're not saying it is right, and it is most definitely unfair, but often there is pressure in the lifestyle for a guy to be very straight. You will see a few men being honest about their bisexuality, but most bisexual men keep it on the down low. The exception is the younger crowd of swingers who tend not to be judgmental if a guy wants to be bisexual with another consenting adult. Unfortunately, the younger crowd is a minority portion of the swinging community. If you list yourself as a bisexual man on a swinging website, you will likely have fewer couples contact you. There are some dedicated swinging groups for bisexual men, so you can still find plenty of play partners, but it won't be as easy as saying you're straight.

If you are a bisexual man, don't worry too much. Even though you might encounter unfair viewpoints from some older swingers, you will find there are many bisexual men in the lifestyle … they just might not openly advertise their preference. If you are open about your male bisexuality, you will likely be contacted by couples with "straight" men who really enjoy a full blown bisexual orgy.

For straight men that are reading this section, grab a beer and relax. Too many straight guys are wound up about proving their heterosexuality and miss out on a lot of fun. We aren't even talking about being bisexual. We're just talking about experimenting with that nerve-packed prostate of yours. Don't freak out if a lady wants to massage that prostate while giving you a blowjob. It doesn't make you gay or bisexual, it just makes you cum really hard from a super intense orgasm. The prostate in your bum is basically the g-spot for guys. There are some really experienced ladies in the lifestyle who can make you cum harder than you have ever come before - if you are willing to relax and try something new. Of course, if you don't want to experiment with this, you should tell your play partner and expect them to respect your decision.

If you are lucky you will find yourself in some hot & sexy moments. These moments could be uncomfortable situations for homophobic guys. They might even think it is a borderline-gay situation like standing naked next to another guy, stroking your own respective cocks, watching both your of ladies put on the hottest girl-on-girl show before inviting you gentlemen to join the action. Don't freak out! No one is trying to trick you but often play rooms can be tight spaces. When you are having sexy time with other people, there is likely going to be times when you unintentionally get close to male anatomy. Unless you prefer having sex fully clothed, make sure you can act like a mature adult and be cool with it. The lifestyle is about consensual fun amongst sexy adults. The more you can chill and handle things that just pop-up, the more sexy situations you will likely enjoy.

Ladies Sexuality

Ladies, you have more flexibility than men do in terms of bisexuality. However, you will likely encounter some pressure to be bisexual or at least a little "bi for the team". This generally means willing to play with another lady to increase the excitement level.

You can do as much or as little exploring of your sexuality as you choose. You can simply say "no thanks" if you're invited to play with another woman. But, if you're curious about what it might be like to kiss another woman, go ahead and try it (as long as you ask if it's okay, of course). If you feel compelled to explore another girl's breasts and want to kiss or caress them, go ahead and ask. Many women in the lifestyle are bisexual or bi-curious, and will be open to attention from other ladies. Don't assume anything about another woman, and always ask respectfully before touching.

If you'd prefer not to experiment with other ladies, this is completely acceptable. You may find yourself growing more curious over time as you delve deeper into the lifestyle and open up more to your own sexuality. Some women are just plain straight and will never want to engage with another woman. Others decide they want to experiment for a while then choose whether it's for them.

It's well-known that many men find it extremely hot to watch two beautiful women playing with each other. Many men just can't stop themselves from asking if they can join in before you are ready to stop playing with your new lady friends. Don't be afraid to tell the men to hang back until you're ready. Swinging is a team activity, but ladies tend to act as the coach, steering what happens or doesn't happen. Be vocal about your comfort level. Push yourself as much as you like, but don't feel obliged to let others push you. It's in everyone's best interest for you to be happy so speak up if you want to do something or would rather not do something.

Polyamory – Swinging's Frenemy

Because all this new terminology just hasn't been confusing enough, let's talk about another new word for you: polyamory. Polyamory describes a committed, closed relationship between more than two people. An ongoing threesome, foursome, or however-much-some arrangement where everyone agrees to never play outside of this arrangement would be considered polyamory. One oversimplified way to explain the difference between swinging and polyamory is to say that poly people love everyone in their group while swingers lust after their play partners. Honestly, there are entire books dedicated to polyamory so our brief explanation will not be able to best explain this type of relationship. To all polyamory people we apologize in advance for this grossly oversimplified crash course.

Polyamory and swinging are very different concepts even though they might seem to be similar. Yes, both swingers and poly people can have multiple sex partners. Swingers tend to play with many partners without making a long-term relationship commitment to those partners. Strong friendships may form between play partners, but swingers don't usually form an intense, emotional, loving bond. Swinging is more about physical pleasure and sexy fun, not love.

Poly people, on the other hand, have love at the core of their relationships, so that a closed group of people will openly say "I love you" to each other. For polyamorous folks, emotional connection trumps physical connection. They can be in closed poly groups or open groups or their own variation of it. Poly people can also be swingers and swingers can find friends that evolve into a poly situation.

It's not unheard of for swingers to become polyamorous while exploring the lifestyle. For instance, you might meet a great swinging couple that you really click with. You enjoy their company, and you certainly enjoy playing with them. You want to engage in play without condoms, to enhance the pleasure for everyone. In this scenario, you might choose to enter a polyamorous-style relationship, wherein you commit to each other that you will not engage in play with anyone else.

Of course, once you agree to that, you're less swinging and more entering a poly situation (not that you should worry about labels and just enjoy yourself). But for many people, sacrificing the opportunity to have many new, exciting play partners is worth the benefits of committing to a polyamorous relationship. You won't have to spend time looking for new partners you like and who like you, which can be tedious and frustrating. You don't have to wonder if your night at the swingers' club will be a success or a total bust. You can plan a schedule that works for everyone in the group. You can engage in play without condoms, which most agree feels better. Your exposure risk for STIs will go way down, since you are only playing with trusted people who have been tested. You can enjoy the fruits of an emotional commitment that comes with a polyamorous relationship.

Our Swinging Journal: Inclusive Parties but Exclusive Bedrooms

Another weekend is approaching and we are on the RSVP list for a local swinger club. The list of RSVPs looks pretty sexy and we can't wait. Some of the other couples on the RSVPs send us messages to say hello and introduce themselves before the party. The swinging community is really awesome & friendly like that.

Finally it is Saturday night and we head out to the swinger club. The event is sold out so we know it is going to be packed with fun people. Sure enough as we pull into the parking lot, it is already mostly filled. We park the car and walk to the front door of the club as we navigate the rough surface. Don't ask us why but most swinger clubs have really crappy parking lots with potholes, gravel and sometimes even mud. If your lady is in sexy high heels, it is usually smarter to drop her off at the front door as you park the car. Of course we weren't that smart this night.

So we walk into the club and get our wristbands. We then drop off our play bag in the lockers and drop off our BYOB booze at the bar. Surprise, surprise our friends are already at the bar having fun so we join them. As we are chatting with them a new couple approaches us. Somehow they know our names and then we find

---

out they know a mutual friend. Ok, cool so we invite them to join our group conversation.

It is nothing special, just your typical swinger party. Drinks are flowing, a buffet for nibbling, and good dance music. Just like any other nightclub. To be fair there was some sexy grinding on the dance floor. Oh and there was also the people playing strip pool, and the naked hot tubbing, ok I guess the topless whipcream fights was a little unusual but seriously nothing different than a typical nightclub besides all the play rooms filled with sexy people having naughty naked fun hehehe.

Back to us, we are still hanging out by the bar just enjoying the sexy vibe and friendly company. The new couple is getting a bit fidgety and anxious. They keep trying to engage only us and pull us away from our group of friends. We are having a good time with our group of friends and there just isn't a four way connection with this new couple. They are a good looking couple and fun to party with but we don't feel a sexy vibe on our side so it's a no go. Eventually they need to leave the club to relieve their babysitter.

They email us the next day and say they wish they could have stayed longer and had sexy time with us. So we had to share with them that they are awesome friends to party with but the lack of a sexy four way connection means sexy time isn't on the menu. Mentioning the lack of a four way connection enabled us to communicate sexy time isn't an option without insulting or hurting anyone's feelings. So we ended up being good friends that just don't share bedroom time but party great together.

Swingers are friendly people but swingers are also a bit picky with who we bring back to our beds. If there isn't a good four way connection, it is better to just be friends and not play partners.

Avoiding Landmines

We all have triggers that can ruin our fun. Or worse, ruin our relationship. To keep you and your relationship safe, you'll want to carefully avoid landmines that might be lingering a little below the surface of your happy relationship.

You might be aware of some of these landmines, and think they won't be an issue for you or your partner. Be careful. It's dangerous to assume anything, especially if you haven't talked about it, or experienced it before. Many veteran swingers in healthy relationships, with years of experience, have encountered a landmine explosion at one time or another because you can't always predict how you or your partner will react to every situation.

It's one thing to imagine a scenario, and another thing entirely to live it. Something you thought was in your comfort zone might prove to push you past your limits. Just ask our friend who learned the hard way to never ask a dominatrix to surprise you: just because he liked his dominatrix using a strap-on did not mean he was ready for her to invite a guy to join in. Most people aren't crazy enough to dare a dominatrix to surprise them, and our friend strongly encourages everyone to learn from his mistake.

When you join the lifestyle, you're going to be facing many new experiences that will test how you and your loved one feel. Some people love the excitement of playing with other partners, but might not be able to handle seeing their loved one kiss someone else, so they have a no kissing rule. Another person might love kissing and touching other people, but can't handle seeing another guy's equipment penetrate his wife, so this couple sticks with soft-swap. Other people really enjoy the fantasy of sexy time with different people, but can't stand to see their partner actually flirting in front of them. For these people, it might be better to stay home and privately watch some porn that will help them role play.

You don't want to assume you and your loved one will be okay with every single scenario. Honestly, you won't be 100% sure of what you're comfortable with until you do it. So don't rush in too fast.

Even taking it slow doesn't ensure that you'll always be safe from landmines. Feelings evolve and change over time, so it is possible for triggers to pop up over time. The great way to protect your relationship from landmines is with better communication. You want to be very honest with each other about your feelings, especially about any negative feelings. This will help you identify triggers and address them early, before they blow up into a big, bad problem.

Here are some questions you can ask each other to help spot potential landmines before you enter the lifestyle:

- What types of flirting (visual, verbal, touching, etc.) are in the comfort zone?
- What types of communications (phone, text, email, etc.) are in the comfort zone?
- What is allowed to happen before you meet another swinging couple face to face?
- What can happen after you meet another swinging couple face to face?
- Are any specific acts or body parts reserved just for your own private fun?
- How much money can you spend on the swinging lifestyle?
- How much time do you want to spend in the swinging lifestyle?
- How often do you want to engage in swinging events?
- What triggers your jealousy?
- What types of physical appearances are off limits (looks like ex-spouse, coworker, etc)?
- How much solo action is allowed and how often do you need to loop back in?
- Is there a level of TMI (too much information) outside of your comfort zone?
- Is there a desire for sharing even the smaller details?
- What would feel disrespectful when talking or playing with other couples?
- What responsibility do you have to each other during a swinging event?

Hopefully, those questions help you both understand what is inside the comfort zone and what is outside. Remember that things change. You should reconnect after each play session and openly share with each other. Talking about what you liked and didn't like about the play session will help your partner better protect you and your relationship. Understanding your partner's feelings will empower you to do the same. You know that you're already with the sexiest person in the world and you don't want to lose them, so make sure you communicate clearly with each other. If you do not understand how your partner feels, just ask them to explain. Talking about these topics helps many swinger couples open up and strengthen their relationship. Many swinger couples love to have a sexy debriefing after playing to share with each other their perspectives on the event – the good, bad, and (sometimes) strange.

Issues are better dealt with early and often, before they can fester into radioactive relationship killers. You joined the lifestyle to have a fun, sexy time – communication will help keep the drama at bay so you can focus on the good times instead of dwelling on the bad times. This open communication can even help to strengthen the bond between you and your partner. It is common to feel like you have a "mind meld" with your partner. Many experienced swingers find that they often already know what their partner is thinking before they even open their mouth.

Plus, chatting after your play sessions gives you a chance to relive the hottest and sexiest moments - which can get both of your engines revving! Many swingers have hot sex during a play session and even hotter sex the next day, as they keep reliving their amazing experience with the hottest person they know - their own partner.

While we are talking about relationship landmines, let's cover some common mistakes. You do want to be the best swinging partner you can be, right? You love your better half, and you want them to have the best time of their life. To help you get started on the right foot, pay attention to avoid these mistakes. It will make everyone think you are lifestyle veterans regardless of how fresh you might be in the lifestyle.

Not checking first with your partner

When you attend lifestyle events, you will likely stay together almost the entire time. There will be brief periods of separation when one of you might go to the restroom or grab some drinks, but usually couples stick together and socialize with others as one unit. Being "one unit" is an important concept. You need to remember that you probably shouldn't act without first checking in with your partner. You are probably already good at reading your partner's body language, and with more time in the lifestyle you will likely get so good it will feel like you have a telepathic connection.

Still, you shouldn't make assumptions, especially if you are new to the lifestyle. It is very common for couples to excuse themselves to privately check in with each other. You don't want to accidentally start a conversation with people that your partner may not like. Worse, you don't want to say yes to an invitation for sexy play with someone your partner has no interest in. There's no such thing as checking in too much. Checking in is a safe way to make sure you are both ok. It's also a good way to remember that you're sharing this exciting (albeit temporary experience) together because you love each other.

Ignoring one partner

Ok, let's imagine your partner gave the green light, and you start talking with another couple together. Wow, this is exciting! Enjoy the sexual tension of flirting between couples as you discover if there is a four-way connection. Remember, it is a FOUR-way connection. Before you start flirting, make sure to establish a level of respect for the other spouse. Guys, make sure to be friendly and respectful with the husband before drooling over his wife's sexy body. Ladies, be cool and make a friend with the other wife before you start clawing her husband's chest. All four people in a couple swap need to give the green light, so be smart and connect with the other spouse before jumping into the super sexy flirting.

Trusting and sharing pictures too easily

You are a good-looking couple, and even if you were ugly there would still be a bunch of lonely losers trying to get sexy pictures from you. Think with the brain above your shoulders and not the one below your waist. Real swingers understand discretion and will not be too pushy for pictures or private info.

It is usually best to follow the "need to know" principle. If someone online does not absolutely need to know something, don't share it. You can just sleep on it and share something tomorrow, but you can't put the genie back in the bottle if you give out sexy pictures or private information too soon. Many swingers tend to prefer minimal online sharing so they can maximize real-life sharing. There usually is some level of sharing pre-meeting to make sure there is a likely four-way connection but when someone wants all your private info and pictures without first meeting in person, you should be on guard.

Assuming swingers will chase after you

We know you are a good-looking couple, but so are most swingers. You shouldn't expect the entire swinging community to come chasing after you. When you first post an online profile, or attend a club for the first time, there can be a rush of interest from regulars who like shiny new toys, but that rush doesn't always last. If you want to make sexy connections in the lifestyle, you should be proactive.

Make sure you have a good profile with plenty of information. Then, proactively reach out to other people. There are too many shy wallflowers in the lifestyle, and unfortunately being a shy wallflower will reduce the chances of you having sexy play time. If you want to make new sex-positive friends and have a chance at engaging in some hot play time, then you should take the first step and engage other swingers. Say hello. Introduce yourself. Compliment them. You will have much more fun practicing those three simple steps than waiting for people to come to you.

Taking One for the Team

No matter what your partner feels, you probably should never take one for team. If you don't feel comfortable or don't want to do something, don't do it. If the situation is reversed, don't let your partner take one for the team. It's not worth it. When someone takes one for the team, they can end up having a terrible experience that leads to fighting, drama and resentment towards the lifestyle or each other.

It's much smarter to stay within your shared boundaries, where you are both comfortable and happy. The risk is usually too high and the reward is usually too low when someone takes one for the team. Be smart and don't do it. Don't worry, there are plenty more opportunities for sexy fun in the future. There is no reason for either of you to suffer so the other can have fun.

Pushing past your comfort zone

Ladies and gentlemen, you need to be honest with yourself and your partner about your comfort zone. Keeping yourselves and your relationship safe is a team effort. No one should be pushed out of their comfort zone. There is plenty of time to take it slowly and let the comfort zone naturally grow over time.

There is no reason to push someone out of the comfort zone or to let them overreach. Going too far or too fast is a recipe for trouble. It doesn't matter how much time, money or effort you might have invested. Remember how much you love each other and want to protect each other. It is worth it in the long term to go slow and let that comfort zone expand organically, in a safe and trustworthy atmosphere.

Keeping secrets

You and your partner are a team. You don't want anything to cause a crack in your amazing team dynamic. Keeping a secret from your partner is a quick way to do just that. Yes, you might be having sex with other people, but you are still emotionally loyal and trustworthy to your own partner. Secrets sow doubt in that loyalty and trust. This is why swingers love communication. Each time you communicate, you grow that bond and better connect with your amazing partner. Make sure you focus your efforts in strengthening your relationship and avoid secrets that can cause a rift between you.

Blindly Following Advice

Use your brain and do not blindly follow advice. Yes, even our advice. Each relationship varies. What works for someone might not work for you. It might even work for your partner but not for you, because we are all different. Keep an open mind and take the time to reflect on any information or advice someone gives you within the lifestyle. Following your own path and reflecting on advice so you can apply it in a way that works best for your own personal situation is a smarter idea.

The swinging world is a big place with many different people. If you travel around you will find that it can change significantly from region to region. The American swingers' community is a bit different from the

European scene. Even within the USA, you will likely find different ways to engage the swinging lifestyle depending if you are visiting the West Coast, Midwest or East Coast.

Be smart, don't hesitate to ask for advice, and then apply the advice in a way that makes sense for your personal situation.

Our Swinging Journal: Not all swingers are good people...

Another weekend and another party to attend at our local club. It is such a rough life we have attending sex parties with fun & friendly swingers :) Seriously it is not always smooth sailing or 100% drama free. This night was especially cringe-worthy to us.

There was a couple who had been flirting with us for a couple of months but we had no interest in playing with them. She looked great physically. She worked out religiously & it showed all over her body. He didn't look so great. His body showed no signs of having ever been inside a gym but the real issue was that there was no spark between us. Maybe there could have been but we will never know because he barely spoke to Dr. G. You don't need to look like a supermodel but if you can't even talk then it is hard to build a sexy four-way connection.

So late one party night, the wife chats up Mr. F while Dr. G. is in the bathroom, which Mr. F doesn't mind because hey she is a very hot lady. She tells Mr. F that her husband is really into Dr. G but has zero flirting skills. She also says that her guy doesn't have to get in the way of all fun as she is available to play by herself. Enticing but Mr. F tells her that is not our plan for the evening. She keeps chatting & explains they entered the lifestyle with her husband kicking & screaming because he was afraid of losing her if he denied her better dick. Uh, repeat that? Yup, she said that & went on complaining & insulting him. Yikes! Luckily Dr. G rejoined & saved Mr. F from that marital drama.

This was a great reminder of how lucky we are to maintain a healthy relationship, largely due to awesome communication and teamwork. We aren't perfect but we do love each other so very much.

Understanding Romance vs. Lust

We all want a fairytale ending to our own personal love story. You might be surprised how many people in the swinging lifestyle have already found their fairytale ending with their lifelong partner. And the single people in the lifestyle are likely hoping to find their own fairytale partner worthy of a Disney film.

But even if there's a lot of romance between individual swinger couples, the lifestyle is not about romance. Love is actually a four-letter word to many people in the community. We generally don't want to love our swinging partners – we want to lust for them, and have them lust for us. Remember the difference between swinging and polyamory: swinging is a temporary sexy play time for you and your lifelong partner. You arrive with your partner and you leave with your partner.

Many people new to the lifestyle are worried about protecting the romance they share with their partner. Newbies fear that someone in the swinger community will wind up stealing their spouse. The thing is we all love our partners. We want to stay with them and don't want anyone else to "steal" them. When swingers engage in play with other swingers, they're focused on the lustful, sexy feelings – not romantic feelings. Even if you find another couple you really like and want to play with often, remember that these are play dates and not romantic dates.

The swinging community hates drama. Veteran swingers often can sniff out newbies who lack the solid foundation their relationship needs to thrive in the lifestyle. When swingers notice a couple fighting often, or on the verge of a break-up, that couple is often politely ostracized while they privately deal with their drama. Relationship drama is a headache that doesn't belong with the sexy, fun vibe of the lifestyle. Successfully nurturing our own relationships is hard enough without inviting in extra drama; so there is no need to worry about people in the swinging community trying to steal your partner.

What about single swingers? Sure, there's a healthy number of singles in the lifestyle, but they're still a minority. And single people in the lifestyle are likely to be some of the best people you'll meet. People who are rude, disrespectful, or trying to stir up trouble will quickly be alienated from the community. Singles in the lifestyle are looking for a good time, just like everyone else; they're looking for someone sexy to play with, not their soulmate. Drama gets in the way of sexy time, and that doesn't benefit anyone!

Of course, we're not saying that the lifestyle is perfect. There have been break-ups and divorces. But there are break-ups and divorces in the vanilla world, too. Most countries have a divorce rate over 50% - swinging couples aren't exempt from those kinds of statistics. Divorce actually tends to be less common among swingers depending on which research you read. This is probably because swingers have above-average communication skills. Swingers know that communicating is the best way to prevent drama and keep everyone happy, smiling, and sexually satisfied.

Speaking of being sexually satisfied, it's hard to find time to cheat on your partner when you're attending these awesome, sexy swinging parties. Still, you don't want to take any chances with your relationship, and you probably want to know how to protect your romance from potential damage. Here are some steps that have worked for many in the lifestyle:

Step 1: Make sure to honestly communicate with each other.

Don't hold back your real feelings and opinions. No one should be "taking one for the team"; you should both go at the speed of the slowest person. One of you might want more, but remember that any sexy fun is better than no sexy fun. There's no need to rush it!

Step 2: Keep external communications on a group level.

When emailing, texting, messaging, or communicating in any way with someone outside your relationship, make it a shared experience. Avoid secrets or surprises. By sharing your lusty communiqués with each other, you can make sure everyone is comfortable and playing within the rules. It is very easy nowadays to arrange group texts, group emails or group calls, so there's no excuse for skipping this step if it might help your relationship.

Step 3: Playing together can make it easier to stay together.

Choosing same room play over separate room helps keep you both connected. Separate room play can be really fun, but it does increase the risk of something not going well. Many swinging people prefer to keep it simple with same room play. If you're engaging in same room play, don't go giving each other hall passes. It sounds exciting, but letting your partner go away on their own is definitely raising the chances of rocking your relationship rowboat a bit too much.

Of course these are just suggestions based on what many other people in the lifestyle find to be helpful. You should talk with your own special someone to figure out what makes sense for you.

Balancing Religion With Swinging

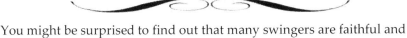

You might be surprised to find out that many swingers are faithful and religious people. We all have our own personal positions and opinions on religion. So how can faithful religious people balance out their sexy swinging with their religious obligations?

First let's remember that a big, underlying theme in the lifestyle is not judging others. We are all different people and what works for one person might not work for another. Swingers tend to follow "a live and let live" philosophy style. You don't need to worry about other swingers, just worry about your own religious situation.

There are some fringe religious groups and houses of worship that embrace consensual non-monogamy. However, most religious leaders probably wouldn't endorse this sexual lifestyle, and would likely advise against it.

In 2014, Pew Research Center conducted a survey of more than 35,000 people from all 50 states and found that about 71% of Americans identified as Christian, about 6% followed a non-Christian faith, and roughly 23% were unaffiliated with any religion[2]. You'll find a similar breakdown in the lifestyle. Of course, the percentages will more likely reflect the religious breakdown of your own local region. Swingers are not just "scary atheist heathens". There are many friendly Christian, Jewish and Muslim swingers.

It might sound hypocritical to be religious and engaging in consensual non-monogamy. If you think about it, swingers are honest, or as honest as society allows them to be. Considering up to 60% of marriages are touched by nonconsensual infidelity, we kind of think those other people are the hypocrites that should be more worried about how they will be judged than judging swingers. It would probably be better if everyone focused more effort on respecting others and less effort judging adults who engage in consensual fun.

Let's focus first on Christianity & swinging since it was the biggest religious group in that Pew research. Christians love to follow the example made by Jesus. We are going to take a moment and remind everyone that if they follow the WWJD principle aka "What Would Jesus Do?" then tossing tables, whipping people and hanging out with prostitutes is a very real possibility. We are taking that a tiny bit out of context but Jesus was definitely all about loving & respecting each other and that fits in very well with swinging.

One of the most common conflicts that Christian swingers encounter is the fact that the bible says adultery is a sin. However, adultery is not clearly defined in the bible, so you need to reflect on your personal definition of adultery. Is adultery simply looking at other sexy people? Doubtful. Is adultery when you kiss someone besides your significant

---

[2] http://www.pewforum.org/religious-landscape-study/

other? Maybe, maybe not. Is adultery having sex with someone other than your one spouse? Then how do you explain all the people in the bible with multiple wives?

Maybe adultery is when you are lying and cheating on your spouse? In that case, swinging is not adultery because you are not cheating or lying. You are exploring your sexuality together in an honest and upfront manner. You are not divorcing or leaving your spouse. You are still faithful, loyal and honest to your partner who is sharing this swinging journey along your side. Many Christian leaders would disagree and say that any sexual contact outside of your marriage bed is adultery. So if you are a Christian you need to decide for yourself. Many of the Christian swingers that we have chatted with try to live life based on loving principles and not the exact letter of the law which can be taken out of context and distorted from its original purpose.

The bible has many rules that you probably break on a regular basis. For example, in the bible Timothy 2:9 says women can't have elaborate hairstyles or wear gold, pearls or expensive clothes. How about Leviticus 11:4, which says you can't eat any pork - including bacon. Proverbs 23:2 says you need to slit your throat with a knife if you are given to gluttony, which would make for a very big mess after your family's next Thanksgiving dinner. Let's not forget Corinthians 14:34, which says women should remain silent in the churches and must always be in submission. There are other parts of the bible that explain it is ok to rape a woman if you are married to her, or kill someone by stoning to death if they worship a false god. Yikes!

Let's remember that the bible has been translated and reinterpreted countless times over 2000 years. These parts of the bible were also taken a little out of context. We don't want you to think we are attacking the bible. The point we are trying to make is that the bible is not an easy document to blindly follow. It is often best for each of us to reflect on the underlying principles and how we can best apply them to our lives in the spirit that God intended them.

If you believe in a loving God that wants you to honor your spouse and share your life together, there is no conflict with the swinging lifestyle. The bible does say to love your neighbor as you love yourself. Swinging can help improve your communication and enrich your relationship by introducing exciting and fun experiences that you can enjoy together.

We have many friends who go out swinging on Saturday night and get to church every Sunday morning. Some of them are very devout and even religious education teachers. Honestly, we have no idea how these people find the energy to wake up for church, let alone be in a positive spirit to share their religious teachings with kids so early in the morning. It would take a true miracle for us to have the energy to do that.

There are also many Jewish people in the swinging lifestyle. If it has been a while since you were in Hebrew School, let's recap the Jewish position on sex: it's a good thing - yay! Sex is not something that should be viewed as shameful or obscene. It is a natural human instinct like eating and sleeping, and should be shared between husband and wife for their pleasure. Generally, sex is seen as the Jewish women's right and not the man's. One rabbi even thinks it is mandatory for men to make the lady orgasm before he can have pleasure.

Many rabbis are going to say that sex should be exclusively limited between husband and wife. Of course, many different rabbis will have many different views. If you are Jewish, you need to decide how kosher you want to be. Are you willing to share the mitzvah of sex with a gentile? Is sex forbidden if you have a same room full swap, because you are still sharing it with your spouse? Is soft swap still allowed because you aren't having full penetration? We aren't going to judge you. There are many Jewish people that have made their own personal decisions to explore the swinging lifestyle and we support you to decide for yourself.

We focused on Christianity and Judaism, but there are many other religious people that like to swing. There are sexy Mormons, Buddhists, Muslims, Hindus and many other religions that you will encounter in the swinging world. It doesn't really matter what religion you follow. You should think about how strictly you want to follow the words of your spiritual book as opposed to following the spirit of those words. Ultimately, it is up to you to pray and reflect on your personal religious beliefs to determine if they conflict with the principles of swinging.

There are many different levels of swinging. So you might find that some levels of soft swap are more acceptable with your religious beliefs. You might also feel that all levels of swinging, including full swap, are ok since you are honest and together with your spouse. We aren't here to decide for you. This is something that you should think about and talk about together so you can feel comfortable with whatever decision you make. The world is not a simple place and we aren't going to judge anyone for deciding how they want to live their life when they aren't harming anyone else.

Our Swinging Journal: Religious services at a swinger resort...

It's morning and we are still exhausted from last night's party. We were at Temptation Resort in Cancun and the DJ had us dancing all night long. The ladies were dancing so much that "accidentally" all of their dresses fell off so they kept dancing in just their g-strings to the loud cheering of the other dancers. The ladies looked so sexy with their hot dance moves and the guys definitely enjoyed dancing alongside their sexy naked ladies. Things quickly got too steamy and we needed to take a naughty break inside a nearby room but I'm getting off topic...

So what were we talking about? Oh yeah, it is morning and the bright Mexican sun is blasting us through the ocean view balcony doors (it's a rough life but someone needs to enjoy it). Those doors were left open because after our naughty rendezvous, we came back and had some romantic fun by ourselves on the balcony and forgot to close it. That's a good thing since we needed to wake up anyway and head down to the pier for the fabulous Cancun Boobs Cruise party.

So what does any of this have to do with religion? Well you see, swingers may live a bit of a debauched lifestyle but we also love to live a generous and caring lifestyle. A well known former Temptation staffer who is now the MC for the Cancun Boobs Cruise had cancer and the swinging community sent thoughts and prayers but we also sent donations to help him. Matter of fact, the donations were so generous that after he recovered from his cancer he was able to send kids he met that were also battling cancer to Disney.

So before a puritanical person judges the swinger community, they might want to actually look at how swingers live their lives. This welcoming community truly loves to help others be happy, healthy & safe. Isn't that really what religion is trying to teach their followers to do?

Sharing Your Swinging Interest

Before we cover this topic, we need to remind our dear readers that you can't trick or coerce your partner into swinging. Too many people are in unhappy relationships and are trying to make their partner into something they aren't. You will have about the same success rate in "convincing" your unhappy partner to be a swinger, that reading this book has in turning you into a homosexual. You either are or are not homosexual, and your spouse is or is not a sex-positive person that might be attracted to the swinging lifestyle. You aren't going to convince them to change who they are, and tricking someone into the lifestyle is often a super quick way to have a bad time.

The preceding paragraph was for men, who are interested in asking their partner to join the lifestyle, and for women, who may be discreetly looking this up. Gasp … what do we mean? Women? Yeah, that's right, women can have a healthy sex drive too! Swinging wouldn't be nearly as fun if that wasn't true, so get over it. If you want to learn how to introduce the possibility of swinging to your sex-positive partner so you can openly communicate your preferences, keep reading.

Hopefully you are in a great relationship. You love your partner and the sex is amazing. Maybe you watched a movie and saw a swinging scene and now you are wondering what it would be like. You've thought about it for some time and think it would be great for your relationship. So how do you start the conversation with your partner? Carefully, very carefully!

Wait a minute. Didn't our kindergarten teacher say that honesty is always the best policy? First of all – this isn't kindergarten. Secondly, honesty can be good, but being too blunt isn't helpful. When you bring up the swinging lifestyle to your partner, some confusing and worrisome thoughts might go through their mind. Here are some of the more common landmines that you need to carefully disarm, or risk damaging your relationship.

Jealousy – When you love someone you greatly value them. It is very natural to feel jealous when you are asked to share what you love most in life. If they didn't feel a little jealous, they might wonder just how much they truly cherish you as a partner. You want to reassure your partner that they are your #1 priority. You are doing this together and coming home together. Your swinging experience is temporary, but your relationship is everlasting.

Insecurity – Your partner may start to wonder why you want to play with others. Is it because they're not good enough for you? Everybody has some insecurity about their body, sexual performance, and other things. You should remind your partner that they are perfect for you.

Reassure them by more frequently complimenting them and verbalizing your feelings about their sexy body. Try giving them the cooking analogy from earlier. Having the best steak for dinner is awesome, but sometimes it's nice to have a cheeseburger for dinner - just for the sake of variety. The cheeseburger isn't better, but it's enjoyable because it's different. Plus, it reminds you to appreciate your amazing steak!

Seeking Greener Pastures – Another big concern your partner might have is that you are trying to use this to find a replacement for them. Swinging can be a safe way to protect your relationship while adding variety to your sex life. The swinging lifestyle is filled with other happy, long-term couples. They aren't looking to run away with you, even if you were to beg them. Playing with other swinger couples helps protect you from singles or recently divorced people that may be looking to form an emotional attachment. The single people in the lifestyle are awesomely grounded and respectful of couples otherwise they would have been politely ostracized.

Fear – Even if you have been clear about how much you love and value your partner, and they feel confident in your relationship, there is still the fear of being outed as swingers or the health risks of having sex with others. Therefore, you should proceed slowly and work together. Between your two smart minds, you can make this happen in a safer manner that adds to your relationship without damaging it. You can take precautions, like agreeing on safety rules. For example, you may have a rule that you won't play within 50 miles of your home or office. You both can read up on safer sex practices to minimize your health risks. We'll chat more about how to minimize your risks so you can maximize the excitement.

It is usually smarter to proceed slower than you want. You need to move at a slow pace that will not endanger the great relationship you have. Swinging is not for everyone, and when you are done with swinging you want to still be able to enjoy your great relationship. Remember that swinging is not a replacement for your relationship! It is one possible avenue to enhance it - assuming (and this is a big assumption) that it is the right match for you and your loved one. Since swinging can be a scary idea, you might want to wait before bringing up swinging directly. Instead, enjoy some indirect sexy communication.

So, how do you communicate your true feelings with your loved one? Let's take a step back and be honest. The communication in your relationship can be improved. Even great relationships can use some improvement when it comes to communication. If you want to have any chance of entering the lifestyle, and staying happy in your relationship at the same time, you should make every effort to boost communication with your partner.

The first step might be to set aside private time that is dedicated to communicating with each other. You can start by checking in with each other after shared experiences to compare and share thoughts. Be honest and open with each other. This is a good time to begin discussing your sexy thoughts and desires, without going straight into your swinging fantasies.

The next step, once you've established strong communication skills, might involve watching some sexy movies together. You can share your feelings about the movie afterwards, including which scenes turned you on the most. The next time you're in the bedroom, see if your partner wants to roleplay some of the scenes they enjoyed from the movie. Watching porn together is common even among vanilla couples, and it's a great way to become more in tune with each other's desires and fantasies.

Remember to take this slow. Don't rush it.
The very slow burn is often the more successful path.

All this sexy communication might lead your partner to voice a strong opinion against swinging. Take that at face value, and treat it like a red light. Respect their opinion, and don't push them. Trying to force your partner into accepting something they don't like will hurt your relationship. Being patient and respecting your partner's feelings will reward you in the long term. You might find their opinion about swinging evolves as you continue to explore your sexuality together. You can keep the discussion open without pressuring your partner, which may lead to them eventually embracing the lifestyle. It is common to hear swingers mention how they talked about the lifestyle for years before they finally felt confident enough to take the plunge. So relax and don't rush. There will still be plenty of sexy swingers to welcome you once you and your partner are both comfortable enough to step inside.

If your partner hasn't voiced any opinion on swinging, and doesn't seem bothered by portrayals of the lifestyle in movies or on TV, you can send up a test balloon to feel your partner out. Perhaps you can tell them you'd like to roleplay a swinger fantasy. Even if your partner responds positively to the idea, and enjoys the roleplaying, that doesn't mean they're ready to enter the lifestyle. Don't rush it.

Let your partner progress at their own pace. If you push the conversation too hard, too soon, you will move outside of their comfort zone and the result is rarely a happy one. Be smart and keep being patient. Is it so awful to keep having sex with only one person, when that person is the most amazing person you know? If your partner has an open mind, it's likely that the hot fantasies will turn into a desire to take another step closer to swinging. Assuming everything is a green light, or at least neutral, then keep moving forward – inch by inch.

Before we entered the lifestyle, we liked to watch Swing on Playboy TV. Swing is a reality show featuring experienced, real-life swinging couples welcoming a newbie couple into the lifestyle. It takes place in a private mansion and features some delightful eye candy! The experienced couples coach the new couples to see if they're ready to enter the lifestyle or if swinging might not be a good idea for their relationship.

It's an awesome resource for newbies or curious vanilla couples. It does a good job demonstrating the sex-positive atmosphere you will encounter in the swinging lifestyle. It is super fun to watch, a bit educational, sexy as heck, and a great way to start a conversation with your partner. Even if you don't decide to test the swinging waters, watching Swing is a good way to start a sexy, intimate evening with your loved one.

To watch this show you can sign up for Playboy TV or just Google "Playboy TV Swing Episode" to find it online. Ask your partner if they'd like to watch this interesting, sexy reality show you found. Create a comfortable, sensual atmosphere. Maybe open a bottle a wine, lay out some chocolates or snacks, and sensually cuddle together as you settle in to watch an episode. Take the time to compliment your partner during the show. Let your partner know they look better to you than the sexy people on the screen. The more you reassure your partner that you find them sexy, the more likely they are to view swinging in a positive light without fear or insecurity.

After the episode, keep cuddling or take your partner to bed. When there is a relaxed moment, ask your partner if they were ever curious about what a real swinger club looked like. Would they ever want to visit one, just to browse - without any swapping? Remember, it is usually best to take baby steps. You don't want to spook your partner. Keep thinking of ways that you can demonstrate and communicate how much you love them and your relationship.

If you don't like Swing, here are some other movies & shows you can try:

- *The Overnight*: a 2015 mystery/comedy about a couple being invited over for dinner by another couple that they don't immediately realize are swingers.

- *Dos Mas Dos (2+2)*: a 2012 comedy about two couples getting bored on a vanilla double date, and one of the couples reveals they also dabble in swinging.

- *Real Life Wife Swap*: a 2004 British documentary about wife swapping.

- *Open Invitation - A Real Swingers Party in San Francisco*: this is more of an adult flick than a traditional movie.

- *Marriage 2.0*: a 2015 movie made by the sex toy company Adam & Eve that is more a frank discussion about relationships and less of a porn film.

- *Eyes Wide Shut*: Stanley Kubrick's 1999 drama isn't about swinging, but rather cheating with some sex party scenes. We mention it because people ask about it but we don't suggest it.

After all this communicating and testing the waters, you should have a good feeling about how your partner feels towards the lifestyle. Conversely, your partner probably realizes that you're interested in swinging. This does not mean you or your partner is ready to start swinging. Chill out. There is no rush. There is always another sexy swinging party, so there is no reason to rush into something you and your partner aren't ready or prepared to handle.

When the time is right and you both feel comfortable, you can test the water by trying out some online swinger sites, a strip club, meet & greet events, or a swinger club. We'll go over these options a bit later in the book.

Our Swinging Journal: Cancun + Tequila = Swinging

One of our earliest encounters with swinging was many years ago in Cancun at the Temptation Resort. The weird thing was that this trip was actually a business meeting. Yeah, we are sure you and the IRS do not believe it, but it is true.

Mr. F. worked on a project with some people that were spread across the USA. Occasionally, they all need to fly to one city for face to face meetings. Lucky for us, that time they found a great deal at Temptation Resort. Cancun is about the same travel time from the west coast & east coast plus it was freaking cold in the middle of winter. Not surprisingly all spouses decided they wanted to come along on this business trip.

So the business meetings are during the day while the spouses stayed back and relaxed. This is a super sexy hotel and when you turn on the TV in your hotel room it automatically started on a complimentary porn channel. It just so happened they were showing a marathon of the Playboy Swing TV show. So while some of us were working, all of the spouses were watching the Playboy Swing reality TV show and then meeting up at the pool to discuss the episodes. This spurred some very strong curiosity from some of the couples and a bunch of theoretical debates.

Since Temptation is an extra sexy hotel it attracts a bit of a swinger friendly clientele. So late at night, there were different swinger couples strolling through the bar looking to make new friends. Some of Mr. F's colleagues took them up on their offers. The others politely declined but kept curiously commenting on that sexy TV show.

Sometimes the best introduction to the lifestyle can be a no-pressure opportunity that just falls into your lap like when you visit a sex-positive resort.

While we don't recommend mixing business with swinging, we do recommend enjoying time at sexy non-judgmental places. It is a good way to make memorable moments regardless of how much or how little you participate. Sharing your sexiness with your special someone is a super experience and everything else is just a bonus. You never know what will happen by exposing yourself to new people & experiences even if you are just spectators.

Swinging Rulebook

As with anything in life, knowing the rules will help you be more successful as a swinger. Rules provide swingers a helpful structure and a clear pathway around troublesome landmines. Rules make it easier on you, your relationship, and the swinger community.

First, let's chat about the common swinging community rules. These are rules you will encounter throughout the different resorts, clubs, and house parties. Of course, each venue has its own set of rules or variations on these common rules, so make sure to check beforehand to avoid offending anyone. More importantly, make sure you and your partner are comfortable with the rules before diving in headfirst.

Always Ask.

This simple rule reminds all swingers that just because we are attending a sex party, we should still ask for permission before touching or playing. If someone says "no thanks" to you, you should not ask again during that event. Don't be surprised if someone says "no thanks". There are countless reasons someone might not want to play and many of them have nothing to do with you. A swinger might not want to play because they don't feel comfortable just yet, or aren't attracted to you, or are too tired, or maybe they know they have had too much to drink. Don't assume it's okay and just start groping. That is a very quick way to be kicked out and blacklisted.

Anyone can say No.

As we've said, it's harder to make a connection when you're swinging because you need everyone involved to be ready to play. For two couples to swing, all four people need to have the right connection and feel up to playing. The swinging community wants everyone to feel comfortable and safe, which is why everyone has the power to say "no" (preferably "no thanks", because that sounds more polite).

Illegal drugs are not welcome.

People on drugs rarely make the best decisions, and this leads to drama or worse: the police showing up. Illegal drugs are not welcome in the lifestyle. This doesn't mean that swinging is 100% drug free. Some people really enjoy their drugs and will find a way to sneak them into an event.

A common drug you'll encounter is marijuana. Regardless of how you feel about marijuana use, you probably want to avoid it when you're swinging. The mellow buzz can kill some of the sexy excitement, and the smell can attract police if you aren't in a legal state. You really don't want to deal with police when you are naked and sweaty!

If you are in a decriminalized state that allows marijuana and you're with marijuana friendly swingers, you will still want to take it easy. You don't want to make bad decisions because you aren't thinking clearly when high, or deal with drama when your swapping partners get too high.

Most swinging events will kick you out for any illegal drugs. About the only drugs welcome at a swinging event are ED pills to help guys perform. Many guys are using those little blue pills, whether they admit it or not. Be smart and talk with your doctor before taking ED pills.

Really Respectful

We're all in this crazy swinging community for the same reason - to have a good time. Being rude or obnoxious is not welcome in this community. Make sure to always be polite and respect each other. We all look different and none of us are perfect supermodels; remember to respect others even if they don't look like the sex god or goddess of your dreams.

You should know that in general, others in the community will respect you in return. Most of us will find you sexier than your ego even realizes. Swingers tend to be happier people, which is probably because we get to enjoy a lot more sex than the vanilla world. Sexually-satisfied people tend to just be nicer to be around than the sexually-frustrated meanies you can find in the vanilla world!

Crucially Confidential

You will learn things about other people in the swinging community, and others will learn things about you, as you spend more time together. All swingers are expected to respect other swingers and not share any personal or confidential information with others. Some swingers are publicly open about their swinging status, but most people in the lifestyle prefer not to share this part of their life with the vanilla world.

When in doubt, think about the "need to know" principle. Don't share confidential information unless it's on a real need-to-know basis. Most of the time, that is not the case. Protect any confidential information you might know, and expect other swingers to do the same!

Those are some common rules in the lifestyle. They are important, but they are not as important as your own private rules. These are the rules that you make with your partner to ensure everyone plays within the comfort zone and you go home happy, with your relationship securely intact.

Each couple makes different rules, and those rules will often evolve over time to better match what works for their relationship. Some swingers may not like your rules or you might not like their rules. That is ok. We all respect each other and know that our own relationship takes priority over swinging. At the end of these temporary swinging encounters, we're all going home with our significant other. No one wants to drive home unhappy, screaming about what did or didn't happen during playtime. Play it safe, follow the rules, and only go as fast as the slowest person in the group. Don't pressure anyone to break or bend their rules.

Here are some sample personal rules to talk over with your partner to see if you want to follow them or not.

No "Taking One For the Team"?

This means that neither of you will play if either of you isn't attracted to their play partner (or just doesn't feel like playing). No one is going to suffer through something they don't enjoy just so their partner can have a good time. You should try to learn what each of you likes in a play partner, and figure out some way to communicate whether it's a no-go or full speed ahead. Using codewords or signals can be helpful.

No Kissing?

This is a common rule for first timers, who often drop it quickly once their comfort level rises. If you are a first timer and it makes you feel more comfortable, use this rule. Many people find it hard not to kiss during sexy time, so they may decline to play with you - but that's their loss!

No Full Swap (No Penetration)?

Another very common rule. Some couples prefer to only engage in soft swap. Kissing, caressing, groping and oral – all of which are very hot - is what they want. Many beginners start this way and some veteran full swappers migrate to this rule over time. It can help defuse emotional issues, ease STI worries, and remove a lot of the stress and performance anxiety that come with full swap.

Same Room vs Separate Room Play?

Earlier, we chatted about same room vs separate room play. There are pros and cons for each, and you can decide for yourself what's really a pro and what's a con. You should talk with your partner to figure out what is comfortable for both of you. Some couples are ok with separate play dates, others are only comfortable with the girls playing separately with each other, and still others want everyone involved together at all times. There are lots of possible arrangements, so figure out what you both want. Be ready to change this rule – and any other rules on the list – over time; people evolve, relationships evolve, and feelings evolve. Your rules should evolve, too.

No Anal?

Anal play is much more common in the lifestyle than in the vanilla world because swingers know how to tenderly take advantage of those sensitive nerve endings. There are some truly talented swingers who know just the right way to engage in finger play or anal sex. If your partner has some big male anatomy you might not have liked it in the past, but in the lifestyle you might find some men with just the right sized equipment for you to enjoy it. You might not be ready for this or want to reserve it for your special partner. As always the choice is yours.

No Repeats?

Some couples won't repeat play with the same couple within a certain timeframe (one month, six months, a year, whatever) to avoid any emotional connections. This helps keep swinging confined to physical enjoyment and away from your personal emotional relationship. Other swingers like this rule so they can enjoy more sexually variety in life. You can adjust this rule to fit your liking.

No Solo Communication?

Figure out how to handle communications so there are no surprises or secrets. Often, a couple will have the man manage their online profile(s) so the lady doesn't need to deal with any annoying fakers. Once you make contact with a real couple, how are you going to handle ongoing communication? Some people love online flirting, while others find it causes emotional angst. One solution is no solo chats. You can start up a group text or KIK, which is easier than trying to get everyone on a group call.

Condoms Required?

Chat with your loved one to figure out your condom policy. Do you need condoms for oral? Will you play with another couple who doesn't always use condoms? There are some couples that have sex without condoms in the lifestyle, and you should talk with your partner about your comfort level before you encounter them.

Avoiding or Seeking Unicorns?

Single ladies, AKA unicorns, can be awesome. Single ladies are definitely in high demand in the lifestyle. Most swinging single ladies are amazingly awesome. Some unicorns might place extra requests to help them feel safer and more comfortable with a couple or single guy. This extra work makes some couples not interested in playing with unicorns. Even a super awesome unicorn who does nothing wrong can expose some sticky issues in your relationship, because threesomes rarely end up with all three people having perfectly equal amounts of attention. Some couples prefer to keep things simpler and stick with only other couples so no one feels left out or ignored.

Drinking Limits?

There is usually plenty of booze at swinging parties. Just like illegal drugs, drinking too much rarely leads to good decisions. Drinking too much can also lead to accidental rule-breaking. You might want to set limits on the booze. Most swinger guys naturally drink less, because no one wants to have an alcohol-induced failure to launch when they're surrounded by hot ladies. Newer ladies tend to be more likely to over imbibe as they drink away their nerves. Be safe and watch your alcohol intake – and keep an eye on each other's intake, as well. You might not want to go home yet, but if your partner has had too much to drink, you're probably better off taking a time out or leaving early.

These are just some of the rules that couples will have. Don't be surprised if some couples break their own rules mid-play. It can certainly happen when you are caught up in the moment, but you should never encourage someone to break the rules. You should always respect their rules just like you want them to respect your rules.

There is no right or wrong set of rules. You should think about what will work and won't work for your relationship. It is common for couples to reduce their rules as they spend more time in the lifestyle, and replace a strict rulebook with a few basic principles like play safe, have fun, take care of each other.

Swinger Pact

Some couples like to sign a swingers pact or contract between each other when they enter the lifestyle. It can help make sure that both people understand what they are about to do together. If you are worried about divorce, you might want to rethink if your relationship is strong enough for this and chat with a real lawyer for a proper contract. We aren't lawyers and this is not intended to be a legal document. This is more intended as a tool to help couples honestly communicate with each other. Here is our sample document for you to modify as you like. You can find a printer friendly version of this available on our website www.SwingersHelp.com.

Our Swinger Pact

Being romantically committed in our sexual mind & body, we agree to jointly embark on a sensual experience during which we will temporarily rescind the rules of our monogamous relationship. We promise each other to be open, honest and loyal at all times during this experience. We will not lie or mislead our partner. If we feel jealous, confused or another unpleasant emotion we will communicate with our partner. We will check in with each other during this sensual experience every ___ hour(s).

This pact permits both of us to freely explore our passion and lust, free of the limitations of a traditional relationship. We freely permit each other to engage in sexual exploration with other couples, males, and females. During this sensual experience we agree to not form any emotional attachments with any of the people we meet. We will respect the comfort level of our partner and abide by the rules outlined below. If a rule is broken, this pact can be immediately terminated by either of us.

Together, we will strive towards non-judgmental exploration of our sexual desires. We will support each other as we venture only as far as we are both comfortable. Regardless of what happens, we agree that our primary and ultimate goal is a better relationship between the two of us. We both love and value each other above all else. Together we want to enjoy and share as much of life as possible.

Our Agreed Rules

Allowed	Not Allowed		Special Note(s)
_____	_____	Emailing	_____
_____	_____	Calling	_____
_____	_____	Flirting	_____
_____	_____	Touching	_____
_____	_____	Kissing	_____
_____	_____	Oral Sex (giving)	_____
_____	_____	Oral Sex (receiving)	_____
_____	_____	Male/Male Play	_____
_____	_____	Female/Female Play	_____
_____	_____	Soft Swap	_____
_____	_____	Full Swap	_____
_____	_____	Same Room Play	_____
_____	_____	Separate Room Play	_____

Extra Rules

_____

_____

Signature #1 _____

Signature #2 _____

Relationship Toolbox

Now that we are clear on your rules, let's take a moment to empower you with good tools to safeguard your relationship!

Communication

You may be tired of reading the word "communication" by now. Honestly, it really is a very important thing for your relationship as you enter the lifestyle. If you don't have great communication skills, think twice and take a step back. Good communication is how you stay connected and avoid mistakes.

We aren't saying you need to communicate everything or constantly check in with each other every 5 minutes. We all know those couples and it's great if it makes them happy but most of us would consider that behavior to be oversharing. You don't need to text your partner about what you are eating for lunch but you should make sure to communicate the more important things, like bumping into your ex-fiancé at lunch.

For everyone that has been in a relationship long enough, you will eventually realize some things can cause more trouble than they're worth, and shouldn't be brought up. Maybe your partner doesn't want to hear about your ex-fiancé and they already communicated that preference to you. Be smart and talk with each other so you know what should or should not be shared.

If you ask a marriage counselor, they will tell you countless tales of how bad communication sabotages relationships and ultimately makes many divorce lawyers rich. Be smart and communicate with each other. Talk about how you both feel about your relationship, and where you want it to go. Share your honest feelings about the lifestyle and ask your partner about their feelings. Communication is a magical potion for sexy relationships, so use it often.

Honesty

All the communication in the world is not going to help if you aren't honest when communicating with each other. If you don't trust your partner enough to be 100% honest, then you should probably look for a new partner. Your partner loves you and wants to support you. They can't support you if you don't honestly share your feelings and concerns with them.

Have enough faith in your partner to share your innermost thoughts. Some of those thoughts may lead to short term disagreements, but in the long term it is much healthier to be honest. You will be more strongly connected knowing that you're both being fully honest with each other.

Guys, if she asks you how she looks and you always respond with the same generic response (like "you look fine"), it won't help reassure her.

Being honest and letting her know she looks better in one outfit or another will help her trust and rely on you.

Ladies, if he asks about your comfort level, be honest. Don't lie and let your emotional discomfort grow until there is a massive blow up.

You should both be smart and honestly share with each other.

Boundaries

Now that we are honestly communicating with each other, let's talk about some of the more important aspects in the lifestyle … boundaries. The best part is that you make your own boundaries with your partner. You should decide together what is too special to be shared and will be reserved just for yourselves.

Some couples set physical boundaries. These boundaries can be soft swap versus full swap, or no kissing allowed, or backdoor play only with your spouse. Talk with your partner about what physical boundaries you both need to feel secure and safe in your relationship.

You can also set emotional boundaries. These boundaries can include no private communications with other swingers, just doing group communications. Another example would be to only play once a month, so swinging doesn't take over your relationship and vanilla friendships.

Supporting Each Other

You both want to demonstrate to each other that you are their biggest cheerleader. Passively listening to them is nice, but proactively taking steps to show they are your #1 priority in life is even better. Yes, you might be visiting a sexy lending library and playing with other people, but swingers are not your favorite book and never will be your favorite book. Make sure you use your actions each day, and at each swinger event, to demonstrate to your partner that they are your priority.

Talk with each other to identify your common preferences and work together to build a strong synergy towards those goals. Remember to be patient with your partner. If they need extra time, give them all the time they want.

Be loyal to each other. When you are chatting with others, always make sure to mention the many fantastic things about your partner.

Share your passion for each other. Don't wait for swinger events to be passionate. You love your partner the most, so show them just how passionate they make you feel on a day-to-day basis.

Demonstrate how much you care for your partner. If you are at any party, make sure your partner is your first priority. Think about what they might enjoy. Is their favorite dance song playing? Then bring them to the dance floor. Is their drink almost gone? Then get them another drink. Doing nice things for each other is a great way to let your actions scream how much you care about your partner.

Avoid being judgmental or overly critical of your partner. Life isn't easy and you are both trying your best to make each other happy. Focus on the positive. Being thankful for all the positive things your partner brings to your relationship is important.

Surviving Your Fight

We all want a life that's free from drama, but very few of us get to have that life. For the vast majority of people in relationships, mistakes will be made and those mistakes can lead to misunderstandings or fights. Remember you both love each other very much, and you're both very passionate about your relationship. You can get past it and use it as a learning experience to make your relationship even stronger.

The first step in getting through your fight is to calm down. Often, there is a trigger for the fight that pushes us well past our comfort zone. We want to avoid escalating the misunderstanding to a full blown fight. Focus first on calming down. Try taking deep breaths. If you need to leave the room for a few minutes, do so. Count to ten before you say anything.

After you calm down, you can work on communicating with each other. Talk through the series of events that lead to the misunderstanding. Why did you or your partner find yourself outside your comfort zone?

Once you understand what caused the situation, you can work together to make adjustments that will better protect your relationship and both of your feelings. Success in the lifestyle comes when you can enjoy your desires within your mutually agreed boundaries. You might need to make new rules, adjust old rules, or take a break from swinging.

If you have a bad fight and can't handle it on your own, seek out a therapist to help. When looking for a therapist, seek out a sex-positive therapist. They can help you figure out if the lifestyle is a good match or if it is better staying in the vanilla world. Some traditional therapists can be too judgmental and not open to different options.

Our Swinging Journal: Fight Club!

Another weekend and another swinging date with some friends of ours. We have had some really great times with this couple unfortunately lately it was more of a rocky patch with these swinging friends. The swinging community is generally friendly but misunderstandings can happen. We were in the middle of one and needed to act mature before we could focus back on sexy fun.

To help smooth things over, the four of us decided to have a vanilla dinner so we could talk about things & clear the air. Dinner does the trick and we all feel like we have successfully pushed the reset button. The focus is definitely turning to sexy fun as the flirting picks up. Our poor waiter just couldn't understand why each spouse was now openly flirting with the other person as we seductively licked our lips and ran our hands up the inside of thighs. It was getting hot and we needed to find a private place.

We all jump into one car as the guys try to find a hotel room while the ladies keep distracting them with sensual touches and seductive kisses on their necks and earlobes. Unfortunately, everything was booked, so we decided to just take a walk into a nearby park for us to have separate good night make out sessions.

After a good long time of saying good-bye with our lips & tongues, we are back in the car and driving home by ourselves. Dr. G asked Mr. F about his sexy time and discovered that Mr. F's make-out sessions didn't involve much of his lips but rather his male anatomy being kissed which led to a fight over the unclear play boundaries.

We did not communicate clearly enough about our boundaries &
expectations since we this was an impromptu vanilla dinner. Our
magic mind meld failed that night. We clearly aren't perfect and
make mistakes. The good news is we rediscovered that even in
bad situations, we are both 100%%honest with each other and
committed to our relationship. We both felt bad for the
miscommunication & inspired to work even harder for mistake
free fun.

Mistakes happen because life isn't perfect. The secret is to
keep the mistakes small and fix them before they grow out of
control.

Handling Your Feelings

Most of us don't handle our feelings and emotions in the best way. We enjoy the good stuff and ignore the bad stuff until it blows up in our faces. It may be normal or natural, but it sure isn't healthy or smart! Since our driver licenses say we're adults, we're going to pretend to be mature about our negative feelings.

You are not the first person to feel a certain way –jealous, insecure, guilty, resentful – and you won't be the last. But you can be the person who's smart enough to defuse that bad feeling before it blows up. Life, your relationship, and your sexy swinging fun will all be a lot more enjoyable if you maximize the good feelings.

Before we dive into these emotions, let's remember yet again that successful swinging is a team effort. Like any good team, we should step up to take care of each other. If your partner is having a problem, you should consider it a team problem and stand by their side, tackling it together. Your partner's feelings are your responsibility, and vice versa. Working together as a team makes it easier to overcome these obstacles.

Here are some ways you might find yourself feeling as you enter the lifestyle:

Guilty

Guilt is a very common emotion in the lifestyle. Most of us have been raised to believe that certain things are or are not acceptable. For example, it is not acceptable to be a "slut"...unless you're a young, single man, and even then there's only a small window of time before you become a "dirty old man". Judgmental vanilla people will say sleeping around with lots of people is "dirty": it's immoral, it's irresponsible, it's hedonistic...you get the picture.

These ideas are drilled into us by family, friends, and religion. People who believe they are the authority on the right and wrong way to live think they're doing you a favor, trying to shape your opinion to match theirs. All those people who try to make you feel guilty never stop to consider the values you believe in.

Of course swingers have ethics and values. Swingers can be religious, swingers can be charitable, and swingers can be incredibly kind. Swingers don't steal, cheat, or murder (well, not any swingers we know!). Swingers can be great parents, hard workers, loyal friends and loving siblings.

What sets swingers apart from the people who want to judge them? Swingers understand that you can enjoy sex with a new person and separate it from the love and trust you have with your long-term significant other. Swingers have no problem visiting the sexy lending library, enjoying a new book, then going back home with their favorite book.

Swinging can be especially liberating for women, who too often experience intense pressure to be "good girls". It's not that crazy to think that a woman is smart enough to know what she wants from life. She can decide, with her partner, on what relationship rules they want to follow together. If she likes sex, and he likes sex, and they're comfortable with their boundaries, there is no reason why they should prevent themselves from enjoying life to the fullest. Life is too short to worry about what other people think, especially people who never took the time to try and understand your perspective.

For consensual, informed, sex-positive adults, swinging can be good fun. Your only moral responsibility is to be honest with yourself and with your partner. If you're feeling guilty about enjoying yourself so much, stop and ask yourself: what is there, really, to feel guilty about? Are you harming anyone? Are you harming yourself? Are you betraying anyone's trust, or being cruel? The answer is probably no – you're just having fun, and what's life without a little fun?

Nervous

It's normal to feel nervous when you try something new. You were nervous when you tried to ride a bike, or went on your first date, or started your new job. Swinging is likely extremely new to you – probably more foreign and new than that first bike ride or kiss.

Your nervousness is natural, but it doesn't have to overwhelm you. Here are a few simple steps to help you overcome your nerves:

#1 - Prepare Together - Reading this book and doing some online research will help you better understand the lifestyle so it's not a total mystery. You'll know what to expect, and will be ready when those situations arise. Talk with your partner and make sure you understand each other, so you can better support each other as you begin to explore the lifestyle. The more you talk, the more you will connect, and that's a wonderful thing! You aren't doing this alone – lean on your partner, and let them lean on you.

#2 - Visualize - Imagine all the different possible scenarios and how they could unfold. This will help you avoid surprises (and could also lead to some very hot role playing as you and partner help each other visualize). This joint-visualizing further reinforces your connection and helps ensure you're on the same page. It is assuring to know you are a strong team, working together so you can have fun together.

#3 - Enjoying Excitement - Yes, this is exciting and awesome - so enjoy it! The lifestyle is a no-pressure environment. You can enjoy as much or as little of the excitement as you want, and stop at any time. There is no rush. You can go as slow as you like and reconnect with your partner each time as you relive the excitement until your next swinging dabble.

Insecure

Even veteran swingers get insecure sometimes. A 2014 study found that 36% of men and 60% of women had negative thoughts about their appearance on a weekly basis![3] And that's just insecurity about appearances: people also feel insecure about their sexual performance, the size of their paycheck, their athleticism, their fashion sense, how popular they are…the list goes on and on. When you consider all the things people can feel insecure about, the number of people who feel insecure about something in their life is likely much higher.

Those insecurities can be compounded and made much worse by vanilla society. We are constantly surrounded by freakishly good-looking celebrities, photoshopped models, and completely unrealistic standards for what is beautiful and sexy. Companies make money off our insecurities: think of the diet and make-up industries. Women must have long lashes, plump lips, and no wrinkles - and they must buy make-up to achieve this unrealistic image. Everyone should be thin and muscular – and a new exercise machine or diet pill offers the solution. But all the make-up in the world, and every diet pill on the market, still won't make you look like that model in the magazine – the picture is photoshopped so much that the model doesn't even look like that model in real life!

And the swinging world has its own particular sources of insecurities. Are we good at flirting? Are we performing well in bed? Do we make our play partners want more of us? Will our partners still prefer us after playing with other people? This is why insecurity is a very common problem even with veteran swingers.

---

[3] https://www.aol.com/article/2014/02/24/loveyourselfie/20836450/

The first step to battling insecurity is to ignore that negative inner voice in your mind. Instead, feed your positive inner voice. Focus on all of the amazing things about you. If anyone is bringing negativity into your life, minimize your exposure to him or her. We want to surround ourselves with lovers, not haters.

The second step is to communicate with your partner so they can better understand and support you. Strong swingers will be great cheerleaders for each other.

The third step is to make a plan to improve yourself so you are better each and every day. You don't need to solve anything in a single day – and you'll likely find it's impossible to fix those insecurities in 24 short hours - but you want to take at least one step forward each day. One little step each day becomes a big change after a month, and awesome improvement after a year. It all starts with taking just one little step forward each day. Moving forward is how we all become even more awesome.

The truth is that we're not all equal. But we are all awesome. If it helps, think of yourself as a french fry. Who doesn't love french fries? French fries come in countless ways. There are curly fries, seasoned fries, shoestring fries, steak fries, cheese fries, and much, much more. And even the same type of french fry is going to be different than the other fries: shorter, crispier, saltier, longer, softer, or more oily. When you're eating french fries, do you dislike them if they're bigger, smaller, salty, seasoned, or something else? Doubtful. You might prefer curly fries to steak fries, but you probably still enjoy steak fries. You're a french fry: awesome, no matter what. Plus, out of all the different types of french fries, you're someone's favorite french fry, which is pretty special!

Remember to communicate & focus on the positive things about you. There is so much positive to think about that you'll have no time to dwell on the negative!

Jealous

We know that we've already talked about jealousy, but it's such a big potential issue that we want to revisit it. There's no such thing as too much communication when it comes to jealousy issues.

Even veteran swingers with years of experience and plenty of sexy self-confidence can find themselves brushing up against a jealousy issue at some point. You want to work with your partner to quickly identify, communicate, and defuse those triggers before they blow up.

Let's say that you are handling the jealousy between you and your partner just fine. What about being jealous with your play partners? This is a commonly overlooked pitfall. You might develop some close swinging friends, then one night they choose to play with someone else. This is a regular and natural occurrence in the swinging lifestyle, and it can cause some jealous feelings inside you.

You need to remember that swinging is more about recreational sexy time, less about emotional commitment. If you aren't careful, a swinging relationship might slide into a blurry mix of polyamory. This isn't necessarily a bad thing; it just means that you click with each other on an amazing level. If you can't handle the jealous feelings you encounter with other couples, you might find it simpler to create a rule that you will only have repeat play every two, three, or four weeks (or months, or whatever works for you.) This can help you avoid getting too close to any one couple and accidentally building possessive feelings towards them.

Our Swinging Journal: Always leave them wanting more....

Another weekend and another swinging date but this was a special one. We were surprising our friend for his birthday. His wife told him they were having a family birthday dinner with his mother in law. He wasn't exactly excited with this birthday plan but soon became crazy excited when we slid into the restaurant booth. Dinner was great and we had an awesome time chatting but all of us wanted to move on to the sexier dessert course so we grabbed the check and headed   back to their place.

The birthday boy got a fire going and we all lounged together sipping champagne on the floor. Things become even hotter as we started kissing. It was a bit like high school as we each had an hour long make out session. Sensual kissing is sooooo enjoyable. Most surprising thing is that somehow we didn't break a single champagne glass despite the flailing arms and legs during an hour long makeout session.

Ok, kissing is enjoyable but everyone needs a proper release so we head to a bedroom with a massive king size bed. We pair off and start having a rocking time, as all four of us made that massive bed move a good bit. We didn't last long because we were all too amped up after kissing and grinding for an hour but wow was it hot. Mr. F heads off to grab some water bottles from the kitchen and more importantly to give the ladies a chance to give our friend his birthday present - a double blowjob. The double blowjob turned into a surprise girl play

---

session. As the ladies were having sexy fun with each other, the guys hung back for a little bit enjoying the hot show. Then the guys couldn't just watch anymore, and they helped form the sexiest sandwich. As each guy thrusted it just drove the ladies bodies further and further into each other. So surprise, surprise it wasn't too long that before the guys couldn't hold out anymore.

It's getting late now and we are thinking of heading home but they just pulled out a fruit platter and trust us, a chilled fruit platter really hits the spot after a hot and steamy workout. Of course when you are lounging around naked and feeding each other fruit its only a matter time before the caressing and kissing restarts. Which inevitably turns into a fresh round of sexy fun. We commend the bed manufacturer because the four of us gave that bed a thorough workout.

Now it's really late and our friends want us to watch some TV with them with the not so subtle hope for another round. We are sexy people but we not all powerful sex gods so we make our excuses and head home with the biggest and most satisfied smiles. We learned a long time ago that it is smarter to leave your swinging partners while everyone is still wanting more. No one wants a fun play session to end but it is better to stop when you still have energy to get home safely and before you pull your groin (but that story is for another time).

Managing Time

Swingers like to joke that it's called the "lifestyle" because it can take over your life. Having fun with your swinger friends can take up all your free time, and even steal time from other responsibilities if you aren't careful. What takes up so much time?

Personal Upkeep - Swingers want to make sure we maintain our sexiness, so we spend a lot of time going to the gym and working out. We want a sexy body, but we really want great fitness so we can keep up with those hours-long sex marathons that can keep us up until sunrise. We also spend a lot of time pampering ourselves with haircuts, manicures, pedicures, hair removal, facials, and anything else that makes us feel good and look good. Even guys spend time pampering themselves, because smart swinger guys know that looking great leads to sexier playtime - and don't we all want more sexy playtime?

Online Flirting – Many swingers have an online profile, and some have multiple online profiles on different websites. We need to check these profiles every day, or at least once every few days, so we can quickly respond to messages from other interested swingers. You can be as active or inactive as you like online, but the more you participate on swinger websites, the more chances you have of making sexy connections. Once we do make a new connection with another friendly swinger, we can spend a lot of time talking on the phone, texting or chatting via kik with our new swinger friends.

Social Calendar - There are real-life swinger events just about every day and night, even during the week. Most of the events happen on the weekends, and for most swingers there is a busy social calendar to manage. You can easily keep yourself busy signing up for a hotel takeover, or going to a swinger club, or having fun at a house party, or going on a private date, or taking a weekend off and staying home with your favorite person.

So how can you manage all of this without going crazy? Divide and conquer!

The swinger lifestyle really does improve communication, and not just when it comes to feelings and issues. It's really invigorating to chat with your partner about which naughty event you're going to enjoy the most. Having so many enjoyable options to choose from is a really nice problem to have!

We suggest setting some limits early on, so you don't become overwhelmed. Some veteran swinger couples will go out every week, and sometimes even attend multiple parties in a weekend. This doesn't mean they are playing at every event, it just means they like attending sexy swinger parties, making new friends, and reconnecting with old friends. The lifestyle is a great way for adults to make a new batch of non-judgmental friends.

If you are new, you might only want to go out once or twice a month. This way you have plenty of time for your vanilla activities. More importantly, you have plenty of time to reflect and debrief with each other after each new step into the lifestyle.

After you figure out what limits work for you, it's usually helpful for the guy to become the caretaker of your online profile. Guys: it sounds like fun, and it is, but it isn't all fun. You are going to be the gatekeeper to prevent creepers and picture-collectors away from your sexy lady. Ladies, you should still participate by taking sexy pictures and adding some information in your own words, so other couples can get a good sense of your personality. For many ladies, that is the extent of their participation online. If a couple contacts your online profile, the male half usually handles the initial screening before getting his better half involved in the decision-making process.

Ladies, just because your man is babysitting the online profile doesn't mean you have nothing to do. Many ladies in the lifestyle take care of the social calendar, which can be very tricky. You need to juggle work time, family time, vanilla commitments, and swinging parties. Sometimes we wish rocket scientists could help us figure out our schedules, because there are too few hours and too many sexy swinger events!

Many first-time swingers find themselves dealing with angry vanilla friends. You used to always be available, and now your vanilla friends are having trouble arranging time with you. They don't know it's because you're busy attending all of these awesome lifestyle parties. Scheduling time for your vanilla friends on a Sunday morning can be a bad idea, because you can find yourself leaving a sexy Saturday night swinger event around 3AM. Be careful with that social calendar as you juggle everything.

Most importantly, you should make sure to schedule private time for just the two of you. As much fun as you both have in the lifestyle, it is important to reconnect with each other. You want to be reminded how lucky you both are to enjoy such a great life together. As much as we may enjoy the novelty of a new play partner, a swinger's ultimate pleasure comes from sharing these temporary experiences with their all-time favorite partner.

Our Swinging Journal: Communicating Clearly aka Secret Signals Help

Hey honey, look we just got a message from that local swinger couple we have been emailing. They invited us over for drinks in their hot tub. Sounds like a great time, let's do it. So we make plans. The day arrives, we grab a bottle of wine & head out.

We pull up and go over a few signals to help us discreetly figure out if each other is up for some sexy play time and walk up to the front door. They open the door & no big surprise they don't look as sexy as their online photos. Sigh! Too many swingers just don't update their pics. But they are super nice and cool, so let's see what happens.

We walk in and there is a sexy roaring fire which makes it nice & toasty ... all the better for us to relax and enjoy cocktails with some fun conversation. We share stories & tips about different clubs and swinger vacation spots. Things are heating up, figuratively & literally so we give each other the GO signal for sexy time and then ask about their hot tub. This immediately gets us invited to test it out with them.

We all strip down in the living room still feeling very toasty from the fire. Things are looking up all around, if you know what we mean as we all enjoy the sexy sights. We head out to their hot tub. Thankfully the neighbors aren't too close so we can enjoy ourselves our skinny dip in their hot tub.

Soon after getting into the hot tub we start kissing and then seeing who can give better kisses on different body parts. Wow, this is escalating pretty fast so let's head inside. We all go into the master bedroom and start to have fun on the bed. Unfortunately the fun doesn't last too long. The other wife is not really responding to the attention to her boobies and keeps saying to go rougher. The other husband keeps going too hard on the boobies. In hindsight, they clearly are a great match for each other because they both like crazy rough boobie play. The problem is neither of us realizes the problem the other person is having. So after a bit of time, Dr. G says "I want to play with you" because she is looking for relief. Mr. F responds "I'll play with you at home" because he wants to get out of this accidental BDSM moment. Dr. G thinks she is getting blown off and keeps suffering till she says she isn't feeling well and needs to go home. Mr. F is thankful and wondering what took her so long to agree to go home. Needless to say we had a very interesting chat on the ride out of there as we headed to the local pharmacy to get pain relief ointment for those poor mistreated boobies.

Bottom line, you can never communicate enough and secret signals can help.

Looking Your Best

We all want to look good regardless if we are in the vanilla world or the swinging lifestyle. Let's spend some time to boost our sex appeal by fixing up our body and wardrobe. We are going to bring up the things you are afraid to ask and the stuff other people are thinking but too polite to tell you. This should help you attract more swinging friends and make your special someone desire you even more!

Frisky Fitness

No matter your fitness level, there's a place for you in the swinging lifestyle. There are overweight swingers, bodybuilding swingers, marathon-running swingers, and everything in between. You can and should be your natural self.

We encourage you to be your best because you want to make a great first impression. How many people are really at their physical best? Life is busy: between work and family, most of us don't have the time to visit the gym – or the motivation. As much as you love being sexy for your partner, it's easy to get complacent and put on a few pounds when you've settled into a long-term relationship. The lifestyle is a great

125

motivating tool to get yourself back in shape! You will enjoy the lifestyle much more if you boost your fitness level.

We're going to be completely honest here: if you want to engage in sexual play with hot, sexy people, you should try your best to become a hot, sexy person!

Most women are already in good shape, or at least better shape than their men. It's common in the lifestyle to see an attractive lady who clearly takes pride in her fitness, accompanied by a man who hasn't spent enough time working on his fitness. Many men overvalue their attractiveness, and don't see the ways they can improve their fitness. They look at their smoking hot wives and think that they must be smoking hot, too! In reality, some of those men are barely smoldering.

So, guys, please take our advice: get into better shape so you can match your lady's sexy body! You certainly don't have to look like a model, but you want to make it clear that you take care of your body and stay up on your fitness.

Improving your fitness isn't just about looking good. Men with a 42" waist are 50% more likely to have erection problems than men with a 32" waist. Yikes! It takes a lot of stamina and energy to keep up with swingers: play sessions can last hours at a time. You might be fully capable of performing for 5-10 minutes in your bedroom, and have a great time for those 5-10 minutes. But can you keep rocking and rolling for hours?

Viagra can help, and so can using a condom that dulls sensations for guys, but if you're out of shape you might just find yourself tapping out halfway through a play session. You don't want to be out of breath and tired after just 10 minutes – not only will you miss out on a ton of sexy fun, you also probably won't be invited back to play with those people.

A good step in improving your shape is to look at your diet. A simple way to start being healthier is to drink more water. Drinking water is great for your body: it will keep you hydrated when you hit the gym, make your skin look sexier, help fight bloating (sounds counterintuitive, but it's true!). Drinking water before meals helps you feel fuller sooner, and if you replace soda with water you'll cut a ton of sugary calories.

Try to eat more fruits and vegetables, and less processed foods. Check with your doctor about developing a diet that will work for you. You don't have to starve yourself or cut out carbs or stop eating red meat – you should be able to find a diet that makes sense with your lifestyle and helps you feel and be healthier.

When it comes to working out, you should focus more on aerobic exercise and less on strength training. Strength training is fun, and ladies often enjoy being picked up and pleasured. Women with sexy, toned muscles can perform amazing pole dancing feats. There's nothing wrong with plenty of strength training – but your aerobic level is much more beneficial to your stamina during play time. Running, cycling, swimming, and other aerobic activities will help improve your lung function, stamina, and heart rate, so you can perform during a marathon swinging sex session!

Again, no one needs to be a supermodel to have sexy fun in the lifestyle. Often people you'll meet will be carrying a few extra pounds, and maybe a wrinkle or two. We all have our flaws and the parts of our bodies that just never look right to us. The point is to take pride in your body and work out so that your batteries are super charged for sexy time. It's a real buzz kill when your muscles cramp up in the middle of a super sexy play session, especially when you're just two orgasms short of an all-time record! Bonus tip: bananas are high in potassium, which helps to fend off muscle cramps during a three-hour romp...oh, the swinging lifestyle can be so much fun!

To get the most out of your swinging experience, try to achieve your best level of fitness. The sexier you look, the more confident you will feel, and that will make you more comfortable while you're playing. Hit the gym, take care of yourself, and be prepared to use your new, improved body to achieve some truly amazing, orgasmic feats!

Gorgeous Grooming

Just like you want to make your body as fit as it can be, you also want to take care of it in other ways. It is very important to make sure that your first impression is your best impression! This means you both need to step up your grooming game.

For many swingers, they've been in long-term relationships for so long that they can barely remember being single. All those little tricks you used to employ to attract someone at a bar have been lost in the day-to-day of your relationship. Your partner loves you and thinks you're sexy. They overlook the over-grown hairs, the red skin, the slightly-greasy hair. They may even have grown to like your B.O. – or at least not notice it!

Potential play partners, on the other hand, don't already love you, and they might not find those little flaws so easy to overlook. Swingers tend to take really good care of themselves and expect the same in potential play partners. People in the lifestyle would much rather go home and play with their own sexy hot partner than go slumming with slobs.

The most obvious question many new people have is simple: what about hair? Down there, everywhere – we all have hair. In the swinging lifestyle, hair below the shoulders is usually on the endangered species list. That goes for men and women. Women will usually have smooth legs and a smoother pubic area. Oral sex is much hotter without any hair getting in the way! That goes for men, too. Going down on a hairy guy isn't usually fun.

Most swinger guys will be smooth all over. This includes getting rid of most chest hair, back hair, and pubic hair - or trimming it extremely short. If you want a visual idea, check out an online porn site and watch the videos. You'll see most of the male porn stars are clean shaven or very closely trimmed. The sasquatch look aint super sexy to most people.

By the way, the hairless trend is making crabs a thing of the past, so you have one less STI to worry about! Do your part and groom that body hair!

Here's a quick grooming guide to help you fit in with other swingers, who already know how best to present themselves in the lifestyle.

Hairstyle – Most people have a contemporary hair style and that is good. Some people are still rocking a hairdo that was in fashion 20 years ago. If you haven't updated your hair style in a long time, ask a hair stylist for suggestions. If necessary, find a new, trendy salon or barber shop to visit. If the same person has been cutting your hair in the same way for 20 years, they probably won't have fun, fresh ideas for your new look!

There is no need to go crazy, just freshen up your style and show that you are staying current. Think of it this way: a dated hairstyle might hint at dated skills in the bedroom, and you want to show other swingers that you're up to date with the latest trends and open to trying new things!

Grey Hair – Having some grey hair can be a big bonus in the lifestyle. Of course, this doesn't apply if you are in your early twenties and trying to connect with other young swingers. Typically for the rest of the swinging community, some grey hair is a positive sign that you are old enough and mature enough to play. Swingers tend to avoid immature play partners because they bring more drama and are less likely to be able to handle swapping situations. Think about how you want to represent yourself and what type of swingers you want to target before messing with any grey hair. If you do decide to color your hair, read the fine print and ask your hair stylist about how it will handle the chlorine in hot tubs & pools, which are common at swinging events.

Facial Hair – Regardless if you are clean shaven or have a mustache or beard, make sure your face is neat and clean. This means no messy stubble. A tickly beard or mustache can be nice if it's well-kept, but stubble is rough. No lady wants you rubbing rough sandpaper against their soft skin, especially if that soft skin is between their legs! You want your face to be soft and smooth if you want the best chance to get close to another swinger.

Eyebrows – Don't get obsessed about your brows. Obsessed people usually end up plucking their eyebrows till they have nothing left and that isn't sexy. You can trim any extra long hairs with a scissor, or use a tweezer to pluck them away. Just don't go crazy.

Nose Hair – Buy a nose trimmer or have your partner carefully use small scissors to trim away hair peeking out of your nose. Don't overreact. You don't need to go deep in the nose. Most likely, no one will be looking way up there, and going too deep will just result you in being injured. A bleeding nose aint sexy!

Ear Hair – Just like your nose. You don't need to go crazy but you don't want to ignore any crazy long hairs.

Teeth – You want a good looking (and smelling) smile if you want any chance to attract play partners. Talk to your dentist about teeth whitening, either at the dentist office or with a DIY home kit your dentist recommends. Beware, as some DIY teeth whitening products can damage more than they help. Make sure to regularly floss or use a Waterpik. Do not floss or use a Waterpik immediately before a play date because you don't want inflamed gums. That can possibly increase your STI risk and no one likes kissing bleeding gums.

Right before a play date, brush your teeth and use mouthwash. When you go on a play date, bring a tiny travel size mouthwash bottle and breath mints - and use them. When you go to the bathroom, refresh your breath to make sure you are giving the best impression. If you are a smoker, try using nicotine gum on play dates so you can wait to light your cigarettes after the play date. Many swingers feel it isn't sexy kissing an ashtray and will avoid people that they see smoking, so it is up to you to decide how you want to represent yourself.

Chest Hair - You can use a body groomer to make it manageable and that is usually good enough. If you want a super smooth chest, you probably will want a wax treatment instead of shaving. Shaving your chest can be hard and result in ingrown hairs and other problems.

Back Hair - Try going to a spa for a wax treatment. The sasquatch look hasn't been sexy for a very long time. You might even want to think about laser hair removal treatment to permanently deal with it. Another option is to have your partner trim it down with a body groomer.

Underarm Hair – Ladies, you already know about shaving this. Men, you need to realize it can be unsexy for ladies to discover a jungle in your armpit. Use some scissors to trim those bushes back to a manageable amount. While you are at it, make sure to use an extra coat of underarm deodorant. Hot sex can get sweaty and you don't want to start becoming stinky in the middle of a hot play session. Unscented deodorant is a safer bet because a heavily scented deodorant might not smell well to everyone you meet.

Pubic Hair – You will find many different preferences on pubic hair but in general, less is more. You want to be extra careful in this area because it probably isn't used to being groomed and it is a very curvy (and sensitive!) area to handle. Start with a body groomer to get rid of the heavy stuff. Then if you want, you can shave the rest, but be very careful and shave well in advance of playing. Shaving irritates the skin and irritated skin does not combine well with bumping and grinding. If you don't want to shave, you can get wax treatment at a spa.

If you don't want to wax, there are chemical hair removal products but many of them should not get anywhere near your pubic hair (unless you want to explain a chemical burn to the ER staff). Men, after you groom around your sword don't forget to take care of your dangling family jewels. Since you have probably never completely removed your hair down there, you should know that it can be very itchy when the hair grows back from being bare. You are going to want to keep it bare or just keep it trimmed to avoid that inbetween itchy regrowth.

Being clean shaven down below is not mandatory. Generally speaking the less hair down there, the better chances for oral fun.

Bum Hair – We want to look sexy no matter what, and different angles can give people unique perspectives of your body – including seeing some things we never expected anyone to see! So take care of your bum. Don't worry. You don't need to go bare back here but you should trim back excessive hairs so they're not distracting. Using a body trimmer is a useful tool for this.

Nails – Don't overlook your nails. It goes without saying that you want smooth nails, but you also want to trim them back as much as possible. You don't want to accidentally injure your play partner with a jagged fingernail. A long fingernail can be just as painful when you are rubbing and grabbing someone's most sensitive body parts. Less is more, even for ladies. Avoid nail extensions, they are just going to break during a frisky play session and long nails can scare away potential play partners.

Some guys in the lifestyle will get manicures (without any nail polish or a clear coat) to make sure their nails are in perfect shape for sexy time. Even the manliest man will enjoy it because swinging ladies really do pay attention to your nails. Plus, you get an awesome-feeling hand massage at the nail salon!

Perfume/Cologne – Just like a sexy bikini, less is more. You want to smell nice and feel confident so use whatever will make you feel confident and sexy. Just don't over-spritz. You might love that smell and it might drive your partner crazy but other people might not like it. Swinging is about attracting new play partners, so you probably want to worry more about what will work best for the most people. It is usually smarter to have no smell or a very mild smell. If you go too heavy with a smelly perfume, lotion, or deodorant you might scare away potential play partners that may not like your favorite scent.

Charming Clothes

You probably know how to dress for the office, for a wedding, for a vanilla night out, and for a casual lunch. But you probably don't know how to dress for a swinger event. Hint: definitely not like any of those events!

Your vanilla wardrobe will probably need some updating before you enter the lifestyle. Making the best first impression goes beyond fitness and grooming. This doesn't mean you have to wear clothes that make you uncomfortable: you can show as much or as little skin as you like and still be sexy. To best represent your sexy side, pick clothes that are currently in style and have them tailored to your body.

We know you love that favorite old shirt and that it's comfortable, but to everyone else it looks like you're wearing a puffy, stained garbage bag. You're a good-looking person, and everyone should know it! Avoid the baggy stuff and go with slim or fitted cuts. Worried that fitted clothes won't suit your body? Well, a baggy sweatshirt certainly won't make you look skinny! Baggy clothes just make you look bigger.

You should realize that your clothes are speaking for you before you even open your mouth to say hello. You want to convey the right message. The right clothes will show people that you're sexy and have your act together. This goes for men and women.

A lot of women are in tune with fashion, and go out of their way to look sexy on a daily basis; men, not so much. Let your clothes help communicate your mood and swinging goals. If you're looking for action, wear more revealing and daring clothes. If you're not looking to get involved physically just yet, dress a bit more conservatively so people get the message.

It may sound prejudiced, but guys are usually the deal breaker when it comes to wardrobe. Women in the lifestyle often complain that guys don't care enough about their appearance. In general, ladies in the lifestyle do an excellent job looking hot. They pick awesome outfits that make them look even more incredible than their usual hot self.

Too many guys don't care and they show it by picking bad, ill fitting, out of fashion, wrinkled, dirty clothes that are torn or ripped. No woman is going to take one for the team and agree to play with a sloppy dude. She and her partner will walk right past you and go for the well-dressed couple who look like they know what they're doing.

Many guys need to upgrade their wardrobe when they enter the lifestyle. You want to build a wardrobe that will appeal to most ladies and help you present yourself in the best light. Don't fight it, embrace it and thank your wife for helping you look half as good as she does.

Every swinging event is different, so here are some clothing suggestions for the different situations you might found yourself (later in the book we'll explain these different situations in more detail). When in doubt, you can always contact the event organizers for suggestions.

Meet & Greet Wardrobe

These tend to be more subdued and hosted in vanilla places so save your crazy, sexy outfits for another time. Go with a more polished and sophisticated look. Imagine what people would wear to a Las Vegas nightclub. Ladies, this can be a sexy dress with some cleavage or a sexy leg slit. You can also wear nice pants that shows off your derriere and a silk blouse. Let's not forget the shoes. Bust out your sexy heels! Ladies have many options, so pick the outfit that makes you feel most proud of your sexy body.

If the Meet & Greet is in a private place, don't be surprised if many ladies go topless as the night progresses. When picking your top, you want to think about how it will transition if you choose to join the other topless ladies. Of course, you can always hand your top to your guy. For some reason men seem to always be more than willing to help when a sexy lady wants to show off her breasts.

Speaking of men, it's time to polish up. Imagine business casual with a sexy twist. It's probably best to skip jeans and go for some fitted chinos. Make sure the pants have some spare room, just in case those topless ladies encourage some growth below the belt. If it is a good Meet & Greet, you are going to want to feel comfortable when things get hotter –

and you get harder. You will probably have better luck picking a collared shirt over a t-shirt. Skip the sneakers and go with smart-looking loafers - easier to slip off & on, which is a good thing. Imagine yourself on the cover of GQ.

Of course, this all depends on who is organizing and attending this Meet & Greet, and which people you are hoping to attract. If it's a pool party, then a more casual approach would be appropriate. If you do go with a casual look, make sure it doesn't look sloppy. Sloppy aint sexy. No matter the location and atmosphere, you want to communicate to other swingers that you care about your sexy appearance.

Swinger Club Wardrobe

Each club is different so ask the club organizers about appropriate attire. Ladies should usually be wearing a long coat, so they can enter the club and reveal their sexy attire (which may or may not be street legal). You want something that is sexy and easy to take off. This could be a lacy lingerie outfit, a sheer blouse and hip hugging pants, a sexy cosplay costume, or your sexiest nightclub attire. You can show as much or as little skin as you like.

It is usually sexier to not expose all your best parts. Covering up a little bit helps leave something to the imagination. As for shoes, you want sexy shoes that are safe for stairs after you have had a few drinks. You might want to go with sexy boots or wedges to make it a little easier navigating any possible stairs.

Some clubs have play areas where no clothes are allowed, so you and your partner can decide if you want to enter those areas. It is very common for ladies to bring a second or third sexy outfit to wear, like a

robe or lingerie, so they can get even more attention looking hotter &
hotter as the night progresses.

Guys, it is much simpler for you. You are basically following the same
guidelines for a Meet & Greet. If you want, you can go with silk pajama
pants, but you don't want to look sloppy. If you haven't already
upgraded your underwear, you should do it before going to a swinger
club because you'll likely find yourself walking around in just your
boxers or briefs at some point. Don't go crazy with the underwear and
skip the zebra stripes and speedos. Almost every guy will look good in
Calvin Klein or Hugo Boss black modal boxer briefs.

Theme Night Party Wardrobe

If you are attending a club or party that has chosen a theme, embrace it
and get creative. Just remember that whatever you put on should also be
easy to take off. This might mean you don't wear the best outfit you
have. For example, if you have an amazing full body corset that takes 20
minutes to be unlaced, it's probably not a good option if you are hoping
to play with others. Also avoid face paint because it is going to look
horrible after making out with your new friends. Guys, make sure your
outfit compliments your sexy lady's theme outfit.

House Party Wardrobe

Ask your host for suggested attire. Usually a bit of flexibility and
dressing in layers will be best here. Show up wearing street legal clothes
for a sexy Meet & Greet. Ladies, think about a fashionable jacket over a
silk shell that shows a bit of cleavage and a very sexy bra underneath the
silk shell. This enables you to quickly adjust your outfit so you can be
anything from a fully-covered, tasteful tease all the way to a sultry siren
in your sexy lingerie. This will help you feel more comfortable and in

control, which is very nice if you are about to meet a bunch of new people at a swinger house party.

The energy of house parties can start slowly as people show up. Once most people have arrived be prepared for the night to quickly escalate. Therefore, we suggest dressing in sexy layers to give you flexibility in matching the vibe of the house party. Men have it simple: dress up just like a meet & greet but make sure you have sexy underwear and polished shoes.

Hotel Takeover Wardrobe

This depends a bit on whether it's a full or partial hotel takeover. A partial takeover party is when you share the hotel with vanilla people, so best to treat it like a house party. You can wear something sexy, but it should be appropriate in case you bump into families on the elevator. You can still pack some very sexy and revealing lingerie to change into if you invite others back to your room.

Thankfully, a bunch of hotel takeovers are full takeovers where you have much more wardrobe freedom. Full hotel takeovers allow only swingers past the reception area, so you can often wear very revealing outfits. Full nudity might even be allowed in the hotel hallways and pool area (definitely make sure you check before strutting out in your birthday suit!). The hotel bar & restaurant areas will require a little bit of clothing.

We like to start with something comfortable to travel in. Then pack some outfits for the day time. There are often sexy demonstrations and guest speakers during the day. You want to make many connections during the day so you can have a fun time at night. Some possible day time outfits can be a bikini with a cover-up, plunging shirts, or sexy yoga pants with a crop top. Most people don't play during the day at hotel takeover. Daytime is usually more for introductions and light flirting, so save your super sexy stuff for later. Guys remember not be sloppy. Casual is fine as long as you keep it polished. Remember we want to be making a good impression to the new friends we are about to discover.

There is usually a big party at night with a DJ or live music. You'll see most people wearing sexy club clothes or lingerie. Some people will leave the party midway just to change into a sexier outfit. Since you will have your own hotel room, pack a bunch of different outfits. We all have a bunch of sexy stuff that we don't get to wear nearly enough. This is a golden opportunity to show them off to a crowd that will truly appreciate it!

Also make sure to pack some comfy clothes for breakfast the next day. If everything went right, you will have worked up a huge appetite from the sexy shenanigans of the previous night. Again, guys have it very easy. During the day, wear a casual fitted shirt with a collar. This can be a polo shirt or a buttoned shirt. Save the t-shirts for your pajamas. At night, break out some nice jeans or dress pants with a fitted buttoned shirt. Loose fitting clothes will not show off your physique. T-shirts will look sloppy and make people think you don't care, which just isn't true. No matter what, always make sure to look good.

Our Swinging Journal: Agent Provocateur? Not so much...

We met a real nice couple that was relatively new to the lifestyle at a swinger event. Unfortunately the event was really packed and we didn't have time to privately chat with them. So we exchanged emails which led to some hot flirting and eventually a date at a trendy local restaurant. Everything is going well and they invite us back to their house where they opened up a special bottle of whisky. Dr. G was in heaven but Mr. F didn't understand the big deal because he is not a whisky aficionado. He almost spit it out when he realized that just his glass contained about $300 of rare whisky. Whisky that good shouldn't be wasted on him so Dr. G graciously volunteered to help out.

After such a nice meal & special after dinner drinks, we moved on to the fun stuff. Clothes start falling off and the other lady looked amazing in her Manolo Blahnik high heels and Agent Provocateur lingerie. Now a sexy outfit like that is something for which Mr. F definitely holds aficionado status. The heat and passion is building but the lady starts worrying about her shoes. So we stop to take them off. We restart getting hot & heavy but then she worries about her silk stockings. So we stop & take them off. We restart yet again, and then she worries about her lingerie tearing.. After so many false-starts nothing much happened more than kissing before time ran out of. It just wasn't a great time. The lady never felt relaxed because she tried to make the best impression by wearing expensive things.

The problem is that expensive things can come with the stress of taking care of them. We learned a while ago the lifestyle is more fun when we don't bring our nicest things. We like to only wear and use things on swinger dates that we can afford to be lost or damaged, because we want the focus to be on sexy fun. We cherish the crazy passionate moments where the clothes are flying all over the place, lube is flowing all over, and sexy people are fiercely convulsing from mind blowing orgasms.

Hot sex often can cause wardrobe casualties so plan accordingly. It will help you replace anxiety with heart pounding arousal.

Online Swinging Sites

After you both agree to take the next step towards swinging, you will probably want to learn more so you can feel comfortable approaching the lifestyle together and getting the most out of the experience. This book is an amazing resource but we can't answer every question, so you will want to check out online forums dedicated to discussing the lifestyle. These sites have huge archives of questions that have already been answered, so make sure to search through the older pages.

If you want a fresh opinion or haven't found an answer to a specific question, feel free to create a throwaway account to post under. Grab a free email address that can't be traced back to you (gmail, yahoo, etc). Pick a random sexy username that doesn't identify you in any way. Remember you can always share more later on, but you can't un-share something once it is online.

There are over 25 different national swinger community sites just in the US, and quite a few regional ones plus several international sites. None of them are perfect. They all have problems. The frustrating thing is that the newer swinger sites have excellent features, are easy to use, have sexy designs, and address the complaints we have with the older swinging community sites. But they can't attract enough members. The more established swinger sites have huge numbers of active swingers, but they look and act like they were built by a high school kid. We are going to focus on the three most popular swinger websites. If you ask local swingers, you can quickly find out which sites are the best for your local area and for the type of people you are seeking.

SwingLifestyle.com - One of the bigger swinger sites in the USA, also referred to as SLS. The site doesn't always perform well and the design is old, but if you want to meet swingers in the USA this is a good place to start. They skew towards the 40-50 year-old crowd, but it's so big there are still plenty of 20-30 year-olds. There are online forums and calendars of swinging events. It allows members and event organizers to write certifications for member profiles to help you sort out real swingers from the fakers or newbies.

SLS had a security issue in 2014. It allowed anyone to manually change the URL to gain access to private photos including face pics and naked pics. SLS quickly fixed it, but it is a good reminder to be very careful in what you upload to any website because mistakes can happen.

SLS offers free and paid accounts. Create a free account, double check to make sure there are plenty of swingers in your area, then upgrade to the paid lifetime account. You don't need to buy a paid account at all the different sites, but this big site is often the top option for US swingers.

Kasidie.com – This site is newer than SLS and skews towards the younger swingers, ranging from 20-40 year-olds. Unfortunately, it does

143

not have as big a membership pool, so it might be harder for you to find swingers in your area.

Kasidie also had a bit of security problem in 2016. Apparently, a fake profile tricked some of the real members into granting access to their sexy private photos. The fraudster then stole these images and uploaded them to an amateur porn site. This wasn't widespread and the stolen pictures were eventually taken down. I think we can all agree that it is smarter to think twice before granting someone access to your private pics.

Kasidie offers free & paid accounts (aka elite accounts). Go ahead and sign up for a free account. You can then see how many people are in your area and if it is worth it to pay for an elite account. Kasidie does offer a reduced fee for some parts of the USA where they have lower membership as a way to grow their community.

SDC.com - This site is also known as Swinger Date Central, but most people just call it SDC. It is usually the best site for finding swingers outside of the USA. The membership profiles are very, very detailed with many different data fields. The awesome part is that you can perform a search for these different data fields. For example, you can search to find people that have tattoos, or people who place more value on intellect than beauty. It has a really big community, including many people in all different age groups but it is not as big as SLS for most of the USA. Just like the other sites, they have free and paid accounts, so you know what to do.

Craigslist Ads - We liked to call it CringeList because it often lead to nightmare stories that would make you cringe. Anyone could post here for free, including horny guys trying to steal sexy pics, scammers asking you to join paid sites, catfishing pranksters, drama-filled couples, and clueless newbies who rushed into this, get scared, and end up not showing. As much as we bash it, there were some real couples on it and for some areas it was a viable option. For better or worse, Craigslist turned off this section due to changes in the US law so this is not an option anymore for US swingers.

Other Swinger Websites - There are new swinger websites popping up all the time. Most of them have better features than the sites we just mentioned, but we aren't going to spend time talking about them. Why not? These new swinger websites tend to be missing the most important piece of a swinger community websites … the COMMUNITY. These sites tend to have much smaller membership counts. As much as we would love to use these new sites with their shiny new tools, it is rarely worth the time, effort, and money to join these sites just to end up talking to yourself. Hopefully this changes. If you are really curious, here are some alternative swinger websites that you can explore: Quiver, OkSwing, FabSwingers (UK), C4P (Kansas area), SwingerZoneCentral (Ohio area), FetLife (huge site but focuses on bdsm/fetish).

Bonus Tip - Be careful listening to advice on which paid swinger sites to join. Many swinger sites give big commissions for referrals, so there is strong incentive for some sex sites to promote poor sites. If you can't try a free version first, avoid blindly following online advice.

Whichever swinging community website you end up using, you will want to make sure you properly fill out your online profile to attract more friends and potential play partners. We've said it before and we'll say it again - don't overshare. You can always share more information later, but you can't un-share something. If you are like most swingers, you're doing this privately, without telling your vanilla friends and family. You want to avoid outing yourself.

Your screen name will be one of your first methods of introducing yourself in the community. Pick a screen name that is easy to spell so swingers can more easily remember how to contact you after meeting you at a swinger event. Make sure the screen name doesn't reveal your personal identity. You can do a mashup of your favorite color and your favorite animal or another mashup of your choosing, just keep it simple but still unique and relevant to you.

Good Username Examples:

Coolkissers - easy to spell and remember

txfuntime - Assuming you are permanently going to live in Texas, it is good

Not so good examples:

T1meforfunz - Good luck having friends from the club spell this correctly to find you later

BobNJaneSmith - Sharing too much personal info like your full name is rarely a good idea

Ok, you have your screen name, now let's talk pictures. Take some new pictures without anything personal in the background. You don't want someone to recognize your living room or have your kid's picture in the background.

Absolutely do not reuse pictures from your vanilla world. If you are like most people, those pictures are most likely too old and not an accurate reflection of what you look like today. We are sure you looked great on your honeymoon, but you want to accurately reflect how you currently look when trying to connect with other swingers. Trying to pull a bait & switch using old photos will likely result in you getting embarrassed in real life as the other couple will pass right by you.

Furthermore, there are online reverse image searching tools that are creepily effective. People can take your photos and plug them into free websites that will match up your pictures and faces with any other public site that also has them. We don't want anyone to be able to use your swinging profile pictures to track back to your real-world Facebook profile. To avoid accidental outing, there should be no crossing the streams between your vanilla world and your swinging lifestyle.

Many swingers only show body pictures with no faces. Later, if there is a connection, they will share face pictures directly with the swingers who are interested. Of course, you should do whatever you both feel comfortable doing. Just remember you can't un-share something online that you have already exposed. Be smart and think twice before sharing once.

While we're discussing pictures, let's talk about a major mistake many couples in the lifestyle make. While we all agree that ladies have much more beautiful bodies than guys, it's important to include some pictures of the man in your profile. It's tempting to focus on the sexy lady, but other swingers (specifically females) will want to know what to expect from a new male play partner.

Focus on the body, and skip the pictures of his junk. Glorious as that junk may be, swingers usually want to see the guy's general physique and, eventually, a face picture. Many swinging ladies veto profiles that don't show enough of the guy or only show his equipment. It's only fair for each partner to know what to expect from a potential connection. How can swinging ladies know if they're attracted to a man if there are no pictures of him? Worse, if there are only pictures of the female, it might be assumed that the male doesn't measure up physically. Save the more intimate pictures for later, and put your best photos forward!

The best swinger profiles will have many different photos showing many different poses. Show off your best parts by striking sexy poses that accentuate and flatter a lady's curves or a guy's muscles. While you don't want to be fake or misleading, there's no shame in being proud of (and showing off) your best features!

Here are some basic tips for taking great photos that show off your sexy body.

- Minimize belly and maximize bust by seductively stretching your arms upwards
- Show off your cleavage by pushing your elbows into your boobs
- Wear high heels to boost your legs
- Pop up your muscles by pumping some weights right before the pictures
- Pick the right lingerie. Corsets can improve weak abs or boost cleavage, while a teddy can help hide a bit of jiggle in your belly.
- Arching backwards turns bulges into sexy curves
- Lie on your back with your legs up in the air to hide the belly and focus on the legs
- Laying on your stomach and arching backwards shows the booty and pops the cleavage
- Looking upwards stretches out that double chin

- Use good lighting to make your skin look better and your eyes sparkle

Feel free to search Google and Youtube for more help and inspiration; there are tons of resources for how to take great boudoir style pictures.

Once you've got a good batch of sexy photos, you can move on to filling out the details. Be honest and upfront, without oversharing. You don't want to waste time with mismatched connections that lead nowhere, so make sure you accurately state your situation and give some details about what you hope to find and experience. If you aren't sure what to write, take inspiration from other profiles.

One or two sentences probably won't be enough to adequately tell your story; try for at least four or five sentences to increase the chances of finding a connection. People like to be well-informed, and swingers are no different. Longer profiles that give the reader a good sense of who's behind the screen are much more likely to receive attention from the swinger community. Personality matters, too, so try and be yourself in your profile.

Avoid negative statements and focus on the positive – talking about what turns you on is much better than talking about what turns you off. Of course, you should mention any deal-breakers you have – politely! But know that if you have a lot of deal-breakers, you'll probably come off as high maintenance, which isn't very sexy at all. A good rule of thumb is to say at least three positive sexy things for every one negative thing you mention in your profile.

Here are some questions to try to answer in your profile:

149

- What do you both look like?
- What is your lifestyle experience level?
- What do you both want to happen?
- What do you find extra sexy?
- How do you have fun outside of the bedroom?
- Where will you to go to meet new people?

Feel free to bend the truth a little about your personal details to hide your identity. For example, you might change your hometown to another town nearby, or fib a bit on how long you have been dating or married. As long as the changes are minor, and you don't think you're misleading anyone, these little white lies can help afford you a little more personal security. Swingers do not like dishonest people and will quickly turn from a person or couple that seems deceptive. One thing you don't want to do is tell a big lie about your age. That's a good way to upset other swingers and alienate yourself from the community.

Protecting your job and your families in the vanilla world is important, but there's no excuse for purposely misleading people when it comes to major facets of your personality or identity. You are likely going to have many conversations with many different swingers and you don't want to get caught in a lie. Keep the details simple and as close to reality as you can. Use common sense, and if you aren't comfortable sharing something you can always skip that part of your profile and return to it later when you're more secure.

Personal Ad Advice

In addition to dedicated swinging sites, there are many personal dating sites like PlentyofFish, OkCupid, AdultFriendFinder, etc where you can find people that might be open to swinging fun. To have the best chance of success with your online person ad posting here are some ways to stack the odds in your favor.

Step 1 - Look for multiple areas that you are willing to visit for meeting people. Don't just limit yourself to your home area. If you can post to two geographic areas you are basically doubling your chances of success.

Step 2 - Expand the categories that you are targeting. Don't just think about casual encounters. Depending on the site, you might want to consider selecting other categories like long term dating if you are open to long term friends with benefits. You can often find open minded people in other categories that might be open to what you want.

Step 3 – Consider multiple profiles. Instead of using one profile to post one ad, imagine profiles on three sites posting three ads. You have just tripled your odds of success.

Instead of 1 ad in 1 place, we are now using 3+ profiles in each, covering 2+ geographic areas and open to multiple types of relationship categories. 1 ad vs 6+ ads is how you sway the odds into your favor.

Here are more online posting tips.

a) Make sure to include a picture. A picture makes your posting more attractive. Some users only read postings that contain a picture. To have the most people read your ad, add a picture. You don't always need a personal picture. Sometimes you can use any sexy image that matches the theme of your personal ad.

b) You will need a great amount of patience. As much as you are concerned about creepy people online, the people responding have the same fear. Take it slow and move one step at a time. This prevents spooking them and helps you avoid rushing into traps.

c) When you think you have made a connection make sure your first meeting is in a public area. Preferably in a fun place that you will enjoy by yourself because many people will get nervous and no show at the last minute.

d) Don't send pictures of your junk. It is rarely the sexiest view of you. Show off your self control and do not send uninvited pictures of your junk. Often it looks even better when covered with sexy underwear. Double check that your background also looks good & clean. We also don't want to see other people in the pictures. That can make people think you are not discreet and careless. Make sure you remove the hidden meta exif data from your pictures that can expose personal data (you can google a free remover tool).

Ok best of luck with your online posting! Now let's move on...

Blogs & Podcasts

The online swinger community websites offer great resources and the chance to meet other swingers but there are many more swinging resources online. We are lucky to have some really amazing blogs & podcasts run by swingers for swingers. Some of them are long time lifestyle veterans and other are newbies that are documenting their journey and letting you follow along.

The blogs & podcasts tend to be more information sites and not interactive communities. Actually that isn't really fair. Many of the swinging hosts welcome questions and spend a huge amount of their time responding to audience requests. These hosts are incredibly nice and helpful. You can learn answers to questions you didn't even know you wanted answered.

To find these swinger blogs & podcasts, just check out the current list on SwingersHelp.com.

Online advice can be very helpful but you should be careful to consider the source. For example, relationship advice from a single 20 year old has a bit different perspective than from a married 50 year old. Keeping in mind the different sources can help you better absorb their opinions for your personal situation. Every day there are different topics being discussed on these sites and people sharing information to keep each other up-to-date.

Remember these blogs & podcasts are run by real life swingers. Just like your real life, these people are often busy with their real job & family. So they sometimes just don't have time to record another podcast episode or write a new blog post. That is a shame because many of these people are incredibly talented and entertaining swingers who you will really enjoy.

We enjoy downloading podcasts and listening to them as we get ready for a swinger party and then keep listening to them as we drive over to the party. It can be a real treat to listen or read and feel connected with the swinger community when most swingers can't share this secret with the people in their vanilla world.

Our Swinging Journal: Anything can happen during an orgy...

We were lucky enough to be invited to a swinger house party. That sounds exciting but take a tip from us, it is a very smart idea to always ask about who else will be attending. We have learned from our house party experiences that the other attendees might not be who you are expecting.

This house party was everything on our wish list. It was close, so no need for a long drive. It also had seven friendly & attractive couples who liked things that we also enjoy. So we had high expectations for a fun time that night.

On the (short) drive over, I mentioned that we might end up in an orgy depending on where people end up playing. You know what? That is exactly what happened. It started with a sexy stripping escapade. Everyone was so hot after watching so many sexy people strip, we all started playing in the same room.

It was quite a sexy ball of kisses, touches and more. My play partner wanted to enjoy some cowgirl riding and I was more than happy to oblige. While I was helping this cowgirl, another lady wanted to practice her mouth to mouth resuscitation with me. Being a gentleman, I again obliged. I am cherishing my charmed life as I am playing with two sexy ladies at the same time. That is when life throws me a curveball.

I feel a third person sucking on my toes. I can't see the person because I have a lady kissing my face and even if she stopped I had another lady practicing her saddle riding prowess on me. I am a big believer that swingers should always ask before touching me and my toe person did not ask. I didn't want to make a scene and disturb the other ladies so I rationalize it is just toe sucking and try to ignore it. That was a mistake.

It just feels weird. I haven't had my toes sucked much in my life and it was very distracting to me. You probably think this is crazy but wait it gets crazier. The person sucking my toe starts moaning. I still can't see what is happening to my defenseless big toe but I do immediately realize that the person sucking on my big toe isn't using her mouth. I squirm enough to get a peek over cowgirl's shoulder and discover a lady having sex with my big toe. There is just no manual for how to handle crazy situations like this.

On one hand, I was pleasuring three ladies at once, which I guess is impressive. On the other hand my big toe was violated. Fast forward to the drive home, I am debriefing with my wife who was on the other side of the crazy large bed and missed this moment. I explain to her the toe incident. My helpful wife tries to correct me when I say it was my toe. I clarify I didn't misspeak and she just gives me this priceless WTF look that just can't be described. So learn from your triple lady pleasing friend and be prepared to say no thanks if the unexpected happens while you are in an orgy. I still laugh (and cringe) thinking about my big toe has literally had more sex than some of my single guy friends in recent times.

Wanna Go Swinging?

Let's uncover the many options for those people that are interested in actually swinging with other real life swingers in the flesh! Don't worry we'll start slow and build up to the more intense events. There is no right or wrong way to enter the lifestyle. You can pick & choose which options work best for your personal situation. Enjoy and happy swinging!

Dress Rehearsal at Strip Clubs

If you're ready to take a step towards the lifestyle but not yet ready to deal with other couples in person, you can try visiting a strip club together. Make sure you choose a classy strip club; believe it or not, strip clubs don't have to be creepy and disgusting! Some are, but lots are sexy, fun, and reputable. There are websites dedicated to providing reviews of strip clubs; study them to choose the best one in your area.

Once you've chosen a club and decided to go, make sure you treat the evening as a sexy date night. Get dressed up and look hot for each other. For all intents and purposes, it is a sexy date night – much sexier than a steak dinner at a restaurant, or an action movie. You and your partner are going out together for the express purpose of having a sensual, intimate time. The goal is to enjoy the excitement of the strip club until you just can't wait to get back to your bedroom.

We are going to assume that all you upstanding boys and girls have never stepped foot in a strip club. Let's go over some of the things you're likely to encounter.

There are generally two types of strip clubs: all-nude establishments without a liquor license, or topless bars where you can order alcohol. Depending on the local laws of your state or city, you might find a club that deviates from these two types but these tend to be the more common options across the USA.

You'll likely have to pay a cover charge and/or order a specific amount of drinks. Those drinks – even the non-alcoholic ones – will probably be mind-bogglingly expensive. Don't be surprised if you find yourself holding a $9 bottle of water – we wish we were joking! Be sure to tip your waitress (generously, if possible) – a happy waitress will help you out later. There are some strip clubs that allow you to bring in your own drinks but they are more likely to have a high cover charge or very insistent strippers pushing lap dances because they need to make money somehow.

Once you have your drinks, you'll be able to take a seat at a table. Many clubs also have seating right alongside the stages. There will be strippers walking around and approaching everyone, asking if they want a dance. This is good practice for curious newbies to talk about which dancers they find sexy and why. It's also good practice for swinger newbies to learn how to be comfortable saying "no thanks." Trust us, there will be no shortage of girls asking if you want a dance, and you'll quickly get very good at turning them down politely.

A lap dance usually costs $20 or more, and will last for one song. During the song, the stripper will grind their almost-naked body against your fully-clothed body. You should not touch the stripper during the dance. It's not allowed, and you risk getting thrown out of the club. When the dance ends, the stripper will likely whisper in your ear, asking if you want another dance – which puts another $20 in their pocket.

Most strippers will happily give lap dances to ladies, and some strippers are lax about the "no touching" rule when it comes to a female customer.

If you pay for a few dances, the stripper will try to upsell you into the VIP champagne room. These rooms are private, or semi-private, and have much looser rules about what you can and can't do with the stripper. Of course, you have to pay for this privilege: usually several hundred dollars, and sometimes over a thousand dollars! And don't be too excited about that champagne. There's almost never champagne in the champagne room, and if there is champagne it's probably not worth drinking. The champagne room is not about drinking fine bubbly stuff.

If you opt for a visit to the champagne room, you can have a light threesome session with the stripper. With looser "no touching" rules, your dancer may allow you to touch or possibly even kiss her. If you're in a classy club, you'll be expected to remain fully clothed throughout the session. Those review sites we mentioned earlier often provide very clear hints about what happens in the VIP room at a given strip club, so use those as a guideline when you're looking for a club that will meet your needs.

You might never make it to the VIP room; after all, you're in a very sexy club with your very sexy partner, and the heat level can ramp up quickly! You might find yourself rushing home with your loved one to relive the night through a sexy roleplay or straight-up passionate sex.

The next day, you can debrief about what did and didn't go well. Don't be afraid to talk about your negative feelings. Did either of you feel any jealousy, insecurity, or resentment? Talk about those feelings and isolate the trigger points so you can avoid them in the future. The more you talk through issues before they arise, the smoother your swinging path will be. Strip clubs can be very useful for new couples to test how they might react seeing another person touch their partner in a sexy way.

Another Step: Meet & Greet Events

You've made your online swinger profile, and maybe you've spent a sexy night at a strip club together as a couple. You might be ready to take another step and meet other swingers in person; the perfect place to do this is a "Meet & Greet". These events are dedicated swinger events, where people who are curious about the lifestyle can meet active participants.

Meet & Greets are social networking opportunities for swingers that don't include any onsite play. You get dressed up and get a good look at other swingers in your area. You can ask any questions that you have about the lifestyle or community and get personal, informative answers. There's no pressure to take the plunge into physically playing with other swingers. Some swingers limit their involvement in the lifestyle to Meet & Greets; they find the sexy conversation and social aspect enough to fulfill their needs. You can attend as many Meet & Greets as you want before taking the next step to swinger clubs or onsite swinger parties.

Meet & Greets can be held privately in someone's home, a rented-out club, or a hotel suite. They can also be held publicly in a bar or a coffee shop. When you attend a public Meet & Greet, you'll probably be told to wear a specific color or to ask for a fake, vanilla-sounding group name. This helps everyone find each other without needing to draw attention to the fact that it's a swinger meeting. You wouldn't want to accidentally chat up a vanilla person and possibly out yourself or someone else! It's usually not that hard to spot swingers in a crowd of vanilla people; the swingers will be the friendly, sexy group of people who clearly care about their appearances and are enjoying a fun time together.

You can find Meet & Greets in your area online by setting up a free (or paid) profile on a swinger website and checking out the calendar of events. The Meet & Greet organizers will post the location and RSVP information on these community websites.

Why should you attend a Meet & Greet? It's a fantastic way to dip your toes into the lifestyle without taking the full plunge. Chatting online can be very hit or miss. You never know who you're talking to, and many people established in the lifestyle don't bother checking their online profile every day. Things online can get lost in translation. You can't sense body language or "vibes" online.

A Meet & Greet allows you to interact with many different people in the lifestyle without any pressure of playing. Meet & Greets are less about finding a play partner for that night (although that can happen) and more about making lifestyle connections that can become helpful swinging mentors, sexy play partners, or whatever else you choose. It is much less scary to attend a group event with no pressure than it is to go on a private swinging date.

When you meet swingers in real life you quickly realize they are just like you. We all just want a good time while being in a sexy and safe atmosphere. We want to feel comfortable mingling and mixing with awesome new friends who embrace sexiness instead of rudely judging others.

So you've decided to go to a Meet & Greet. The next step is to get sexy! Think about what you would wear if you were headed to a club looking for someone to date or hookup with. Feel free to ask the organizers about the dress code if you're not sure. These people are organizing a Meet & Greet for a reason: they want to help newbies and established swingers alike meet and have fun!

Just because there's no onsite play at Meet & Greets doesn't mean you should slack on your sexy primping. There are often many opportunities for offsite play right after the Meet & Greets. Even if you don't make a sexy connection to play that night, you'll likely head home for some exciting, inspired sexy time with your partner afterwards. Make sure to take care of your grooming and wardrobe as though you're treating your partner to a night of pleasure with your sexiest, hottest self.

Now that you're looking good, smelling good, and feeling good, you're ready to attend the event. You might be struck with nervousness or anxiety right before you enter. That's normal. Take a deep breath and go for it. Do something crazy: walk up to another couple and say hi! Trust us, they won't bite and will likely be very relieved that another couple is talking to them. You most likely aren't the only people in the room who may be feeling a little nervous.

A Meet & Greet can sometimes feel like the first day or school, where everyone is a little bit shy, checking out everyone else and wondering who will be the first to break the ice. Find a couple that looks interesting and say hi. Start a conversation just like you would at any other party: give them a compliment, or ask them a question. Maybe you want to know where she bought her sexy outfit, or how long they have been swinging, or which swinging sites they've found most helpful. Swingers are very friendly and helpful, and will be receptive to almost any question you can think of.

161

Avoid questions that get too personal, like where they live or work. If someone asks you something that's too personal and you don't want to answer, politely decline. You can say something as simple as "sorry, I'm not comfortable sharing that." Swingers are great at respecting boundaries because we value discretion and want other people to respect our boundaries.

If you've found a couple – or a few couples – that you really connect with, you'll likely want to swap contact info. You can give them your screenname, or your e-mail address, or your phone number. Whatever you feel comfortable giving out. You might want to set up a dedicated e-mail account for your swinging life versus your vanilla life email. If you want, you can get a separate phone line dedicated to swinging fun. Prepaid cell phones or the Google Voice app are great ways to keep your identity private while staying connected.

Try to talk to many different couples, instead of latching on to the first couple you speak to. Politely disengage from the conversation by saying you're going to get another drink, and mingle with some other guests at the party. Meet & Greets are really relaxed and no-pressure. If you don't find anyone that interests you, that's okay. You can still have fun and enjoy a sexy night out, looking good for each other and enjoying lively, sexy discussion.

Different Meet & Greets can cater to different types of people, so you might need to try a few out before you find the best crowd for you. You will also find that the crowd can change at the same Meet & Greet from week to week. Veteran swingers won't usually attend Meet & Greets every single week, because they've already networked and made swinger friends to spend time with. Plus, every week brings in new swingers dipping their toes in the lifestyle. There are usually many fresh faces for you to discover at each Meet & Greet.

On Premise Swinging Parties & Clubs

So meet & greet events are "off-premise" affairs since you meet & the party but the sexy stuff happens off-site. "On premise" is when the sexy stuff is happening on site. At on-premise events you show up, party, and socialize with other swingers. Of course if you make a connection you can have some sexy time right there at the swinger party.

Usually most couples play together. Of course you can play separately but that is less common. Most often one sexy couple finds another sexy couple and they swap.

House Parties

House Parties are one form of on-premise swinger parties. They are held in someone's private home. The host couple usually provides some light finger food & drinks. When you arrive they'll give you a tour of the house and explain which areas are for partying/socializing, sexy play time and if any areas are off-limits. If you aren't sure about something, please ask the hosts. Your host couple may or may not ask for a donation to help cover the cost of the house party. If they don't ask for a donation, it is always nice to bring them a little gift to thank them for doing all the work it takes to prepare, host & clean-up from a house party.

House parties can be a small affair with just a few couples or they can have over a few hundred people. You can find available house parties listed on the calendars of the online swinger membership sites. Every house party is different because each host couple has a different way of running their swinger house party. To get a better sense of a house party you can ask the host couple any question you have.

Usually but not always, the crowd shows up a bit late and brings their own preferred alcohol since it is often BYOB (bring your own bottle aka supply your own alcohol) style. There is usually some party music playing as people enjoy drinks and introductions. There might be an ice breaker game or you can do your own ice breaker with the people you happen to be chatting. If you find a sexy connection and are ready for sexy playtime, then you can head over to a play area. The play area(s) could be the bedrooms or a finished basement or some other space in the house. The play areas can be shared or private depending on the house. After you have had enough fun, please clean up after yourselves before you head home with the best looking person at the party – your special someone.

Swinger Clubs

Swinger clubs are another on-premise option. Just like house parties, and regular vanilla bars & clubs, every swinger club is a little bit different. Some swinger clubs don't allow public nudity, a few are all nude and others have mixed areas. Swinger clubs usually have hospitality couples aka ambassador couples. These couples are like host couple at the house parties. They can give you a tour, explain the rules, show you were you can store your party supplies and introduce you to some regular attendees.

Many swinger clubs are BYOB since it is usually too much of a headache dealing with a liquor license for a sex club. The bar can be self-serve or they might be a bartender to handle your BYOB alcohol supply. If there is a bartender, it is nice to tip them each time they help you even if they are serving you your own alcohol. The bartenders can also help steer you towards other attendees that might be a good match for what you are seeking.

Swinger clubs come in all sizes & shapes. They might have a handful of people attending or several hundreds of sexy people depending on the venue and weekend.   They often have private play areas but sometimes they only have shared play areas.   There is also a wide range of amenities depending on the club like indoor or outdoor swimming pools, hot tubs, sex dungeons, stripper poles, shower rooms, lockers, massage tables, and much more.   You should do some online research to make sure you pick a swinger club that has just what you want.

While you are researching the swinger clubs, you should also pay attention to their calendars.   Clubs often host different parties with different rules on different nights.   In other words, Friday nights might be couples only, Saturdays might allow single men to attend and Thursday nights could be reserved for BDSM/fetish people or they might have a calendar of special themed party nights like Mardi Gras or Schoolgirl Night. Make sure to check twice before picking the right night to attend the swinger club so you get the type of party that you want.

Anyone that walks around politely smiling and saying hello will make new friends. These new friends are just friends - there is no need to sexually play with anyone. If you really like a new friend you can ask that couple if they are interested in playing with you.

Most couples do not separate at a swinger club. This is not a high pressure or "everyone fends for themselves" situation. This is more of a friendly party atmosphere with couples, who if the spark feels just right might get friskier than your craziest New Years Eve party.

Don't worry, just because other people at the swinger club are inclined to play, it doesn't mean you have to play.   You can attend and be a wallflower enjoying the party vibe.   If anyone approaches, you can politely let them know you aren't playing that night. They will probably still want to chat with you if you don't mind, because swingers are a friendly bunch. You are in the driver seat and control how much or how little you do at a swinger party.

You will probably see more skin than you have ever seen. Ladies in swinger clubs know they are in an appreciative environment so they tend to wear revealing outfits. You are likely to see a few ladies take their top off. If there is an open play area, you might even see some real life sex.

Swinger clubs follow the "No means no" rule. If anyone asks you, you can just say no thanks. There is never pressure to sexually play with anyone. Touching is not allowed without asking.

Regardless of how or where you decide to go swinging, you have the power to proceed as fast or as slow as you want. Relax and enjoy a fun time knowing that whatever happens you are guaranteed to go home with the sexiest person in the room – your own partner!

Our Swinging Journal: We meet the nicest dominatrix...

We are signed up for a hotel takeover. Like many other swinger hotel parties, this one has some learning demonstrations that you can attend during the day. We were going to attend them because it is always fun to pick up a new trick to enjoy but we ran into some friends who pleasantly distracted us from the schedule.

Later that night we head down to the ballroom for the big party. The dance floor was great but it was a bit too great.

The music was so loud, we couldn't hear each other and forget about trying to flirt with any of the sexy couples on the dance floor. So we take a break from dancing and move from the ballroom into the lobby area.. Thankfully it is a full takeover so Dr. G doesn't worry about her lingerie looking dress being too risqué. We sit down and start talking with another couple. After some quick introductions we find out these were the presenters for the BDSM presentation. She is the dominatrix and he is her loyal submissive bringing her drinks while we chat.

We have a very pleasant conversation about the weather, summer vacation suggestions and oh yeah which leather makes for the best whip. We ended up having a nice but surreal two hour conversation that causally kept moving back and forth between mundane topics like what is the best cheese to serve with red wine and crazier topics like how best to suspend your slave using fish hooks. The dominatrix and her submissive husband were incredibly pleasant & helpful sharing tips. We bought the cheese but skipped the hooks.

You just never know who'll meet in the lifestyle or what you may learn. It was a bit extra hard to keep a straight face when we were asked at work if we did anything special that weekend. How do you explain that you learned the right and wrong way to suspend a human using hooks?

Your Lifestyle Travel Agent

Looking for a travel destination to play in the lifestyle? Maybe there aren't good clubs near you, or you've decided to only dabble in swinging when travelling or you just like to travel. Whatever your reason, there are plenty of sexy hotspots for you to enjoy.

A typical day at a swinger resort includes sleeping in or heading to the gym (swingers love staying fit). Then showing up for a nice breakfast, sleeping a little bit more in your room or poolside after breakfast. You can grab lunch while the entertainment staff does something fun and crazy to help shake off the previous night's sexual stupor. Casually making friends over poolside drinks or lounging in the hot tub until dinner – we'll admit, the daytime activities at a swinger resort are crazier than Spring Break but pale in comparison to what happens when the sun goes down!

After dinner, people change into their evening clothes (maybe some sexy lingerie, or a costume for the theme party) and the fun really begins. You can find live entertainment at the nightclub and make a sexy connection for that evening! Swinger resorts often offer play areas for guests to enjoy, or you can bring your new friends back to your room. Once you've worked up an appetite, you can indulge in some late-night snacks and drinks at the 24-hour restaurant before you finally crash and get ready to do it all again the next day!

While it sounds like fun, you shouldn't expect a non-stop, all-day, all-night orgy. Everyone – including you – needs some time to relax and recharge.

While you're at the resort, be sure you leave your camera and phone in your room unless you want to be on a first-name basis with security. Privacy is very important at swinger resorts, so there are usually zero tolerance policies in the public nudity areas.

Sound like a dream come true? Here are some of your options if you're looking to indulge in a sexy vacation!

(You can find the resort website links & discount codes on SwingersHelp.com)

Nudist Resorts

There are many nudists resorts across the US and abroad. Most people going to these resorts are non-playing nudists, but there are usually a suitable number of swingers also enjoying the freedom. Most nudist resorts allow children, so any heavy flirting or frisky business needs to be kept inside your room.

A general tip for spotting likely swingers at a nudist resort is to look at their bodies and grooming. Nudists tend to let things grow down below, while swingers usually keep things very tidy and groomed. Of course, this is not a 100% accurate, so be careful when meeting new people at these resorts. The ratio of swingers tends to increase on the weekends, so plan accordingly.

Some of the more popular swinger-friendly nudist resorts are Freedom Acres in California, Rooftop Resorts and Caliente Resorts in Florida, Paradise Valley in Georgia, Live Oaks and Riverside Ranch in Texas, and Cap d'Agde in France. Just remember that these are primarily nudist resorts so don't assume everyone is a swinger. A subtler approach usually delivers better results & avoids upsetting other people.

Swinger Conventions

Yes, this is a real thing. There are a few different conventions, all across the states! There's the Vegas Exchange (in Las Vegas, of course), which attracts a few thousand swingers for a four-day foray into all things swinging. Then there's Naughty in Nawlins, a five-day adventure that's so big they have a full parade of swingers going down Bourbon Street in New Orleans. There are several other swinger conventions, but these are the two most popular ones. Make sure to book early so you can stay at the host hotel instead of the overflow hotels which will have fewer people. Conventions are great learning opportunities, even for veteran swingers, and an awesome chance to see more of this huge, sex-positive community.

Hotel Takeover

A few times a year, a lifestyle party organizer might rent out several floors of a hotel (or an entire hotel) for a private swinger soiree. Full hotel takeovers often allow nudity in the pool area and hallways, since the public isn't allowed inside during the takeover. These takeovers are usually 2-3 days long and cost as much as an average hotel stay. Don't hold your breath waiting for a 4- or 5-star hotel takeover. Those places tend to be too busy to allow takeovers, and party organizers would have a much harder time finding enough swingers who can afford a 5-star hotel. Most hotel takeovers are hosted in 2- to 3-star hotels.

Thankfully, the people attending these events are less interested in the hotel and more interested in making new friends with the other guests. A hotel takeover is similar to the swinger conventions, just on a more condensed scale. There will probably be a few hundred people instead of thousands, with few or no workshops offered. The good thing is that most weekends, if not every weekend, there are swinger hotel takeovers going on. You just might have to travel a bit to get there. If you are a swinger in a rural area, this could be your solution for finding partners.

Temptation Resort

Cancun's everlasting spring break for adults, Temptation is not a real swinger resort. It's more of a lifestyle-friendly topless resort that just happens to attract swingers and swayers. The staff does not allow any blatant sexy playing in public. You need to keep that in your hotel room. The party vibe is top notch. This crowd focuses on some serious partying. As the night gets late, there are plenty of swingers that will be flirting and looking to bring new friends back to their hotel rooms. If you want to party more and play a little, Temptation is a good match for you.

Hedonism Resort

Jamaica's famous clothing-optional resort. Officially it is called Hedonism II but it's the only Hedo resort so don't worry. You can pick a room on the Tame (clothed) side or the Wild (nude) side. Whichever side you pick, you can use either the Tame or Wild pool areas as long as you appropriately dress or undress. Many guests are nudists who want to have a fun, non-swinging time. There are plenty of swingers who will have sex anytime in the public pool area on the Wild side. Singles are welcome at Hedonism, so you may run into a bunch of single guys. Hedonism hosts many swinger takeovers throughout the year, organized by different swinger groups. These takeover weeks cost more, but the swinger ratio is much higher and there are usually a lot of extra activities during the takeover weeks. Hedonism also has some "Young Swingers Weeks", where the crowd skews towards swingers in their 20s and 30s.

Desire Resorts

There are two Desire resorts, and they are right outside of Cancun. Both are pricey and are couples-only but well worth the price tag. No unicorns (except in August) or single men (sorry, no exceptions) are allowed. Desire Riviera Maya is a bit bigger, with a more active scene. Desire Pearl is smaller and people tend to feel it is a bit more elegant. They are all-inclusive and clothing-optional. There tends to be more swingers than nudists at Desire, but it's not a free-for-all play marathon; most opportunities to play take place at night. If the mood hits you during the day you are allowed to play in the pool area, beach beds, & the super sexy Sin Room. Because Desire is a bit pricey, the clientele tends to skew towards swingers in their 40s and 50s. The higher price does deliver a higher service level than you usually find at Hedo. Like Hedonism, Desire hosts a few swinger takeover weeks throughout the year run by different swinger groups.

Swinger Cruises

There are a bunch of swinger takeover cruises organized by different companies. It is kind of crazy, but there are so many swingers looking to party that we can fill up entire cruise ships! If you want to go on a weeklong cruise with 3,000 of your closest swinger friends, this is for you! These cruises cost more than normal cruises, and usually cost more than any swinger resort but you are talking about great service and a huge swinger party so it's worth it. It's like a takeover week at a huge swinger resort: they usually bring on some guest speakers and throw extra-crazy parties with group play areas available on the ship. Since it is a cruise takeover, you can leave the swimsuit at home and not worry about tan lines! With thousands of swingers and assorted lifestylers, there is something for everyone and every age group. Each cruise is different but roughly about 20% of couples are in their 20s or early 30s and that means about 600 young swingers so there is definitely something for everyone.

Whichever swinger travel choice you go with, you might want to look up a nearby hotel that you can give to your vanilla family and friends when they ask where you are going on vacation. Happy travels!

Packing Your Swinging Party Bag

We are going to need some party supplies to have the best time which is why it is very common for swingers to pack a party bag even for local parties. This can be as small as a purse or as a big as luggage depending on what you want. Here are some things to consider putting into your party bag.

Condoms - Bring many more condoms than you need. Condoms break and you'll need to change condoms each time you change partners. You might also want to bring an assortment of condom sizes in case your play partners don't pack enough. This ensures play time keeps rolling along. The wrong condom size can lead to condoms slipping off or breaking off which isn't fun.

Lube - Make sure the lube is compatible with your condoms, toys, etc. There are many different types so make sure to pack the right match. You can buy small lube packets if you don't want to bring a big bottle.

Toys - Most swinging situations are so hot they don't need any toys. Toys are more common for girl/girl playing. If you bring toys make sure to have condoms to cover them up to stay safe and change the condoms for each sex partner because you can get a STI from a toy. Also have a plastic bag to put the dirty toys in after you are done playing.

ED Pills - Many men are using ED pills. If you benefit from them, make sure to properly plan. You want to take your pill early enough so you will be all ready when play time starts but not too soon that the effects wear off before the playing is finished.

Flat Shoes - Ladies those high heels look super sexy but after a long play session you just might want to put on some comfy flats as you get dressed and go home.

Hand Sanitizer/Wipes - Sometimes there is a line for the bathroom, so having cleaning supplies can be helpful. Baby wipes are great for quickly refreshing after a long and sweaty play session.

Cash - Have plenty of cash. This makes it easier to split any bills if you are meeting for drinks, dinner or getting a hotel room. If something goes wrong you can just leave money on the table and leave. More likely things will be going so well, you'll want to just leave cash to pay your tab as you all scurry off for a hot play session. Make sure to bring plenty of singles so you can tip the bartender even if it is a BYOB party.

Mouthwash/Disposable Toothbrush - Most likely you are going to be making out so you want sexy fresh breath. Pack some travel size items to help you keep your breath sexy fresh all party long.

Water/Gatorade - Play sessions can turn into quite the sexy workout. It is very common to bring water bottles or even Gatorade to help you catch your breath before the next session of your sexy workout begins.

Camera - Don't pack a camera unless everyone is comfortable with it. A sexy photo shoot can be a great way to ease into a play session or to fill up the time while the guys recover for the second or third round of sexy time. Some people will get extra turned on with a camera and others will freak out. Don't assume and make sure to ask first.

Spare Underwear - Having a clean pair of underwear in a small zip lock bag can feel really nice at the end of the party.

Swimsuits - Swingers tend to act a bit more like nudists at swinging parties with a pool or a hot tub, so many experienced swingers will be chuckling about this one. At swinging parties you can choose your comfort level and wear a swimsuit if you prefer. Swingers want everyone to feel comfortable, so it really is up to your comfort level (and of course the rules of your swinger party). More likely you will pack a swimsuit for when you have a play date at a hotel. Unless it is a full swinger hotel takeover you will need to wear a swimsuit if you want to use the hotel pool.

Portable Speaker - Load up some sexy playlists on your phone and then play them on your portable speaker. It can help to set the right vibe for your play session.

Towels - Most swinging clubs/resorts will provide free towels but having a spare towel can be very helpful. If you are playing at a hotel, always ask for extra towels as soon as you get in your room so you won't have to wait later in the night. There might be some sexy squirting that needs to be cleaned up or a bunch of sexy people taking showers.

Contact Cards - Some swingers have their screenname & swinger contact info printed on a business card. It makes it easier for people to remember you the next day especially if it is a big party with a bunch of mingling and socializing.

Alcohol - Some alcohol can be a great social lubricant and ease the nerves just don't go overboard. Sloppy drunk isn't sexy or appealing. Feel free to bring extra in case you want to share with new friends.

Candy/Snacks - A bit of a sugar rush can be really helpful after a long play session. It can also be nice to have something for the trip back home if it is a long trek.

Honestly we could go on with a bunch more things that different swingers pack in their play bag. Like hair ties, corkscrew, bottle opener, cups, shot glass, multiple lingerie outfits, tylenol, tampons or moon cup, and so much more. Don't worry and don't go crazy. It's supposed to be fun not stressful. The most important thing to pack is a great attitude. The more you play, the more you will figure out what you like to bring for the different swinging situations.

Our Swinging Journal: Always Be Prepared aka Pack the Lady Gear

Our friends are hosting a house party and they invited us to join. It is going to be an intimate affair with just over 100 of their closest swinging friends. Ok so not so much an intimate affair but still should be a fun time. We are thinking it's going to be more of meet & greet cocktail party with little chance to play because really how are 100 people going to find space to play in a small house. It is exciting as we look forward to this sexy house party filled with a fun sex-positive crowd. We aren't sure what exactly will happen but we do know it is going to be a great party.

Finally the weekend arrives and we are getting ready. We learned a long time ago to bring our play bag whenever meeting swingers. Sometimes lightning can strike causing a super hot spark that leads to a sexy play. It isn't fun saying "no thanks" to hot friends just because we forgot to bring condoms. So we grab our "to go" party bag and head out. When we pull up to the party, we decide to put just the condom bag (a repurposed cosmetic bag) in her purse and leave the rest of the party bag in the car. Yeah, you are probably correctly guessing this was a silly mistake on our part but live & learn.

We enter the party and it is freakishly fun. The hostess is welcoming people with jello shots & shooters. The main floor has the kitchen that is filled with trays of tasty food from a restaurant. Downstairs has been converted into a disco with a full bar where we drop off our BYOB wine. Everyone is just super friendly and getting into the party vibe.

We are chatting with a fun couple and as often happens in the lifestyle, one thing leads to another and it becomes sexy time. We go from complimenting the ladies who look extra sexy in their plunging tops, to seeing who has the most sensitive nipples using our fingers & lips to judge. Yeah, life is pretty good and then it gets amazingly good.

Good luck shined upon us because right as we are all getting worked up we notice one of the bedrooms set-up for play is available. Thank goodness we brought the condom bag! We step in the room and start having a hot time first with our own partners and then we switch partners with the ladies on the bed next to each other as we all build to a volcanic finish. Wooo!

We are catching our breath when the other lady confides that she is straight and isn't curious but the incidental contact when the ladies shared the bed felt really good. Well would you like some more? Oh yeah, she wants more. Now guys, when this happens to you, be smart and get out of the way of the sexy ladies. This is their moment, just relax & enjoy the hot show.

So for a straight lady that is not curious, she is very eager for girl/girl play and it escalates to a super hot scene. Mrs. "I'm straight but hot for a girl right now" is wishing they had a dildo to play with. Mr. F knows where he can get a full arsenal of girl/girl sex toys. So now, it's late at night, and he is running to the car on the street half naked to retrieve the sex toy bag to keep the sexy ladies smiling. Safe to say a new speed record was established that night and crisis was averted.

The ladies had a super sexy time by themselves with the men grateful for the amazing view. After catching their breath for a second time that night, the ladies then pull the guys back in to join them for another round. Oh, it is tough having enough stamina for these sexy swinger parties. So be smart and always prepared because life is much more fun when you are fully equipped.

Safer Sex is Smarter Sex

Staying healthy and safe is a big concern for newbies and veterans alike. The lifestyle is a community, and staying healthy keeps everyone healthy – which allows everyone to have more fun.

According to the United States CDC, sexually transmitted diseases and infections (STDs and STIs, respectively) are still a big problem. Out of the 320 million people in the US, roughly 80 million have had some form of HPV, the most common STI.

Before you get too freaked out, here's some good news. First of all, not all HPV is created equal, and many forms of HPV resolve themselves on their own with no symptoms or health problems. Secondly, STI rates drop dramatically for people over the age of 25. For example, 66% of all chlamydia cases involve people ages 24 and under. People aged 40 and older make up only 4% of yearly chlamydia cases. And third, some studies have found that people in consensual non-monogamous relationships (including swingers) tend to have a lower risk of contracting an STI than the average American but that hasn't been 100% proven just yet.

We know that sounds odd; more sex must mean more risk, right? Not necessarily. When you think about it, monogamous relationships deal with infidelity – which often occurs when people are drinking and making bad, impulsive decisions. Those bad, impulsive decisions include unprotected sex, driving up their STI risk. Even if a cheater isn't getting drunk when they're unfaithful, they may be unwilling to carry condoms or get tested, afraid of their significant other finding out.

Swingers, on the other hand, aren't hiding anything from their partner. Swingers don't need to hide a supply of condoms or get secretly tested; they are open and up-front about how they want to protect themselves and their partners. People in the lifestyle also tend to be a bit better informed about sex in general, which helps them make more informed & safer choices when it comes to STI prevention. Swingers may be having more sex than the average American, but they're doing it in a much safer fashion.

None of this means that swinging is completely safe. There is no such thing as 100% safe sex - this is why we use the term 'safer sex'. Whenever you are exchanging fluids or even making skin-to-skin contact with another person, there's a level of risk. Think about it: you risk catching the common cold or the flu whenever you shake hands with your coworker. Nothing in life is 100% safe!

There are many different STDs, all of which can be contracted in different ways. There's also the risk of pregnancy. You need to talk to your partner and decide what level of risk is acceptable for you, and what rules can help mitigate your risk.

Thankfully, there are many ways to reduce your chance of exposure to STDs, STIs, or pregnancy. Here are some of the more common strategies used to keep swinging safer for you, your partner, and everyone else.

Avoiding Risky Behaviors

The best way to minimize risk is to just avoid risk. Many swingers opt to only engage in soft swap because it carries less risk than full swap. Staying away from penetrative play puts you at a much smaller risk for STIs and pregnancy. Even if you prefer full swap playing, you should talk with your partner about whether or not backdoor play is on the menu. Anal sex does increase your risk of STIs.

Even then, you can have full swap play that includes backdoor access without putting yourself in a high-risk situation. Choose to play only with partners who have recently been tested, and of course use protection. There are many ways to pick and choose your play boundaries to help you reduce the risk of STIs and keep you healthy for a long time.

Preventative Medicine

Scientists are doing some amazing things with preventative medicine. We are not your doctors, and we aren't giving you medical advice. This is just some helpful information to help you start a conversation with your doctor. Always talk to a doctor before trying a new medication. He or she is the best person to help you figure out your personal health situation.

The most common preventative medicine when it comes to sex is birth control. Even if your man has had a vasectomy, birth control might be a good idea. Not everyone in the lifestyle has had a vasectomy, and condoms are not 100% effective at preventing pregnancy. Birth control has evolved a lot over the past decade, and there are many options available: there are hormonal pills, patches, implants, and shots. Some forms, like the pill, are taken daily, while other forms, like the implant, protect you for three years at a time. There are also non-hormonal options, like the copper IUD.

Side effects vary from method to method and from woman to woman, but most women can find a birth control that has limited side effects. Some side effects might even be beneficial – birth control can help regulate periods, make them lighter or disappear entirely. Some birth control options also allow you to control when you get your period, making it easier to make swinging plans or book a sexy vacation without worrying about a surprise visit from Aunt Flo.

There are also preventative medicines for STIs. The vaccine Gardisil is already commonly used on children since so many adults have some form of HPV and it can be spread by touching skin. Some forms of HPV can cause cancer; Gardisil targets some of these nastier strains. Gardisil is marketed towards people under 26, but anyone can potentially benefit from it. Many swingers have already spoken to their doctors and received this vaccine. The vaccine will cost about $500 per person (depending on your location and insurance), which isn't so bad considering the peace of mind and health benefits that come with it.

Twinrix is a vaccine that helps prevent hepatitis A and B. It is used on children and adults alike. It is commonly used by anyone travelling abroad, since hepatitis A can be transmitted through food or tap water in certain countries. It is a series of 3 or 4 shots. The total vaccine treatment will cost about $300 to $500 depending on your location and insurance.

PrEP (Pre-Exposure Prophylaxis) is another weapon in the medicinal toolbox. In 2012, the FDA approved Truvada as a PrEP drug. This daily medicine is about 95% effective against preventing HIV. It doesn't save you from other STIs and can be expensive (about $1000 per month, depending on your insurance). It is more commonly used by the gay and bisexual community.

There is also PEP (Post Prophylaxis) treatment. PEP is more of an emergency backup treatment in case you have unprotected sex with a HIV-positive person. For PEP to be effective you need to take it within 72 hours of exposure. It is not perfect and has many side effects, but it is an option if something goes wrong. The good news is that there are at least options for fighting HIV and more research is being done all the time.

You probably don't want to talk with your regular doctor about this. Maybe you're embarrassed, and don't want your doctor to know about your swinging lifestyle. Suck it up buttercup, and be an adult. Most doctors love helping patients with this stuff because these doctor visits are usually quick and easy – and, frankly, a bit profitable for doctors. Your doctor has encountered things much stranger than an adult being responsible about their sexual health.

If you still don't want to chat with your doctor, look up a local clinic. Most counties across the US have a public health clinic providing these services, and some counties even provide them on an anonymous basis. You can also visit your local Planned Parenthood. You might be thinking that Planned Parenthood just handles that one very controversial procedure, but that isn't true. Over 95% of the people visiting Planned Parenthood are going for birth control, cancer screenings, STI testing, and other non-controversial stuff.

Don't be embarrassed that you are over the age of 18 and having sex. There are too many 40 year old virgins that are crazy envious of you. Be an adult and talk to a doctor to better protect yourself today.

Fluid Bonding

Fluid bonding is more common amongst polyamory couples, but it is certainly an option for swingers. Fluid bonding is when you commit with another person or persons to cease all unprotected sex with people outside of the relationship. For example, most married couples are fluid bonded, since they are monogamous and only have unprotected sex with each other.

In theory, this is great. In reality, it rarely works for a long time in the swinging lifestyle. First, you need to find matching swingers with great connections all around to have the potential for long term fun. We all know how tough it can be to find a four-way or six-way connection, and it only gets harder when you're looking for a connection that will last a long time as opposed to one night.

After you find these magical partners, everyone involved needs to be ready to stop playing with other swingers and form a closed swinger group. Then you'll likely need all the guys to have vasectomies. No modern contraceptive is perfect, and you don't want any surprise pregnancies. Then you need not one but two rounds of testing, because some STIs can take a few weeks before they show up positive in tests. Even after all that, no STI test is 100% perfect and some STIs can show up as a false negative unless the person is having an active outbreak. We don't want to scare you, just inform you so you aren't surprised to discover that fluid bonding is not 100% perfect.

If you really trust your amazing swinger friends and have carefully considered all risks and taken the best precautions, enjoy! Just know that many swingers try this route and find it's harder than it looks to perfectly implement.

Condoms

You'd think that by now condoms would be such a simple concept we wouldn't even need to chat about it, but there's actually a whole lot we need to cover in this section! We love condoms because they are a great way to fight STIs and help keep us healthy for more swinging fun. But condoms aren't perfect.

The sad truth is that some STIs, like herpes or HPV, are passed from skin to skin contact, so you can get them just from hugging or kissing. The other sad truth is that condoms are only helpful when they are used correctly, every single time.

Some swingers play bareback (full penetrative sex without condoms). Sex feels better without condoms; that's a no-brainer. But condoms keep us safer. Even if some STIs can be spread whether you use a condom or not, plenty of other STIs can't breach the barrier of a condom. Some protection against STIs is better than none at all! Imagine a cop not wearing a bulletproof vest because it doesn't keep their legs safe; that's silly, right? So why would you not use a condom that could protect you from HIV, just because it won't protect you from 100% of all STIs? Using condoms is smart, safe, and highly recommended.

What about those bareback swingers? Are they reckless and dangerous? Not necessarily; some swingers only play bareback with a certain group of trusted partners and fluid bonded friends. Those people are responsibly making an informed consensual decision.

Of course, there are people who don't use condoms outside of a closed, fluid-bonded situation. You might want to avoid playing with them to lower your risks. Safer sex starts with avoiding people who put themselves and you at risk. We suggest you play with people who value safer decisions.

Most swinger couples are awesome and play wisely. However, if you're in the lifestyle long enough, you might encounter an unsafe couple. They may try to push you into playing bareback. They may act offended if you ask them to wear a condom, because they feel it implies they are dirty. They may even try to slip in without a condom during heated foreplay. None of this is cool, and you should immediately walk away from these people. If you and your partner made a rule to always use condoms, that rule should hold true even during the most heated, passionate moments.

Most swingers are great people and will respect your rules but mistakes do happen. Another swinger might have had too much to drink. If you suspect a potential play partner has had too much to drink, you should avoid them until they are ready to think more clearly. If you feel pressure from another swinger to do something that doesn't feel safe, STOP! If you are swinging as a couple, let your loved one know immediately and get out of that situation. Don't worry about hurting their feelings. Your first obligation is to protect you and your partner from bad apples.

OK, now that we've talked about why you should use condoms, let's talk about how to use condoms. Guys, we know that condoms don't feel the best and can make it harder to keep an erection. Not all condoms are created equal. There are many different styles and brands of condoms. You just need to find the best match for you to maximize your enjoyment and sensations.

The three biggest differences in condoms are how long, how wide, and how thick. You'll probably want to avoid extra-thick condoms unless you're aiming to delay your orgasm – in the case of men who finish too quickly, or if you're gearing up for a super-heated, multi-hour session, thickness might be a huge benefit. But most of the time, you want to go thinner, so you can experience more sensation. There are many new super-thin condoms that didn't even exist five years ago. Trojan Supra condoms are so thin they are almost half the thickness of a regular Trojan condom.

Let's also talk about the length and width of condoms. Check your ego at the door. Condom companies know that many guys decide on which condoms to buy using only their ego. That's why you see terms like "Magnum" and "XXL" decorating condom packaging. We're going to let you in on a little secret: these condoms can cost almost double the price and are sometimes the same length and width (if not smaller) than standard size. Crazy, right? Condom manufacturers know male egos will pay big money before reading the fine print. Be smart and check out a condom chart, which you can find on *SwingersHelp.com*. It will help you find a condom that is a good match for your size.

A little PSA for guys: your size is a good size. Women like variety, and for most women it's much more important for guys to know how to use their equipment than the actual size of it. To give your play partner the most pleasure, you should make sure to use the right size condom. Condoms that are too big can slide off during sex. No one wants to go to the ER to get a lost condom fished out – yes that happens, but thankfully not very often. Condoms that are too small are more likely to break, which kills the fun as you worry about STIs and pregnancy - and fishing out all the pieces, getting a new one on, and hoping you still have an erection to keep going. Wearing the right size condom will help feel better for you and for your play partner.

Test out different condoms with your partner until you find the right one that fits and still feels good. Get in some condom practice with your partner at home. This will help you better perform in the lifestyle, where you might feel a bit of pressure playing with a brand-new person. Besides, any excuse to have more sexy time with your special someone is always a good thing!

A note about decorum: just because you are wearing a condom does not mean you should orgasm anywhere you want. Be a gentleman and ask the lady where she'd like you to finish, or where you definitely shouldn't finish, before you play. Some people feel comfortable with climaxing inside the body if the guy is wearing a condom. Other swingers will be extremely offended and angry if you climax inside, even if the guy is wearing a condom.

The best way to avoid this potential drama is to communicate. The lady might say you can climax anywhere but it would drive her extra wild if you climax on a certain body part. Don't you want to have extra-hot sex that climaxes in a way that turns your sex partner's heat level to ultra-hot? It's simple: skip the drama and ask about her preference.

Whenever going anywhere in the lifestyle, bring condoms. Bring more condoms than you will ever need. You can plan a simple coffee chat with a new couple and have zero plans to play. Every so often the chemistry is so great you may end up wanting to play with the couple immediately. You always want to be prepared with condoms. If the other guy forgot his condoms, or you need to cover up some sex toys, or you end up swapping partners a few times, you want enough condoms to keep the party rolling. You should also change condoms if you switch from back door action to regular sex, or risk causing a painful UTI for the lady. It is not unusual to go through more than six condoms in a single playdate, so make sure to pack more than enough condoms.

Another tool for safer sex is the dental dam. A dental dam is a flat, square piece of latex that's used to provide a protective barrier for oral sex. It does not replace the need for condoms during penetration. It just adds a layer of safety by avoiding direct mouth-to-skin contact during oral play.

Many of you might be thinking that dental dams are just for going down on a lady, but they can also be used for oral action on the backdoor (this goes for men and women alike). Dental dams are less common compared to condoms, but some couples in the lifestyle do use them.

No, you can't substitute plastic wrap for a dental dam. That cling-wrap in your kitchen is actually porous, and some nasty microscopic bugs can get through it. If you can't find dental dams at your pharmacy, you can use a non-lubricated latex condom by carefully slicing it down one side to create a flat sheet. It won't feel the same as a wet tongue but it can absolutely still feel great when using it during oral. Most people love some oral attention down below and any tool to help keep us safer and healthy is a helpful tool.

Testing

No matter how you decide to control the risks involved with sex, you should include regular STI testing even if you have no STI symptoms. Testing can help you get treatment before any symptoms get too nasty or even show up. It also helps protect your current and future partners.

Don't be afraid of testing. The worst case scenario is that you have a STI, in which case you most definitely want to know what it is and get it treated ASAP. Best case, the STI test comes back negative and you can brag to your next partner how you were recently tested. Many people are turned on knowing they are dealing with a responsible person and not a walking petri dish.

Just remember that standard STI testing does not check for herpes or HPV. They usually don't check because about 70% to 80% of adults already have some version of herpes and/or HPV in their system. Even if you are carrying either virus (which, mathematically, you likely are) it can be hard for the STI test to return an accurate positive result if you aren't currently having an outbreak.

Honesty

The best defense against STIs is honesty and trust. You should be honest with your play partners and expect the same from them. Honesty is expected amongst swingers for this reason. If you ever suspect a partner is not being 100% honest, you should decline to play. Trust your gut and do not take chances. You want to know that you are playing with responsible partners who are not taking unnecessary risks. Their risky behavior could have exposed them to things you don't want to deal with. So if you have any doubt about a play partner being honest, then you should wisely defer on playing.

Just remember to use common sense and think with your big head, not the one that lives below the waist. It can be too easy to get caught up in the heat of passion and expose yourself to a risk. If something doesn't feel right, it's smarter to decline sexy play time. There will be many more opportunities in the future – but only if you keep yourself healthy! It just doesn't make sense to take unnecessary risks that can endanger your entire future as a swinger. Thankfully, there are many ways to have your sexy cake and eat it too!

Our Swinging Journal: All fun & games till an emergency doctor visit...

Ok so we're having a fun time and by fun time we mean several rounds of amazing hot sex. On the last round, something weird happened. The condom disappeared. The other guy was wearing a condom and somehow *poof* it is gone, he immediately stopped and tried to find it. We looked in the bed sheets, and the pile of clothes, all around the floor and still couldn't find it. Dr. G did an internal look about and couldn't find it. So we decided it was best to call it a night, got dressed and headed home.

We tried our best to see if it was lost inside Dr. G but eventually admitted defeat and made an emergency doctor visit to make sure it hadn't disappeared somewhere it shouldn't be. Apparently, magically disappearing condoms isn't a rare thing according to the gyno on duty. She shared a bunch of fun stories about crazy things that people needed removed like pens, veggies, golf balls, hot dogs. So seriously everyone, please stick with appropriate sex toys and don't improvise.

We were assured it wasn't still inside her so we went home to finally relax & rest but not before we ordered better fitting, ultra snug condoms for our friend so this would never ever happen again.

Seriously, how does a condom just disappear?

Fakers and Ghost Stories

Ready for action? Excited to make new connections and enjoy sexy times? Slow down for a second and let's talk about fakers and ghosting.

You will encounter a bunch of people who are not real swingers. Some of them are maliciously faking for their own personal gain. Others might be real swingers but will still frustrate you as they disappear like ghosts when it's time for the real action to start.

Spotting & Defending Against Fakers

Fakers have many reasons for putting up a false front. A faker could be a lonely vanilla person collecting sexy pictures, a married person trying to cheat on their spouse, or something worse. They will set up online profiles or ads hoping to entice real swingers into their trap. Here are some tips for spotting fakers before you waste time on them.

Avoid free websites and stick with dedicated swinger websites like SLS, SDC, or Kasidie. Forcing members to pay for access keeps many (but not all) fakers away. Some fakers will still pay for access to swinger profiles.

Avoid online profiles without pictures. Real swingers know that you are looking for a physical connection and will be happy to share at least a picture of their body, with their faces cropped out. If someone is unwilling to share any pictures at all, it's sign they are likely fake or too uncomfortable to play just yet and likely to turn into a ghost.

Avoid perfect-looking profiles. We all want to stumble upon amazing, god-like airbrushed swinging supermodels, but that isn't reality. If something looks too good to be true, it probably is. You can use a reverse image search engine to see if the images have been stolen from another website. It could also be real swingers who aren't attractive and trying to pull a bait and switch on you, though certifications on the paid websites make this rare.

Make sure to voice verify or read certifications. Most swinger profiles will have certifications/validations from other swingers and party organizers to vouch that they are legit. If you find an online profile that has no certifications from other swingers, you should have the ladies do a quick call to voice verify. This helps make sure the other lady is excited about swinging and not being dragged into an uncomfortable situation. Voice verifying and certifications also protect you from a more common bait and switch situation – a single guy pretending to be a couple.

Skip very short profiles. Very short ads are less likely to be a real swinger looking for a real connection. We want to find good matches and if a profile has almost no information, how show that it is a good match for what you want? Skip the short profiles and go for a profile that has more information.

Don't use your vanilla contact information. Protect yourself from being outed by setting up a different email address and phone number just for lifestyle communicating. There are bunch of free options for email and phone numbers.

Think twice before sharing. Many fakers like to collect naughty pictures. If something doesn't feel right, don't rush to share pictures. Voice your concerns. Start with body-only pictures before revealing your face pictures. Real swingers will understand that new swingers can feel nervous and they will not pressure you.

Ghost Stories

If you've been talking with someone and building a connection, and they suddenly disappear and stop responding to messages, you've likely been ghosted. Ghosting is common among fakers and nervous newbie swingers.

Unfortunately, ghosting can also happen with veteran swingers. If they're having relationship problems, they might unexpectedly disappear from the lifestyle while they focus on their own relationship. If there is a dramatic conversation snafu, like someone bringing up politics or religion, the other couple might run away and cut off all contact. Exchanging pictures can also result in swingers ghosting each other. Before you jump to conclusions, it's not just about your pictures being hot enough. It could be that you look too similar to their family, friends or coworkers.

Even crazier, you might actually be their family, friend, neighbor, or coworker! Yes, this actually happens quite a bit. The funniest story that we've heard so far is when our swinging friends were travelling and unwittingly ended up flirting with another couple who turned out to be one of their identical twins – in that scenario, awkward was definitely an understatement.

There are also false ghost sightings. If you message another couple and do not hear back the same day, don't assume they are ghosting you. Remember that swinging is extracurricular fun, so it often takes a backseat to the rest of life. Many swingers don't respond until they can chat together about your message. If one of them is on a business trip, or busy with a deadline, or dealing with family, or distracted by any other of the many more important priorities in life, they can be slow to respond to you. It is better to be understanding and forgiving while you wait for a response instead of assuming it is a rude ghosting.

The best way to fight ghosting is to focus more on real-life meetings. Spending less time cruising online profiles and more time meeting new friends at swinger clubs will greatly increase your chances of actually playing. If you are going to cruise online profiles, focus on couples that have more in common with you, so you have a better chance of making a connection. Chasing after couples with big age gaps or other significant differences increases the chance of being ghosted. Some swingers just don't know how to politely decline other couples, and think ghosting is easier even though it can be rude and frustrating.

Of course, there is another legitimate reason to be ghosted. If you are turning into a stage 5 creepy clinger, you shouldn't be surprised that you push people away. Be careful not to bury your play partners with too many messages. Swinging is fun, but it's not anyone's full-time job. Many swingers don't have the time or desire to get bombarded with many messages every day. Be cool and don't act desperate. Barraging them with too many emails and texts usually results in a bad time.

How much is too much? Everyone has their own preference, but many swingers will be ok with about a message a day or less. Some will enjoy more and others will prefer less. You can show off your maturity by asking play partners how they prefer to communicate. Seriously, if you are close enough to play a sexy game of "hide the salami", you should feel comfortable chatting about your communication preferences.

Being Stood Up

There are going to be times where you are stood up on a sexy date. Believe it or not, there is a good chance they're real swingers, not fakers. The community often jokes about how swingers have a reputation for being flaky. Honestly, it's not so much that swingers are flaky; it's more about swingers juggling a bunch of stuff in their lives. Unexpected schedule interruptions are not uncommon.

The lady might have gotten her period early. Their kids might have gotten sick or forgot to tell them about a school or team event they need to attend. The couple might be having an argument and don't want to bring their drama out to the public (for which you should be thankful). If they are newer to the lifestyle, one of them might be having a bad case of the nerves. Unfortunate as it may be, there are many real reasons that can cause a last-minute cancellation.

To protect from no-show swingers ruining the evening, stick with swinging websites that have verified profiles. This way, you can minimize the headaches of fakers. Another tip is to arrange first-time meetings at swinger clubs. This way, if something unexpectedly pops up with the other couple, you can still have fun with everyone else at the swinger club. As a matter of fact, you can start partying before they even arrive – so their arrival is more of a surprise bonus than the whole reason you're there.

If you're thinking about booking a hotel room, you might want to wait as long as you can to reserve the room just to be safe, or at least make sure the hotel has a generous cancellation policy. Many swingers will just use a last-minute hotel booking app or website so they get a deal and don't have to worry about cancelling a hotel room due to no-show swingers.

Remember to stay positive if there is a last-minute cancellation with your play partners. Seriously, let's think about this "worst case" scenario. You get to go out on a sexy private date with your fantastic partner, with both of you looking amazing and feeling excited for some extra special sexy fun. When the worst thing that can happen is having hot, sexy fun with your own amazing partner, there isn't much to complain about!

Of course, if something unexpectedly happens to you, please remember that no one likes to be stood up. So be polite enough to send an apology in advance, at least via text or email.

Our Swinging Journal: When life gives lemons, make cocktails...

Your adventurous duo was once again looking forward to another sexy weekend. We met a couple online and had been chatting with them for a few weeks. Their profile was certified and they were paid member so we felt more comfortable than we usually do when meeting fresh faces. We make plans to meet at a bar midway between our towns for a meet & greet.

We get to the bar, order our drinks but don't see them anywhere. We text them and they say they are running just a few minutes late. Ok, that is common in the lifestyle - no big deal. We'll just order another round and chill out. Another 20 minutes pass, and they still aren't here. We text & email them again but are now getting no response. Now they are over 40 minutes and we have no idea what is going on and our glasses are empty - so we hop in the car and drive away from those ghosts.

We spent a good bit of effort to look good & arrange our schedules for a fun night so we wanted to party, Dr. G fires up her smartphone & finds the closest open swinger club..

We pull up to the club, pay the admission fee and head inside. We made a big of a mistake in rushing to this backup plan. We didn't think to grab some booze on the drive over and we didn't have booze in the car since the original plan was for a meet & greet at a vanilla bar. This means we are now showing up empty handed to a BYOB swinger club.

Oh well, booze can be fun but we really were fine just drinking cola and making new friends. Oh boy, did we make new friends! The swinging community can be so freaking welcoming. It was a smaller club and that just made it easier to mingle with different people throughout the night, sharing jokes, giving sexy compliments and just being awesome to each other. As each couple heard about us getting stood up, they kept offering to share their own booze with us. Mr. F was the designated driver, but Dr. G just couldn't bear to be rude & decline any of the cocktails, or champagne, or yummy jello shots. Yeah, the community can be really friendly & with great taste in booze.

There was a bit of flirting but nothing too crazy. Just run of the mill stuff like the women giving impromptu stripper pole performances, hot grinding on the dance floor and some topless body shots - like we said nothing crazy or out of the ordinary for a swinger club. We didn't play that night and honestly that wasn't our goal. It had been a long week, and we just wanted to blow off some stress having a fun time with a friendly people that appreciated the sexier side of life. Despite the earlier snafu, that night was awesome. We made many new friends that night that led to sexier nights and opportunities for us to return the favor of sharing our favorite drinks with them.

Conversing and Cliques

You will likely make a bunch of new friends in the lifestyle. It can seem a bit intimidating when you first start. You might feel as nervous as a kid transferring into school during the middle of the school year. You might encounter a bunch of cliquey groups when you show up to an event. Don't be intimidated. Swingers are usually very friendly and open to new people, but sometimes we get too excited seeing our old friends and naturally clump together with our old friends. Here is a good game plan for working the room when you don't know anyone.

Step 1

To welcome new faces, some swinger clubs and parties will have special host couples, or the party organizers will do this job. These are swinger couples who are veterans of that particular swinger event. They will give anyone that asks a tour of the place and answer any questions. Remember, you often need to ask for a tour – they won't seek you out and offer one.

At smaller events, the party organizers will give you a quick overview as you show up. This is a great time to ask about the vibe and usual flow of the party so you can better enjoy the fun – you should have done this research before you showed up, but you may have forgotten, or you may not have understood what you read. Host couples are very useful for first-time swingers, but they're also great for veterans who are new to that venue. Worst case scenario, you will at least get introduced to the host couple and they will likely introduce you to a bunch of other people as you get the tour.

Step 2

Hopefully, you were able to take a tour with a host. If not, give yourself a tour. Walk around the room(s). Say hello and acknowledge anyone that looks your way. It's ok if you don't know them, swingers are friendly so just say hello. Be prepared for some close hugs and kisses on the cheek. Swingers can be a very friendly crowd. Don't be surprised if you see a quiet couple look your way and turn out to be scared first-timers. They will be very grateful for a friendly hello, so be generous with your hellos, handshakes, and hugs. After you walk the room(s), head over and get a drink.

Step 3

While getting a drink (or pouring your own drink since many swinger events are BYOB), check in with your partner. Figure out which people looked the most exciting to both of you. Once you know who you want to approach, it's time to actually do it! Yes, you can wait a few minutes as you enjoy your drink and let the alcohol sooth your nerves, but remember you came here to have fun. If you wanted to stand alone in a corner, you could have stayed home. Get excited! Let's do this!

Step 4

Head over to the people you want to approach. Wait for a lull in the conversation and jump in. Don't know what to talk about? You're not alone. Many swingers haven't been in the dating game for a long time, and it's easy to forget how to start and hold fun conversations with strangers. We got your back, and will clue you in on what and what not to talk about. If there is already a good conversation flowing, go with it. Don't try to hijack the conversation and change the topic. If you need a new conversation topic, here are eight possible icebreakers for you to pick from. Use the pneumonic "Stretch" to help you remember.

1. **SPOUSE/PARTNER** - How did you two sexy people meet? How do you juggle private romance time with the lifestyle?
2. **THEMSELVES** - People really like talking about themselves so embrace this. You look great tonight. How did you start in the lifestyle? What's your favorite swinger event? Which other sexy places do you like? People love to talk about themselves. When in doubt, ask them an open-ended question about themselves.
3. **RECREATION** - Are you following the game on TV tonight? Which teams do you like? Have you been to any music concerts or seen a movie recently?
4. **EXERCISE** - You both look super. How did you get into such great shape? What is your workout routine?
5. **TRAVEL** - Have you been to any of the swinger cruises or swinger trips? We are looking for tips on where to travel for lifestyle fun. What swinger trips are most interesting to you?
6. **CLOTHES** - Hi, we love your shoes. Where did you get them? Any tips for how to build a better wardrobe for the lifestyle?
7. **HOBBY** - Cool looking drink/beer, what does it taste like? Do you like mixology/ microbrews/cooking?

So now you know what to say, but what about what not to say?

Don't get too specific

Some swingers may not want to get too detailed for fear of outing themselves. Make sure to stick with general questions and avoid specific questions. For example, you can ask what industry they work in, but it's usually best if you don't ask which company they work for. You can ask what area of town they are from, but don't ask about specific cross streets like you are trying to uncover their real address. Being nosey or creepy is unsexy.

Don't engage in politics or religion

Don't bring up politicians, elections, religion or any controversial topic. This is a fast way to kill a sexy vibe. If someone mentions anything close to controversial, don't engage. We repeat - DO NOT ENGAGE. Change the conversation or just excuse yourself to get another drink. Even if you are both in the same political party, you could be very opposed on specific topics or the other swingers around you might not agree. Swinging is about coming together for sexy time, not dividing people into a controversial debate.

Don't share other people's info

Trust is super important to swingers. If you blab sensitive stuff about other swingers to your new swinging friends, you are basically telling them you can't be trusted. You can share stories of your friends or previous swinging experiences, but leave out any names or other identifying info. Demonstrate to your new friends that you respect other people's secrets and are trustworthy.

Don't hate

You might not feel comfortable with people who are different than you. That is something you need to work on privately - do not share that shortcoming with others. The swinging lifestyle is a very big tent with plenty of room for people of all sexual orientations, races, religions, and nationalities. Remember that swinging is about coming together for sexy time, not dividing people.

Don't bring up your kids

We all love our kids and have a bunch of funny kid stories. Save those stories for your vanilla friends or your long time swinger friends. When trying to generate a hot sexy vibe with new swingers you just met, talking about kids and parenting can be a big buzz kill. The only time you should come close to mentioning your kids is when you say "we had a great time chatting with you and you look sexy, but we only have a babysitter until midnight so would you like to come with us for some sexy playtime?"

Ok, that is a lot to remember. Don't stress, there aren't any swinger police that enforce these tips. These are just helpful suggestions to increase your chances of success when chatting with swingers.

Dealing with Cliques

A very common complaint in the swinging lifestyle involves cliques. You will show up to an event and find the swingers clumping together in tight groups with seemingly little interaction between the separate groups. Don't view cliques as being intentionally exclusive. Swingers can sometimes get too caught up in chatting with old swinger friends; just like any other group of people, talking to people you already know is easy and swingers like to know how their friends are doing. Be confident, not intimidated, because most groups will welcome you into the conversation if you politely make the first move.

One way to make the first move with a group of people is to wait for someone to leave the group to get a drink. While they are getting a drink, you can ask them one-on-one if their fun-looking group is a private party or if you can join the chat. This usually results in the person introducing you to the group. On occasion, that fun-looking group will be a private celebration with plans to play within the group. Even then, it's a win-win situation. You will either make new friends or learn they are not available to play, which will save you time so you can go meet other people. The only way you can lose is by being a wallflower, too scared to chat with others.

Remember that everyone going to a swinger party is looking to make a connection. If they wanted to be alone, they would have stayed home. Once you realize this, you will feel more comfortable and confident making the first move and starting a conversation.

You can chat with anyone, even if you're not interested them sexually. Chatting does not mean you want to play with someone. It just means you want to chat. You should feel comfortable talking with anyone in a group. Of course, everyone's ultimate goal is to have some sexy fun, so be careful with your time management. The more you talk with someone you don't want to play with, the less time you have to build a sexy connection with a potential play partner. Prioritize your conversations, and enjoy your sexy new friends!

Etiquette AKA Polite Phucking

Your teachers probably never taught you the proper etiquette when it comes to having sexy time with another person's partner. We don't know why they skipped this very important lesson in life, but it's time we rectified that mistake. Here are some tried-and-true etiquette lessons to help you minimize your embarrassment and increase your fun.

When meeting fresh faces...

Engage both people when meeting a couple. You want to show that you respect both of them, no matter what naughty thing is running through your mind about one of them. Showing respect now, is your way of showing that you can be trusted to respect their rules and boundaries later on in the bedroom. If you are at a swinger-only event, you can greet with a cozy hug and a light kiss. In more vanilla settings, you'll probably want to stick to handshakes.

How to approach a new couple...

Usually, swingers will have the ladies approach each other to start the conversation. Yes, guys can make the first contact - just remember to engage the man as well as the lady. Too many guys think they are in a bar trying to pick up single women, and that attitude just doesn't work in the lifestyle. Be very careful that you don't accidentally come across as an aggressive male, unless you like rejection and getting kicked out.

Be polite and show respect to both people in the couple. Compliment them on something and then ask them an open-ended question. If they are in a group talking with others, wait for a lull in the conversation. Apologize for interrupting and ask if it is a private conversation or if you can join. Then quickly compliment them. Everyone loves compliments, so give freely!

When attending a free party...

Bring a present for your hosts and make sure to seek them out when first arriving. It takes a lot of work to arrange a party, so be thoughtful and bring them a bottle of wine or sexy lube along with your own booze (if it is a BYOB party). It's hard to say which gift they'd like best, but they'll appreciate the thought behind the gesture!

When attending a paid party...

Do your best to avoid last minute no-shows. Swinger events often sell out and being a no-show prevents another couple from being able to attend. Be a respectful attendee. Make sure to tip the servers. There are many costs involved in running a swinger party. Organizers usually do this as a service for the community, since the profit margins are often razor thin. Don't ruin a good thing: be respectful of the venue and the organizers.

When getting a hotel room...

Wait as long as you can before booking a hotel room since swingers can be flaky and cancel at the last minute. Expect to pay for the room yourself. It is polite for the other people to offer to split expenses, but often they are so excited about sexy time that they forget. If you are the other couple, make sure to contribute towards the room. If your play partners won't take money then bring some snacks and drinks to share.

When not playing with others...

You can most certainly attend any swinger event and not play with others. Just be upfront and open about your plans so there is no confusion. If anyone asks if they can join your sexy play, politely decline them and keep having your private fun.

When watching others...

Keep a respectful distance from the action and don't distract them. If they can touch you, smell you, or hear you, then you are too close. You are not a porn director so mind yourself. Some people really enjoy putting on a hot show for you, but no one likes getting distracted and derailed from their hot, explosive finish!

When changing partners...

Make sure to always use a fresh condom. Then ask your new partner about what they want. We are all unique and have our own preferences. Don't just assume and start doing your thing. It's is much more fun when it is a joint effort.

When finishing...

Guys, before you start playing, ask where you should finish so you know what is and isn't allowed. Many full swap swingers assume they can finish inside, but others feel this is taboo and will be extremely upset.

Ladies, when you get close to climaxing, try your best not to claw your guy. Remember, this is a lending library and you need to return him in the same condition you got him, so no bite or nail marks. If you are a squirter, you should give the guy a heads up before you start to play because it can freak some guys out (though many will find it hot!). Both partners should give some warning as they get close to finishing so there are no surprises and everyone can better enjoy each other's sexy explosion.

After you have played with a couple...

Send them flowers...just kidding! Many swingers would freak out if you knew their full name and street address to send flowers. It's nice to send a "thank you" text or email the next day. If you would like to play again, offer it. Don't turn into a stage-5 creepy clinger. If they don't respond, don't stalk them. We all have busy lives and they might just be extra busy right now.

How to decline another couple...

You are going to have some couples asking if you're interested in playing with them. Be polite, honest, and don't overshare. Just say "no thanks". You don't need to defend your rejection. It would be nice to compliment something about them first and then say "but we just aren't a good match" If you want to give a reason, keep it general to avoid hurting anyone's feelings. You can say you don't feel a four-way connection; they don't need to know that you think one of them is hideous or maybe one of them is so hot it is causing possible jealous feelings.

How to react when you see swingers in the vanilla world...

Act cool. If they are with people, keep your distance. If they are alone, you can cautiously approach for a very discreet vanilla greeting. You don't want to accidentally expose someone as a swinger or make them feel uncomfortable. When in doubt, don't approach them and just say hello with your eyes from a healthy distance. You can privately message them later without risking anything.

Our Swinging Journal: Waking up Sleeping Beauty

Most swinger stories you hear are just not completely honest. They will focus on the exciting action & never admit our bodies do have limitations. Thankfully for you, we have no shame & laugh about our limitations. We hope you'll share this laugh with us.

So on a dreary Monday morning, one of our favorite couples reaches out to us about our upcoming weekend plans. This question was a no-brainer for us. If our good friends wanted to play they just had to pick a time & place. So we quickly plan to meet at a swinger club Saturday night. If this was a regular swinger couple, that would probably end the conversation for us. But we click so well, that it kicks off five days of heavy online flirting & fantasy sharing that would make Hugh Hefner blush.

Thank goodness the weekend finally arrives. All of us happily agree to meet early at the club. None of us are silly enough to pretend we don't want to play so the night is on a sexy fast track. We immediately all head to a play room for a giggly good time. Ok it wasn't all giggles because there was so much moaning happening. But seriously how can you not have the widest grin on your face when you find yourself in the middle of a super hot sexcapade?

The sexy crazy hot outfits, the tingling caresses over our bodies, the hot dueling tongue action - oh my! If you haven't enjoyed a three way french kiss, you just gotta do it. So all of this leads into some intense action. Bodies are flying all over as we change from one hot position to another. The guys have a friendly competition to see who can outlast in this blissful moment. Thankfully the men are soon put out of their misery, because no one mortal man can last for long with that much bliss.

While the guys are recovering, the ladies just don't want to stop and use this as a perfect opportunity for some luscious lady loving. They truly enjoy themselves and become oblivious to their husbands who are enjoying a super hot live porn show. With such a sensual display, it doesn't take long for the guys to rise up for round two.

We pull out the fantasy wish list from the week long flirting and start checking off the list of sexy ideas. Thankfully it was round two or the guys wouldn't have lasted as it felt like we did the entire Kama Sutra but all good things eventually end or should I say climax again.

Somehow it is three hours later. We are ridiculously sweaty, hungry and thirsty. Time to head to the shower and then see what refreshments we can find. A bit of time passes and the ladies aka energizer bunnies are full of energy are ready for round three. No man is foolish enough to turn down this hot offer so we head back to play.

We grab another play room and keep it simple this time...ok simple for a swinging playtime. We are playing with our own partners on side by side sex swings as the ladies play with each other. You know just a typical swinger play date. This hotness works its magic & the guys climax yet again so the ladies quickly get back into lady loving.

Now at this point, it is very late and it has been many hours of some sexy physical grinding. We mention this to help explain what happens next, Mr. F closes his eyes and takes a nap while the lady loving turns into an all play session without him. That's right he took a nap instead of playing! He was too pooped out! Make sure to get a good night sleep the night before so you have enough energy for those non-stop party times otherwise you might end up napping like Mr. F :)

Safeguarding Privacy

Swinging is a private decision. It should be your choice who knows that you swing. Thankfully, the swinging community appreciates privacy and serious swingers work very hard to respect each other's privacy. Here are some security tips to help you keep your swinging life and vanilla life separate.

Your name

You will probably encounter people in the lifestyle who use fake names. How will you know this? Because given enough time, they will slip up and use their real names. It is too hard to use totally different names all the time. To protect your name without going totally crazy, just don't give out your real last name and spell your first name differently.

You can even have your credit card company print up a spare credit card with this different spelling of your first name and a fake last name. Simply fill out an online request for an authorized user on your main credit card. If you want to be extra safe, leave the credit cards at home and bring a Visa gift card and cash.

Your address

Most swinger websites ask for your city and state when building your online profile. This is to help you connect with other nearby swingers, which is great. Some towns are very small, which might make it too easy for people to trace your swinger profile back to your real-world life. You can pick a nearby town to help safeguard your privacy. Just be prepared to entertain in the town you pick, because swingers in that town and visiting swingers will likely get in touch with you.

Your phone/email

If you like your privacy, don't use your vanilla contact info. Set up a new phone number and email address just for swinging. There are plenty of free and paid options. You can have your swinger phone calls and emails forwarded to your vanilla accounts so you don't need to monitor extra stuff. Once you have this set up, make sure to test it out with your partner so you know you have it set up just right to conceal your identity without missing out on sexy communications.

Your pictures

You will have your vanilla photos and your swinger photos. Those two groups of pics should never, ever overlap. Your swinger photos should not have anything identifying in the background. For extra safety, don't show your face in your naked pictures. Take pictures in a hotel room and not in your living room, which could possibly be identified. You can blur out identifying tattoos, jewelry or other markings using a photo editor.

Once you have taken your swinger pictures, make sure to delete the secret exif data. Exif data includes stuff like GPS coordinates and other potentially identifying data that your phone or camera automatically adds to the electronic file. You can google "exif data removers" for free online tools to handle it.

When you want to share pictures, you can upload them to the swinger websites and place them in password-protected galleries. No website is 100% safe; even billion-dollar websites get hacked. A safe option would be to only upload body pics with no faces.

When someone wants to see your face pics, ask them to share their pics first. This way you can avoid people you know in real life (which can happen but is unlikely). Then, you can send them G-rated face pics using kik, or send them to a link to a G-rated gallery on a photo hosting site like Imgur.com. You can delete those images after they've been shared, so you never have face pics regularly available online. Reverse image lookup is a real thing and becoming more powerful each year, so don't be lazy with your picture security.

Don't store swinging pictures on your phone. Many people like to swipe through other people's photo gallery on their phones. You don't want a vanilla friend who is over eager with photo swiping to accidentally browse into the swinging gallery on your phone.

Internet Usage

Always use incognito mode on your internet browser. This way none of your websites, screen names or passwords will be saved in your history. You never know when someone might ask to borrow your smartphone or laptop to look something up. It's best to just keep it clean so there is nothing for your kids, in-laws, or friends to accidentally find. You should also Google "how to enable auto-closing of incognito windows".

This little trick will close your browser and get rid of the evidence after a set period of inactivity so you can be safe even if you forget to logout.

Facebook

For starters, never share your Facebook login if you want to best protect your privacy. If a swinger app asks for your Facebook login, and you want for maximum discretion don't walk away – run! There are some really good swinger apps that require a Facebook login but you are risking a certain level of your privacy.

If you want to be as discreet as possible, make sure you max out your privacy levels on your Facebook profile. Facebook has some super-advanced facial recognition methods for auto-tagging pictures, and other creepy stuff that might put your identity at risk. Don't upload your picture from a swinger party or from your swinger profile to your Facebook page and risk your name being auto-tagged onto it. Yes, that newbie swinger move sounds obvious and silly, but many people make mistakes like this including swinging veterans. Beside auto tagging face pictures, Facebook can also connect you with a common phone number or email address. Protect yourself and max out those privacy settings! For the best privacy protection never cross the streams of your swinging lifestyle with your vanilla Facebook life.

Pay to Play

Avoid free sites and free profiles. There are too many picture collectors, troublemakers, time wasters and drama queens. Thankfully, most of them are too cheap to pay. Sticking with paid profiles greatly reduces your risk level and reduces your frustration. Even if you find a good match using a free tool, these tend to be less reliable people and more likely to turn into ghosts when it comes time to play in person.

Helpful Hesitation

We all want to make a sexy connection. Sometimes, when we've had a little too much alcohol and the flirting gets a little too hot, mistakes are made. Remember that you can always share more later, so be hesitant when sharing specific personal details. Is there a real "need to know"? If not, change the conversation and think about it later when you aren't horny, drunk, or both.

Don't Swing With Friends

Make friends out of swingers, don't make swingers out of friends. It is easier and safer to make friends out of swingers. If you swing with friends, it can end badly. If those friends are hurt, they might blab your swinging secret to all your other friends. Your friends may seem cool with swinging in the moment, but first timers can have regrets after the fact - especially if alcohol or drugs are involved. Why risk it?

Even if your friends are veteran swingers, it is still safer not to play with them. Better to keep your friendship safe and use them for swinger advice then risk it all for one night of fun. There are too many hot swingers to enjoy, so focus on those who don't transcend the barrier into your vanilla life.

Vanilla Cover Stories

You are going to have some crazy awesome times in the lifestyle, and you probably won't want to share what you really did over the weekend with your office coworkers. You'll need some cover stories. You should keep your cover stories as simple as possible, so they're easier to remember and less likely to be exposed. You can say you met old college friends, then ask them about their weekend. People love to talk about themselves, so try to shift the focus back to them. If that won't work, just say you had a sexy time with your spouse. That will shut most people up – they won't want to hear the details because that wouldn't be proper.

If you are going to a swinger resort, just tell your vanilla friends that you're staying at the Hilton or whatever hotel is nearby. No one calls the hotel front desk anymore, so just answer your cell phone and email and you'll be ok. You can take some pictures at the airport, inside your hotel room, and in the resort restaurant without revealing that you were visiting a swinger resort.

If a vanilla friend hints that they are doing something exciting, or want to do something exciting, don't take the bait. It is very unlikely they are up to your level of excitement and you don't want to expose yourself. Remember it is much safer to make friends of swingers than the other way around!

Discretion is a two-way street

As much as you want to protect your privacy, you should remember that other people in the lifestyle expect you to practice a high level of discretion. This is super important to the swinging community. Most swingers do not want the vanilla world to know about their involvement in the lifestyle. You are probably thinking "DUH!", but there are some people who need to be reminded of this and you probably don't even realize just how discreet you should be.

Never detail your previous exploits.

Congratulations on having sexy fun! If you want to keep having sexy fun, don't "kiss and tell" on other swingers. Yes, we know you still can't believe that you are making your sexual fantasies a weekly reality. You feel like you just need to share this with someone. You probably can't share it with your vanilla friends, so you blab to other people in the lifestyle.

Sharing general details is fine as long as you don't say anything that could possibly identify your partners. If you mention other couples or give clues that might expose them, other swingers will likely start to avoid you. Smart swingers realize that next week it will be their names or identifying details in your stories. Some swingers absolutely do not want that. Respect everyone's privacy and do not expose anyone, even to other swingers, without their permission. You should never assume you have permission to talk about another couple's intimate details. Demonstrate how much you understand the need for discretion by practicing it when talking with other swingers.

Keep quiet in vanilla settings

Imagine you are a World War II spy. You wouldn't dream of discussing your secret mission in public while you are behind enemy lines. Talking about swinging in vanilla settings is basically the same scenario. It is very easy for a customer, waitress, or bartender to overhear you, and vanilla people love to gossip about swingers. Some of our swinger friends got outed while they were travelling because a waiter from their hometown overheard their friend with loose lips bragging about them in a restaurant. Trust us, it's a freakishly small world after all.

Congrats, you don't need to hide! But others still do

If you are lucky enough that you don't need to worry about being exposed as swingers, we congratulate you! This does not mean you can ignore the need for discretion. Many other swingers absolutely need to be discreet. They might have small children they are trying to shield from bullying at school. Maybe their job is on the line. Even if they run their own company, they can still need to be very discreet or risk losing their customers and going out of business. So regardless of your status, you need to zip your lips when it comes to other swingers. Go ahead and talk about your life but don't expose or drop any clues about other swingers without their permission.

PS - Remember these are two very discrete matters. It is <u>discrete</u> because your comfort with being outed as swingers is totally unrelated, distinct, and separate (aka discrete) from what other couples are comfortable with. Other couples need to be <u>discreet</u> because they need to keep their status as a swinger private and show extreme prudence with this secret. Bet you didn't expect a vocabulary lesson at this point! Keep it in mind when you're writing your profile; you probably want to use the word "discreet"!

Coming Out

Whether voluntary or involuntary, we should talk about coming out as swingers. This is becoming a more regular occurrence as many people in society are reaching a more evolved understanding of sexuality. This enables some swingers to voluntarily share their private choices with certain people in their lives.

Unfortunately, it also happens because mistakes are made that expose swingers. These mistakes could involve trusting the wrong people, or not safeguarding our information well enough. It doesn't matter why. What matters is how you handle exposing your private decisions to minimize the headaches and maximize the benefits.

Family

If you are thinking about voluntarily coming out, you should think about the possible ramifications. It will impact your family, especially if you have children. Kids generally prefer to know as little as possible about their parents' love life, so they won't want to hear the nitty gritty details. They want to know that their home life is safe and stable, and that their parents can be relied upon to help them grow up. When opening up to your kids you will need to decide what is best for them.

There is no magic age to tell your children about this. Some swingers never tell their adult children, and other swingers share some information about their relationship with their young children. We aren't going to judge you, but we will mention that you should proceed cautiously. You might want to share this information when school is not in session so your children have more free time to absorb the information and ask questions. If you decide to only tell your older children, you should be prepared for them to accidentally (or maliciously) reveal the secret to your younger kids, because kids can say the darndest things.

Let's remember that some kids love to tease and bully other kids. If you publicly come out in your local community, you could be exposing your kids to some harsh times with the class bully.

If you have older kids, they might have guessed about your swinging already. Kids would have to be really clueless not to wonder about your over-the-top sexy wardrobe, or the weird packages getting delivered, or the mysterious trips you take, or the weird conversations they overhear, or why you were skinny dipping late at night with your "friends from college".

That doesn't mean your older kids want to know about your sex life, although they also don't want you to insult their intelligence by telling silly lies. Depending on your relationship with your older children, you might prefer a "don't ask, don't tell" policy. Other families might have a relationship where openness is prioritized. You should take some time to reflect on what is best for you and your children.

As for your parents, too many parents tend to be a little less open-minded, especially if they are very religious. You need to think very carefully about how your parents will react. On the plus side, being honest with your parents could make it much easier to arrange babysitting so you can go on more play dates. You can't unshare this secret, so think long and hard who you decide to tell, and how.

Work

You should also think about how being outed will impact your work. If you are retired, then it's an easier decision to make, but most swingers are still working. Even if you never tell your boss, coworkers, or clients, sharing your swinging status elsewhere can get back to them. It is too easy to find out very personal details about people just by going online. It only takes one nosey person to discover your secret then gossip about you.

Hopefully, your boss and coworkers will accept your personal decisions and respect that they are private. But we live in the real world, and too often there is a self-righteous person who goes out of their way to cause trouble. Even if you own your company, you aren't guaranteed to be safe. Someone could start harassing your customers to boycott your business. It just takes one person to threaten your income. It is usually very hard to legally prove that someone broke the law when they unfairly denied you a promotion, raise, or new contract. We don't want to scare you, but we do want to help you think it through and make an informed decision.

Friends

You just can't predict how vanilla friends will react to finding out that you aren't vanilla. Some trustworthy friends will turn into the biggest blabbermouths and spread your secret far and wide. Other friends might distance themselves from you out of fear you will ruin their marriage. They will rethink every conversation, and assume that you were secretly trying to sleep with them the entire time. They will over-analyze everything you do and say, assuming ulterior motives. It is common for ignorant vanilla friends to think swingers are simply out-of-control nymphomaniacs who can't be trusted.

Then you might also find some friends who are curious and ask you a bunch of questions about the lifestyle. You can answer these questions, but you should immediately tell them you only make friends out of swingers and not swingers out of friends. Playing with friends too often results in a bad situation for everyone involved. This explanation also helps you avoid having to turn down your friends who are sexually unappealing but nice people. Your friends can find their own paths into the lifestyle if they choose to do so.

There are other ramifications you need to think about. For example, your neighbors might think differently about you. If you regularly attend religious services, you can expect a few glaring looks from judgy people. You should hope for the best but anticipate the worst from other people.

There are many swingers who are publicly "out". You should try to talk with them first. If you can't attend a swinger event to meet these people, or find these people on the swinger community websites, don't fret. Do some Google searches for "coming out as a swinger". You will find there are many stories online to give you a better sense of what to expect. A common experience among these swingers is you just can't predict how positively or negatively people will respond.

If you think coming out as a swinger is the best option, or if someone involuntarily exposed you as swinger, then here are a few tips to make it easier for you.

Tip # 1- Stay ahead of the gossip. Talk with the people closest to you, so you can protect them from shocking surprises. Kids are much better at handling teasing and bullying if they aren't surprised.

Tip #2- Individually, share with your closest friends, so they don't feel hurt that you hid a big secret from them. This also lets you frame the conversation and calmly explain why you aren't a risk to their relationship. It is best to role play these conversations beforehand, and brainstorm the best and worst case scenarios so you can prepare the right responses for each close person in your life.

Tip # 3- If things go horribly wrong when you come out as a swinger, you can try to go back to secretly swinging. You might need to tell all the vanilla people you are dropping out of the lifestyle and seeking relationship help. To be safe, you should temporarily remove your profiles on swinging websites in case someone gets nosy and tries to check your story. Then, you will need to make a very public show that you are living a "vanilla only" life on the weekends. After many weeks, you can restart a much more discreet swinging lifestyle.

Another option is pretend it was an extra marital affair and not swinging. Everyone's situation is different. You need to do what is best for you. Some couples felt they had to pretend that their spouse was cheating when they were exposed with another swinger. It's an unfortunate truth that it can possibly be easier to pretend an extramarital affair was forgiven than admit you were exploring the world of consensual non-monogamy.

Tip #4 - As much as we value honesty in the lifestyle, all swingers live in different situations. Some of these situations do not allow for public honesty about our private decisions. For example, the US military forbids swinging and regularly prosecutes military personnel who engage in consensual non-monogamy. There are many countries that send swingers to prison. Proceed cautiously and make sure there are no legal ramifications of swinging before revealing your secret.

Our Swinging Journal: Coming out of the closet...

One late Sunday morning as we were recovering from yet another sexually decadent party, Mr F's younger brother came to visit. He seemed more serious than usual and we quickly found out why. He wanted to come out of the closet and share with us that he is gay. We were honored he came out to us and could now share more of his life with us instead of secretly making excuses so he could meet up with his gay friends.

Over the next few weeks he started making jokes that he could help out Mr. F by giving Dr. G some blowjob advice since she wasn't as experienced as him. Little did he know that we also had a secret. So we opened up about our swinging escapades and we came out of the closet to him. They just don't make Hallmark greeting cards for these types of situations..

Being open with your loved ones is a great situation. We understand it is not possible for everyone. We do sincerely hope you all can find as many trusted friends & family who love you no matter what!

Rural Swinging

Having adult fun while living in a small, rural town introduces extra challenges. Don't worry! It's still very possible and done successfully by many swingers! Here are some helpful tips to overcome hurdles that city-dwelling swingers might not face.

Adjusting Your Online Profile

Swingers really value honesty in online profiles, but certain situations require a little bit of bending the truth – and that's okay. Living in a very small town and naming that town in your profile can reveal your identity. Most people reading your profile on swinger websites will be swingers. There isn't too much to worry about unless a curious newbie couple checks it out and has a bad lifestyle experience. They might resort to outing other people, which isn't right but has happened.

Be smart and protect yourselves. Instead of naming your tiny little town, consider a bigger town that you regularly visit. If other swingers reach out, you can meet up with them in the town you list on your profile. Likely you'll be meeting other rural swingers who are doing the same thing, so they will understand your slight bending of the truth.

When writing your profile details, double and triple check to make sure you don't accidentally list details that are too specific and can be traced back to you. There are some hateful people out there who enjoy causing trouble. God forbid an overly-religious person decides they are going to stalk local swingers and expose them. Thankfully these hateful people are rare, but you should still be smart and keep yourself safe.

Maximize Your Online Screening

Swingers are busy people just like everyone else, with work obligations, families to raise, and vanilla friends to visit. To save time, it's smart to do a more thorough online screening. Living in a rural area means you often have to drive many hours back & forth to meet a new couple. That's a big time investment! Give yourselves the best chances of success. Don't let your excitement take over and agree to a real-life meeting too quickly.

Take the time to really check out their swinger profile. Many profiles can be light on information, so feel free to ask a few questions. What is their overall experience level in the lifestyle? What are they looking for? Do they like the same things as you? Do they have any play rules? Do these play rules match up with your rules? Make sure to chat with both the guy and the girl to make sure there is a four-way connection. You don't want to drive out to meet a new couple and find out that one of them is not interested in swinging. The KIK mobile app is a great way to anonymously chat, talk and share sexy pics to jump-start a fun, flirty connection with the other couple.

Playing With Out of Towners

To further protect your swinging secret, you can choose to only play with visiting swingers. If you live in a small town, you can pick the biggest city near you and seek out visiting swingers in that city.

If you check out swinger websites, you can find swingers who will be visiting your nearby city and are looking to play. This will help insulate you from local swingers who might accidentally out your secret. That doesn't usually happen, but if someone drinks too much you never know what will happen. Mistakes happen and vanilla people might overhear something or see something they shouldn't.

Playing with tourists also comes with some great side benefits. The first benefit is that tourist swingers have hotel rooms where you can play. Another benefit is that you don't have to worry about the visiting swingers developing romantic attachments or becoming totally creepy clingers.

If you like chasing long odds, then you can also buy a pair of black rings. Some swingers wear a black ring on the right hand as a secret signal to other swingers. Honestly, very few swingers do this. Many swingers have no clue what a black ring means other than the person likes black jewelry!

Playing on Vacation

Swinging can be harder for people in rural towns. There can be a smaller pool of sexy people. You may need to drive a long way to meet potential partners. It can be costlier, since you might have to buy gas and maybe more frequently get a hotel room.

Sometimes, swinging locally is too much of a hassle, and you might want to limit your play to vacation time. There are many great swinger-friendly resorts like Hedonism, Desire, and Temptation. There are also swinger takeovers on cruise ships, like Bliss Cruise. Add in several adult-only nudist resorts across the US which are open to swingers, and you have plenty of good places to start looking.

You can also arrange mini-vacations to cities with awesome swinger clubs or big hotel takeover parties. This will help protect your small town reputation and keep you scandal-free. It also removes the hassle of trying to find another attractive couple in your rural area. You might not be able to play as often as you prefer, but playing only on vacation will give you a chance to maximize the fun and minimize the hassle of rural town swinging.

Paid Options

Desperate people are not good decision-makers. Some swingers in rural areas have thought about paying for an escort or stripper. This might sound tempting, especially after a frustrating search finds no play partners. You should think twice. Paying for sex is illegal in most places. We aren't going to debate whether it is right or wrong. We are just going to remind you that sex workers are often busted by the police. Police will search the contact list in their cell phone. Do you really want to have to explain why your phone number was in a sex worker's cell phone?

Too many sex workers also have health issues. Many of them will have risky sex if the price is right, unlike swingers who generally value safer sex. Sex workers are doing this as their job, so they tend to lack the passion and joy you will find when playing with swingers. You are going to pay for some escort or stripper to go through the motions and pretend they are turned on. Hopefully they have good acting abilities, but more likely they'll be jaded, bored, and just trying to get paid as fast as possible and leave.

Settling for a paid option might seem like a good idea, but if you have the money to pay an escort or stripper, you should probably consider the swinger vacation options instead.

Underground Secret Groups

The struggle is real in rural areas. The good news is you are not alone. There are many others in similar situations. There is usually an underground network of open-minded people in most rural areas.

These networks are often very careful and overly cautious bringing in new people. They typically wait to invite a new member till they have developed a reputation of being drama-free and discreet. Relax and don't worry. If there is an underground group in your local rural area, they will contact you when they are ready. Till they do, just focus on being a good partner for your special someone and enjoy whatever sexy bonus comes along.

It can be frustrating and maybe even lead to a fight as you try to enjoy rural swinging. You will often work a bit harder to find a sexy connection. Sometimes you might come close to success only to find that one of you isn't happy with some small detail and is unwilling to lower your standards. Be careful not to let your frustrations boil over. Remember this is all just a bonus to your amazing relationship.

Our Swinging Journal: Handling Awkward Assumptions

Anyone that spends enough time in the lifestyle will encounter an awkward situation that they never dreamed they would need to handle. This is one of those situations. Another weekend rolls along & we are invited to a house party. It is being run by friends of friends so we aren't sure about attending. We check out the rsvp list & see a bunch of familiar faces from previous events that we attended, so we graciously accept the invite.

We should probably clarify something before proceeding. When we say friendly faces, we mean friendly people not former play partners. We have enjoyed many lifestyle events without playing because we are strong believers in a 4-way connection before any playing. Neither of us will take one for the team and lower our standards just to play. We may be sluts but we are selective sluts when it comes to playtime. We love to make new friends and have a great time even if that doesn't always lead to a sexy 4-way connection for playtime.

Ok, back to the story. We show up at the party and it is a really fun time. We are dancing, drinking and laughing. We aren't really flirting with anyone just yet because this party is skewing a bit older ... let's be honest most of the people that showed up reminded us too much of our parents and that aint sexy. So we aren't finding any potential play partners just yet.

Then in walks another friendly face. We have known this couple for several months and bumped into them a bunch of times but never played. They are a few years younger than us & in good shape. After a few drinks, we are about to go to the bar for a fresh round of drinks when the other lady loudly announces that they are going to head downstairs and grab a play room for all of us. Uhhhhhhh....... what?

We looked like deer caught in headlights because we weren't flirting or planning to play with them. We were 100% flattered they wanted to play with us but.... even though the guy was younger, cute and in shape, he was as hairy as bigfoot and that isn't sexy to Dr. G so definitely no chance for a 4-way connection.

So we scooped up our surprised jaws off the floor and thanked them for their offer but explained we weren't up for playing. Honestly there is no easy way to reject another couple. It was extremely awkward so they decided they were going to a play room anyway so they could have fun by themselves. Whew, crisis averted.

We go back to the bar, get our fresh drinks and bump into another couple we know, who was late arriving to the party. We have a fun time chatting with them. We find a bunch in common with them and soon start giving each other sly smiles as we all feel that sexy 4-way connection.

We all decide to see if there are any play rooms still available. The other couple leads the way. Most of the play rooms are taken by this time. There is one play room with the door still open. The other couple walks in & we follow them right into the return of the awkward situation. The first couple that we declined was in that room & they left the door open as an invitation for other people to join them. So we quickly bolt out of that room and then explain it might be better to go grab a hotel room.

Honestly we don't know what we could have done to avoid these awkward moments and just try to communicate as clearly as possible. Awkward moments aren't fun but they happen from time to time. You just need to be honest and polite to get through the situation as best as possible.

ED Issues & Performance Pills

In case you haven't realized yet, this book has been written by a PhD and not a MD. So if you're thinking of taking male performance pills, you should absolutely talk to your own medical doctor first. We are about to share some information about ED pills and you should not confuse this with real medical advice from your own doctor about erectile dysfunction. You would be crazy reckless to use any performance pills without talking with a medical doctor. Unfortunately, there are many crazy reckless people in this world. Men of all ages use and sometimes abuse ED pills like Viagra, Cialis or Levitra. These are serious drugs so let's have a serious chat about them.

Guys, if you have enough play dates in the lifestyle, you will almost certainly encounter DDW, also known as "d*** don't work". Go ahead and say it won't happen to you. Every guy says that until it happens to him.

Let's be honest; considering what guys are up against, it's surprising that DDW doesn't happen every play date. Guys are leaving their safe, familiar bedrooms to go to a crazy swinging environment to play with a

235

brand-new person they barely have enough time to make a connection with, and the new lady doesn't know the best way to turn him on. Mentally and physically, this is a lot to handle and a common cause of ED. When ladies get nervous at a swinger party, they can drink some alcohol and relax. Guys who get nervous and drink too much end up sabotaging themselves with alcohol-induced DDW.

Guys, your best bet is to relax. DDW is usually more of a mental issue and less of a physical issue. The great news is that there are many solutions for DDW.

First, stop sabotaging yourself. Quit smoking and dial back on the booze. You wouldn't be smoking and drinking if you were training for a marathon, and swinging is basically an awesome sex marathon. Start doing some cardio exercise a few times a week. Build up to 30 minutes (or more) of cardio a few days a week. Drink more water and eat right. If you want your body to perform at its physical best, you need to properly fuel and prepare it. Make sure you get enough sleep. It's crazy to expect your body to perform at its best if you aren't rested.

Visit your doctor and make sure you are healthy enough for a sex marathon. These simple steps can prevent many DDW situations. Take care of your body and your body will take care of you!

Most swingers are smart enough to do the basic physical prep, so it's often a mental issue that creates a DDW situation. Before you start popping ED pills, try to resolve these issues naturally. Some swingers prefer to only engage in soft swap. It removes the high pressure and stress of pleasing brand new partners, which is a common contributor to DDW issues.

Another preventative measure is to slowly ease into the lifestyle. Go to swinger clubs and just watch for a few weeks. Progress slowly into some public non-swapping play or soft swapping. As you grow more comfortable in the wild atmosphere of the swinging world, your body will relax and you can show that sexy new partner just how good you are between the sheets.

Don't want to wait and ease into things? There's still another step you can take before taking performance pills. Let's chat about vitamin supplements. You should still talk with a doctor before taking vitamins, even though they're available over the counter. Only a doctor can make sure you're healthy enough for a sex marathon. Your doctor can make sure you don't have a heart problem and that these supplements won't interact with any other medicine you might be taking.

The more common performance-enhancing supplements are L-Arginine, Maca root, and ZMA supplements. One of the more popular brand name products is Horny Goat Weed. Some guys report great results with these supplements. Remember that all bodies are different. Some people may respond differently to different supplements, so don't buy a big batch of anything until you test a few different supplements and find out what works best for you.

Don't like vitamin supplements? Let's talk about the ED prescription solutions. There are many different options, and they come in many different forms. There are pills, gels, and chewables. The most common prescriptions are Viagra, Cialis, and Levitra. Viagra tends to have more annoying side effects, like nose congestion, than Cialis or Levitra, but they are all viable options for most healthy men.

Usually your doctor will have you try out different ones to see which prescription gives you the best performance with the least amount of side effects. Your doctor will start you on a low dose and slowly work you up to whatever dose is appropriate for your body. Before you think about changing dosages without consulting your doctor, take a breather. Cheating and going with a higher dose than your doctor prescribes is stupid and dangerous.

Think about a metal hammer. The hammer is as hard as it needs to be. There is no reason to wrap it in extra layers of aluminum foil to make it even harder. Apply that same logic to ED pills. Except while covering your hammer with aluminum foil is just a waste of aluminum foil, taking too many ED pills can land you in the hospital with a painful erection that needs to be medically addressed.

You'll have the honor of being jabbed with a crazy long needle (guess where!). You'll have to hope that the needle can drain the blood fast enough or penile amputation might be required. An estimated 10,000 men end up in the hospital every year because of ED pills. Please listen to your doctor before you become one of those guys.

ED pills aren't necessarily expensive, but they aren't exactly cheap, either. To save money, ask your doctor if he or she will prescribe a higher dosage – then you can split the pills to your recommended dosage. Many ED pills can be cut in half to save money. Instead of buying 20 pills at 50mg each, you might be able to buy 10 pills of 100mg and use a pill cutter to split them in half. Ask your doctor before doing this.

Once you have a prescription, you can get it filled at any pharmacy. Depending on where you live, there might be some legitimate online pharmacies that will offer big discounts, and occasionally there are some coupons you can use at your local pharmacy. If you check out the online swinger forums, you can find out what is currently the best deal for your ED prescription. There might be a free discount card that offers automatic coupons for your prescription. Talk to your doctor about this, too, as they will usually want to help you afford your medication as opposed to not taking it at all.

When facing DDW issues, relax and know you are not alone. You are not the first and definitely not the last. Just about every guy in the lifestyle has had or will have a DDW moment at one point.

Ladies, it's not about you. You are all smoking hot and all the guys want to play with you. Sometimes it's difficult for a guy to juggle all the stress of work, family, and the lifestyle on four hours of sleep. That stress can trigger DDW in the middle of playing.

If your buddy has a DDW moment in the middle of playing, it can be helpful if you quietly go get some water or towels for the group while the ladies stay behind and leisurely give some oral action. Don't put a spotlight on the DDW issue – that will only make it worse.

Taking a step back and relaxing so you can enjoy and relish the moment is often the quickest way to overcome DDW. It can also be helpful to switch back to your usual partners to reduce the performance pressure. If everyone goes with the flow and enjoys the chill sexy vibe, things might just pop back up!

239

Male Insecurity

Guys, you're probably confident – and you should be! You look good, have a bunch of friends, and convinced that hot lady to be with you. Because you are so freaking awesome, your lady feels comfortable enough to enter the lifestyle with you and explore some amazing sexy times together. Seriously, you are scoring some major fist bumps and high fives from the Manly Man's Hall of Fame.

Can I pull you aside for a second to talk dude to dude? I don't know how to say this, but you aren't the biggest guy in the world and you better be okay with that. If you're lucky enough to have some sexy playtime in the lifestyle, you are going to come across guys with bigger equipment than you - so don't freak out.

Bigger equipment does not mean they are better at pleasing ladies. Many ladies avoid men with bigger equipment because it isn't the easiest to play with. It can be harder for oral action, and might even be too painful for any sustained oral attention at all. Many ladies will also say "oh hell no" to any backdoor action for guys with big equipment. Even regular sex is a challenge because the average vagina is just 3-4 inches deep. Big equipment is not as awesome as you might think. If you have big equipment, you already know this and have learned how to use your equipment with the right angles and positions to keep everyone feeling happy and sexy.

Guys, especially younger guys who tend to have trouble understanding that size is not everything, listen up! Your hot lady loves you and is going home with you. You like playing with big boobs and small boobs alike, and at the end of the night you happily go home to play with your lady's amazing boobs. It is the same for your lady. She can play with big equipment and small equipment and will still look forward to going home to play with your special equipment because it is and will always be her favorite.

Swinging enables us to enjoy a variety of new sexy experiences. Relax and be happy that you and your lady can dabble with so many new and exciting play opportunities before going home together. You are both likely to learn new ways to push those sexy buttons from your different-sized play partners, which can lead to bigger explosions in your own bedroom.

If you think you have very small equipment, you're probably underestimating yourself. You probably have more than enough for a super-hot, sexy swinger time. Remember that the average vagina is just 3-4 inches deep. Some of the hottest moments don't even involve a guy's equipment. Most women love, love, love receiving oral attention. Some women will have a more intense climax from talented tongue action than any penetration. It's fun watching a woman try to walk on jelly legs after a long session of moaning and quivering from a super talented tongue.

With more experience in the lifestyle, you will realize that there is a wide range of people. This includes bald guys and hairy guys, tall guys and short guys, skinny guys and chubby guys. Don't freak out over these differences. Most people join the lifestyle because they want to enjoy the sexy variety. Be confident in who you are and enjoy every sexy moment!

Men & Changing Libido Level

Dear men…. rest assured that you are all manly men and the world is envious of your libido and sexual prowess. Ok, now that your ego has been assuaged let's cover things that guys just really don't like admitting – we are all getting older. Things change when life changes. In other words don't freak out if your libido might not be as high as your horny teenage years or even as high as when you were in your thirties.

When ladies enter the lifestyle, many of them may find their libido increases while men may find their libido moving in the other direction. Of course every situation and each couple is different so your experience may differ. For any worried couples, we'd like to explain why this isn't a huge problem.

Generally, ladies face much more pressure from society to be "good" and not sexual. When ladies enter the lifestyle, they usually are greeted with a deluge of compliments and positive encouragement as they embrace their sexier side. This reversal of mental pressure empowers many ladies to relax which helps their libido to flourish.

Now guys often face the opposite situation. Society often encourages men to act more virile and possessive. So men can face enhanced mental pressure when they enter the lifestyle. To complicate matters for guys there are also certain biological issues like dropping testosterone levels as men age which can lead to lower libido. We also think there is a third element that can impact men in the lifestyle - satisfaction. Once you enter the lifestyle, you can more easily satisfy your hottest fantasies. When threesomes or orgies become commonplace in your sexual diary there can be less reason to have a strong libido. You have nothing to prove. Your proud sexual history can make a porn star blush. It can be natural to feel less drive and ambition to simply pump up the numbers to your already impressive sexual history considering you already take home the hottest woman every night – your own wife/girlfriend.

Exploring the lifestyle helps reinforce what we already know that we love & cherish our partners. They are the best lady for us. Even though it is fun playing with others, when you know your partner is the best for you, there is less desire to chase after new play partners.

Many men (but not everyone so relax) have discovered that their desire for other women is not as strong the longer they stay in the lifestyle. This is perfectly normal and nothing to worry about. Between the different mental and biological reasons, it is likely you will feel a change in your libido.

If you feel libido not as high as it used to be, relax and be happy because it is often a sign of good things in your life. Focus on the positive aspects in your life. The amazing lady in your life, your proud sexual history and all the other blessings in your life.

If you are still worried, you can check out your testosterone levels with your doctor. If they find a problem besides normal aging, they can prescribe you some stuff. It would be very wise to improve your diet and exercise. Many men can gain more benefit from improved diet & exercise than from expensive medicines.

As for swinging with a changing libido, there are many options for you. You can consider a MFM threesome or a group play session where there will be multiple men. Many experienced couples prefer these type of play sessions. To them it is not about score keeping but rather a fun & sexy time. For example you would probably feel ok if you swapped with another couple and one of you choose to only have oral while the other choose to have full play. Swinging is more fun when we don't keep score and just let each other choose how best to enjoy themselves. A respectful single guy can make a MFM play session into a great memory for all involved.

Before you tell yourself that you will never consider a MFM situation, take a deep breath and think about it. You may find the longer you are in the lifestyle that your comfort level will grow and you might be open to different opportunities like MFM or group sessions. Why? Well besides feeling more comfortable and confident from your lifestyle experiences it can be the hottest thing you will ever see. Your lady is the hottest person to you, so seeing the hottest & most attractive woman having sex is basically seeing the hottest porn you will ever see in your lifetime and you have the option of joining the action whenever you want. Just imagine listening and seeing your amazing wife show off her sexual body & erotic skills. Ok, go take a break from reading and fool around with your hot lady over that super smoking thought.

Just because some society pressures might imply that every guy should always want to fool around with every woman but that just isn't real life. Remember these are the societal pressures that imply it is wrong for adults to have consensual sex. Don't worry about what society tries to imply is right or wrong. Don't worry about labels or judgments. Worry about talking with your partner to decide what is best for both of you to enjoy life.

Our bodies aren't robots. They will change as time and experience grows. So relax and help reinforce your amazing relationship by being honest with communicating with each other. Libido is a natural thing so like any natural thing it can change over time.

Our Swinging Journal: Why Mr. F hopes to have DDW again...

Let's have a flashback to when Mr. F was dating Dr. G. It was his birthday and Dr. G arranged a great birthday party for Mr. F. She somehow found his favorite wine & surprised him with a case of it at the party. Well, wine is meant to be shared with friends so Mr. F made sure to drink a glass of it with everyone at the party. Mr. F became a little buzzed ... ok, he was joyfully blasted.

Rest assured, Mr. F 's sex drive is so strong he wasn't going to let the inability to stand stop him from seeking naughty fun with Dr. G. He poured on his sexy moves almost as much as he poured the wine that night. Finally she pointed out that he was trying to "push rope" and it wasn't going to work. Mr. F was not to be deterred. Considering his inebriated state, he said a surprisingly coherent & memorable line "What am I too much man for you to handle". We both laughed long and hard and still joke about that funny statement.

Even though there was no sex that night because Mr. F went overboard with the drinking at his birthday party, it was still a great night. We ended up having one of our most passionate make-out sessions and felt uber connected and happily content. There was no embarrassment over this ED issue. DDW can even happen to young, happy & healthy guys when they are a sexy lady. When it does happen it just gives us an opportunity for overlooked sexy aspects like passionate kissing and caressing.

Since we've been in the lifestyle, we've seen many different DDW situations & each time Mr. F gets a little envious of the guy. When DDW has popped-up (or should we say flopped down) the guy with DDW is treated like a king by the ladies. It seems the like fastest way for a guy to be treated to double or triple oral action is a case of DDW. We know no guy wants DDW but being worshipped like a king with extra oral attention is a very nice problem to enjoy.

Ladies & Mother Nature's Calendar

Ladies, imagine you are looking forward to a hot swinger event. You are doing everything to make sure it will be perfect, but surprise! Your period arrives early. Relax. It happens all the time. Mother Nature does not care about your hot dates. As far as she is concerned, if it's that time of the month then it's just that time of the month.

Some women have a uterus you can set your calendar by and just don't schedule playtime when Aunt Flow is in town. Other women are less regular and sort of cross their fingers when making a date. Some women don't want to be touched by anything other than a heating pad while others find themselves almost constantly turned on during their period.

Wherever you fall on the spectrum, keep in mind that your cycle often affects more than just your weekend plans.

If you're going to be in the lifestyle, you're going to need to talk about your period way more often than you could ever have imagined. The good news is that swingers are grownups, and most lifestyle men haven't freaked out over the mere mention of menstruation since middle school. The conversations you need to have depend on your preferences and comfort level. Just remember that you are not the first woman in history to ovulate and think about it as another bodily fluid that might be exchanged --- which means you owe it to your partners to communicate about it. Unless you have already gone through menopause or happen to be the luckiest woman ever in the lifestyle, your period and what it means for play plans will be a topic of conversation.

Here are some options for navigating sexy time with your cycle.

Reschedule or Revise

If you're planning to play and are surprised by your period, reach out to your dates as soon as you can. Some lifestyle women prefer to discuss the sudden arrival of Uncle Red with the female half of the couple, but that is not always an option especially if communicating only through email. The straightforward approach works best. Explain the situation and ask if the other couple would like to reschedule the date. Some will immediately pull out their calendars to make a new sexy date. Some will suggest keeping the date but making it a vanilla night.

Just Flirt and Socialize

You could choose not to do anything to "deal" with your period. There is no rule that says you have to play at every swinger event. You can just enjoy the sexy vibe, make new friends, and catch up with old ones. Sometimes it's nice just to enjoy a party free of all performance anxiety.

Soft Swap Only

You can still have plenty of fun keeping activities on a soft swap level. There are plenty of sexy ways to enjoy yourself without penetration. You can have a hot kissing contest, sensual massages, or use vibrators outside of your sexy lingerie. We don't know a lot of men who would turn down a blow job just because the potential giver is on the rag. This is a great way to build a stronger connection for even hotter sex the next time.

Have Sex!

A lot of lifestyle couples play during periods, but you can't assume it's okay with them just because you are comfortable with it. You have to communicate and establish what is acceptable and what is not. Some men are down to play during spotting or light flow days only while others don't care about the level of flow as long as they won't find their male anatomy awash in a sea of red. Still others don't have sex during periods as a rule.

Sea Sponges

These absorbent little wonders can be a lifestyle girl's best friend. You may have heard menstrual sponges referred to as soft tampons. Like tampons, sponges are inserted into the vagina to absorb blood before it exits the body. Unlike tampons, there is no dangling string and sponges are reusable. Most importantly, you can have intercourse with a sponge inserted. Natural sea sponges are growing in popularity due to their convenience, earth friendliness, and comfort. Synthetic, vegan friendly sponges are also growing in popularity.

Menstrual Cups

Menstrual cups are aptly named. They are small,cup-shaped devices inserted into the vagina that collect blood before it exits the body, similar to tampons. Menstrual cups come in both reusable and disposable forms, and the difference is hugely important. Disposable menstrual cups can be worn during sex because they are designed to sit at the cervix and are made of softer material than the reusable kind. Reusable cups should not be worn during sex because they are positioned lower in the vagina and are made of heavier material that can cause discomfort for you and your partner.

Anal

Some women don't enjoy vaginal intercourse while on their period, but love a good ass ride. If you enjoy some backdoor fun, this is a good time to explore it with the added benefit of not having to worry about removing a tampon and messing up your sheets. Some ladies enjoy backdoor action in the lifestyle because they can partner with a guy that is smaller than their man and more comfortably enjoy the stimulation of all those sensitive nerves in the bottom hole. Keep in mind that there is no medical reason to limit the potentially mind-blowing joys of playing in your back room to one time of the month!

Move Your Period

Okay, this one is pretty drastic and mostly used for really, really big events. This is not for your run-of-the-mill Saturday night out. Some women want to guarantee that they won't need to pack the tampons for a swinger cruise or other big getaway so they kind of fake out their uterus. If you take oral contraceptives, you might be able to shift your cycle by skipping your placebo week to start a new pack right away. This not possible with every type of birth control pill and should never been done without consulting your OB/GYN. Be careful when adjusting and be prepared for some unusual hormone levels.

Ice Breaker Games

You are going to be meeting a bunch of new people and hopefully want to have sexy time with these new swinger friends. So how do you tastefully get from casual chatting to sexy stroking? Don't worry. We are here to help!

Before we talk about the different sexy game options we should take a moment to talk about when is the right time to pull out a game. You should only pull out a game after you have made a connection and everybody is at least open to possibly playing. These games can get a bit intimate so you don't want to spring this too soon in the conversation.

When you are sure you and your partner want to play, you should ask if the other swingers would be interested in playing a sexy game. This gives them the chance to bow out if they aren't feeling the same connection ... which is a possibility. If you are already have been touchy feely and have a bit of clothes off, it is probably not a good time for a game.

Games are meant for pre-heating your oven and if your fire is already raging hot then it is probably not smart to take a step back to pre-heating. A game at that point is more likely to cool down your already raging hot moment. You want to carefully choose when and when not to pull out a sexy ice breaker game.

Here are some sexy swinger games to help you break the ice and start your sexy time.

Naughty Dice

You can pick up novelty adult dice at any sex toy shop or even Amazon.com. They usually come with two dice. One die has different body parts (arm, leg, lips, butt, etc). The other die has different actions (kiss, caress, etc). You each take turns rolling the dice and doing that action on the body part the dice show to the person from the other couple. You can also use regular dice and print out this list (feel free to edit the list to fit your style)

Roll a 1 - Take off an article of your clothing

Roll a 2 - Kiss the person on your right

Roll a 3 - Three-way kiss (pick two people to join you)

Roll a 4 - All couples kiss

Roll a 5 - Kiss the person on your left

Roll a 6 - Take off an article of clothing from someone else

Game of Lifestyle Card Set

This company made up two sets of card for swingers that are very similar style to a truth or dare game. You each take turns pulling out a card and following the dare instructions or ask the truth question on the card. The Ice Breaker edition is a bit too tame for most swingers but if you are newbies it can be a good starting point. The cards in this set are good conversation starters but not the best sexy starters. Their Hot N Heavy edition is much more suited for getting the sexy times rolling. The cards range between kissing to taking off other people's clothing. Each set is $20 and can be ordered at http://www.gameoflifestyle.com/

DIY Sexy Dare Game

If you want to save money or don't want to leave a paper trail buying a swinger game online, we have made a DIY card game for you.

Step 1 - Type the sexy dare list (listed at the end) into a one page document with space in between each dare.

Step 2 - Take a manilla folder (because it is sturdier than regular paper) and slice it along the edge, transforming it into two flat sheets.

Step 3 - Manually feed a sheet of the manilla folder into your printer and print out your page.

Step 4 - Slice the manilla folder page into equally sized slivers with a sexy dare on each sliver.

Step 5 - Place the slivers in a glass.

Step 6 – Get in a circle (alternating boy-girl). Take turns pulling out a dare from the glass. If someone is uncomfortable with the dare, you can let them pick again, to help keep everyone comfortable and happy.

Step 7 - Whenever it gets too steamy feel free to pair off and let nature take its course.

Sample Sexy Dare List

(Customizable printer friendly version is available on SwingersHelp.com)

Demonstrate your oral skills on the fingers of the person to your right

Have someone take an article of your clothing off

Close your eyes, pick out your partner's behind with just touching

Kiss the inner thighs of a new friend for a minute or till they quiver

Give a lap dance to the person on your left for a minute or till they moan

Give or get spanked 3 times with the person to your right

Close your eyes & pick out your partner's chest with just touching

Give a 30 second handjob, removing clothes is optional

Have a three way kiss

Dry hump the person of your choice in your favorite position

Do 15 seconds of your sexiest dirty talk to the person on your right

Make out with a person without any other body contact

Take an article of clothing off someone

Grope your favorite body part of the person on your right

Grope your favorite body part of the person on your left

Kiss the person to your right on their chest

Kiss the person to your left on their chest

Strip Poker or Blackjack

If you already know how to play poker or blackjack, you can turn it into a sexy swinger game. The winner of each poker/blackjack hand gets to take off any article of clothing from any other person they choose. Once someone is naked you can have them perform sexy dares until the passion gets hot enough that you forget about the game and focus on more enjoyable whatever hard things might be popping up

Sexy Jenga

Buy a regular Jenga game. Then write a sexy dare on each wooden block (feel free to use the sexy dare list previously mentioned). Take turns pulling out blocks and doing the dares on each block. If someone knocks over the Jenga they have to strip off all clothes.

Strip Twister

Buy a regular Twister game from any toy store. Take turns spinning. Whenever someone loses they have to take off an article of clothing and becomes the spinner. To speed up the game you can fold under the bottom row or two of Twister dots so there are fewer dots to be used and the game moves along at a faster pace.

Cards Against Humanity

You can buy this fun card game at Amazon or from the Cards Against Humanity site. Their website even has instructions on how you can print you can print your own copy for free at home which some people do so they can laminate it and use it in the pool or hot tub. Then play the game following the normal rules with a slight twist. Each black card you win, you can cash in for an article of clothing from someone else or a sexy act if they have no more clothes.

Watermelon Pool Polo

Have everyone get into the pool and this time we are going to use a watermelon. Not just anyone watermelon but a greased up one. You can use sex lube, petroleum jelly or vegetable oil. Swap partners & form two teams. Place the watermelon in the middle of the pool. Then have each team go to opposite sides of the pool. On the count of three, race to the middle of the pool and bring the slippery watermelon back to your side. The first team that scores 3 points gets to claim a prize (massage, strip show, whatever you like).

Hot Tub Footsie Game

Buy some toy pool rings. These are plastic rings with a little weight in it so it will sink in water & stand up. Have everyone get into the hot tub. Then drop one ring in the middle. The first person that retrieves the ring using only their feet gets to request a favor from anyone in the hot tub. Then they drop the ring into the center and it repeats. To spread the fun around, the winner of the previous round play can't compete. This ensures a new winner each round.

Hot Tub Dodgeball

Get everyone in the hot tub and then open up a pack of ping pong balls. You can't let the ping pong balls touch you and must always keep a foot touching the bottom. Each time someone is hit by a ball they lose an article of clothing or must do a dare that they group decides.

Our Swinging Journal: You never know who wants to swing...

Most people are not active swingers though it is hard to say for sure because swingers are too busy having sex to answer surveys. Anyways swinging is something that attracts all different types of people so odds are good that one or two of your family & friends have been or will be a swinger.

Dr. was out at dinner with her visiting sister-in-law and they started have a girls chat. SIL dropped the bombshell that they were considering swinging. Thankfully the good Dr. has an impeccable poker face and just listened attentively without revealing our secret. The more SIL kept talking it became clear that swinging was likely not the best idea for them because they already some serious emotional stresses in their marriage that needed to be fixed. Not to mention they almost broke up while dating when they tried their first and only threesome. They were totally unprepared and doing everything wrong like not talking about rules & boundaries. They were about to repeat many of the same mistakes except now they had kids and a mortgage.

That experience was a good reminder that swinging isn't for everyone. Plus you never know who you might bump into at the next swinger event and thankfully for us SIL lives 8 hours away.

Hosting House Parties

So you want to invite some swingers over to your house for a sexy time? Great idea! House parties are awesome but they usually require a bit of work. Let us explain…

First, let's talk about free vs paid house parties. Some people charge each attendee a party fee for their house parties. We do not recommend this. Charging money can turn this into a business situation and possibly make your homeowners insurance null & void. When you charge money, swingers tend to raise their expectations. Unless you have experience of hosting amazing parties, it is safer to offer the house party as a free event to your friends and soon-to-be friends.

The next step is to figure out how many people can comfortably fit in your house. Think of the socializing areas (living room, kitchen, dining room, outdoor patio) separately from your play areas (bedrooms, basement, living room). You want people able to socialize without feeling the need to play so you should have designated social areas where playing is discourage. Plus no one likes to visit a buffet line that is within splatter distance of bodily fluids, so keep the play & social areas apart. As for the play areas, you want plenty of space. You can never have enough beds. Air mattresses are ok but a hidden murphy bed is even better and keeps your space versatile when you aren't hosting swinger parties.

Ok, back to our calculations. People aren't going to immediately run off to the play areas so you likely will need a socializing space that is big enough to accommodate all the invitees. You don't necessarily need enough seating for everyone in the socializing space as house parties tend to be more of a standing-up cocktail mingling party style.

Once you know how many people you can accommodate, it is time to start inviting people and announcing the party. Make sure to do it several weeks in advance so people can arrange their schedules to attend. If you absolutely want certain swinger friend to attend, ask them first to ensure they are available. It is helpful to have swinger friends attend since they can be an extra set of hands & eyes helping you. When thinking about who to invite lean towards more social people. The smaller the party, the bigger impact shy people can make on your party. If you only invite three couples to your house party and one of them turns into a shy wall flower, it can be awkward. You might end up chatting with the shy people and never playing while the other couples use your house by themselves and no one is really happy. If you invite new swingers you haven't met, make sure they are certified and/or talk with both of them to make sure they both understand the situation. You don't want surprises or drama at your party. Expect 10-30% of people no showing. The number of no-shows can vary and you might even have everyone show-up but expect the usual swinger flakiness.

When people RSVP, make sure to send them the party rules & any other useful information like directions to the party. It is helpful to set-up a clear marker on your house like balloons or a favorite sports team flag so the sexy people know they are knocking on the correct door and not accidentally bothering your vanilla neighbors.

As for party rules, you should think about your comfort level. Is the entire house available or do you want exclude certain areas like your kids bedroom or your office? Where is nudity allowed & not allowed (does any room have large windows)? Are drinks and food allowed everywhere or limited to certain areas? Are people allowed to smoke inside, outside, or not allowed? Are people allowed to congregate outside or do you have nosy neighbors that are prone to call the police? Can they sit naked or do they need a towel (the answer is always towel)? Are you providing bath towels or should they bring their own towels? When they use your beds, should they replace it with clean sheets (you provide) for the next couple? Is there a time people need to arrive by before you lock the door so you can also play? Is there a hard finish time when they need to leave or can people sleep over? Are there any special parking instructions (more people, more cars)? Any clothing requirements to enter the house or are you ok with topless bikinis walking up to your front door? Do people need to bring anything (condoms, alcohol, food, whatever)? You may think some of the questions are silly. Please trust us, we have seen silly things. The more information & rules you provide, the better everyone can respect your wishes and keep the party rolling in the right direction.

Once all of the RSVPs are received, you might want to let everyone know who else will be attending. You can share their online screen names so they can be contacted while still protecting their full names. It can help jumpstart connections & flirting before your party. The more connected your guests feel with each other, the less likely they be no-shows. Your guests will thank you for helping them making their party experience even hotter. We all know that it is much easier to cook with a pre-heated oven ;)

Before people start arriving you should designate a place for the food and drinks. It is usually helpful to only have easy finger foods that people can munch on while chatting with others. Don't fret too much about the food. Swingers are looking less for elegance and more for functionality. They want tasty, easy to eat and without any lingering breath issues. A fan favorite is petite BLT sandwiches. These two bite finger sandwiches with their tasty bacon give a nice energy boost to recharge after a play session. That's right, we should have mentioned people will often seek out munchies after their play sessions. You can keep the buffet out or switch it with some dessert trays. Your desserts should also be easy to eat while standing – cupcakes, brownies, cookies are all good ideas.

The drink station should have plenty of extra space. You can provide all of the booze but usually hosts just provide glasses, ice (buy extra bags), mixers & water (buy extra cases) and the guests bring their own favorite booze. Some guests might forget to bring enough booze and booze is a social lubricant so try to have a spare supply. The good news is that you will often end up with many half used liquor bottles after the party. Many swingers forget to take home their bottles when they leave. You can store them away and use them as your reserve supply for future house parties or make yourself a drink the next morning as you clean up.

You should start to prepare for the party many hours before it starts. You might be interrupted in your party set-up with last minute emails & texts making it go slower than normal. You want to finish your party prep work early so you have enough time to shower & prep your sexy body and be ready for any early arrivals. In other words you can never start too early prepping for a swinger party. Gather everything that you absolutely love and put it somewhere safe. When you have drunk people, accidents can happen. Speaking of accidents prepare a spill kit before the party. Just in case someone spills a glass of red wine or whatever else. You can quickly handle it and get back to having fun. While we are talking about spillage, let's also protect your bed mattresses with waterproof mattress pads. You don't want to have a mattress ruined with body fluids. It is also wise to place a small garbage can & extra bedsheets in each play area.

Woo-hoo it is party time! People are starting to arrive. Most swingers tend to arrive late and may arrive very late. Don't freak out if people are slow to show up. Try to stay close to the front door so one of you can welcome your guests. As people arrive, have one of you take them on a tour. Show them first where they can drop off their coats, and then drop off their booze, then the socializing areas, play areas, bathrooms, garbage cans (aka condom disposal spots) and off limit areas. The tour is a good time to remind them of party rules.

As the group starts to build in your social area, remind people to keep the sexy play to the appropriate spots when things heat up. To help heat things up, you can play some games. Spin the bottle is cut & fun but risky since not everyone might be willing to kiss everyone else. The "Never, Have I Ever" game is a quick way to uncover hot fantasies and sexy accomplishments without any play pressure.

The party will eventually roll along on its own and you can have your own fun. When people are ready to leave or you loudly thank everyone for coming but explain you need to work tomorrow (hint, hint it is time to leave), make sure they are ok to drive. If someone gets drunk at your house and causes an accident you can be legally liable. Check with your local laws and don't take any chances. Keep everyone safe & alive. As each couple leaves, ask them if they have everything (arrival clothes, play clothes, underwear, alcohol, play bag, etc). Before you open the door to let them out, remind them about your sleeping neighbors. You want to keep your neighbors happy and don't want police responding to noise complaints.

The next day you are most likely going to be very sleep deprived. Swinger parties can easily go until 4am and then you still need to clean up a little, like putting away the food and changing the sheets so you can sleep in a clean bed. You might be going to sleep closer to 6am.

You still need to properly clean the house. There will be several loads of laundry as you wash all the dirty bed sheets and bath towels. You will have a mountain of bottles & cans to collect from around the house and trash that need to be taken out. Let's not forget a sink filled with dirty dishes & trays. You will have to deal with that inevitable spilled red wine that you probably decided to ignore so you could enjoy sexy play time. Swingers are usually a very polite bunch but when the passion is high, silly things can happen. You should very carefully look over all spaces to make sure there isn't something small like a condom wrapper in your potted plant or a beer bottle in your shower stall or a forgotten g-string in your couch cushions. Now go re-check everything before your kids come home from their sleepover.

Congrats and go get some sleep, that was an epic house party.

Of course if you want to throw the ultimate house party here are some ultra advanced, next generation, transcendent level party tips:

- Stripper pole/dancing pole professionally installed. Can be extremely dangerous if not properly installed. You don't want to have to call an ambulance when you are naked.
- Extra mini fridges for water, cut fruit and snacks close to the play areas so you don't need to go all the way back to the kitchen
- Mood lighting (red light bulbs or low lighting) can help. No candles! You are likely going be distracted for many sexy hours and don't want a fire hazard.
- Extra condoms & lube for people that forget to bring enough.
- Empty cubbies (cube storage) are very helpful for people looking for a place to drop off their clothes/shoes/supplies.
- Make sure the sound system is Bluetooth so you can easily change it from anywhere in the house.
- Redundancy - you never know where the crazy play might happen so have party supplies in the kitchen, living room, basement etc so you can be ready for anything.
- Many towels and not expensive ones. There is a good chance you will need to clean up some red wine or bodily fluids and you might want to just throw away the towel afterwards.
- Sex swings - you will need to install it properly using an overhead support beam. Buy fake smoke detectors to hide the ceiling support points when not in use.
- Liberator sex furniture & pillows. They really are great at helping get the right angles and making it comfortable so you can enjoy that angle for a very long time.
- Sybian or similar sex machine. Make sure there are condoms near it. Even though it is a sex toy you still want to play safe.

Younger & Senior Swingers

The swinging lifestyle attracts people from a very wide age range. Honestly, the longer you are in the lifestyle the more you will likely realize that age is just a number.   Here are some helpful tips for the younger & senior swingers so they can more fully enjoy their swing through this lifestyle.

Younger Swingers

Swinging is not just for old folks. There is a growing number of young swingers between 18- and 30-years old. The number of young swingers is a minority in the entire swinging community, but a quickly growing segment. More and more young adults are discovering the pleasure of consensual non-monogamy.

If you are under the age of 21, you are going to have a much harder time finding your place in the lifestyle. Many states don't legally allow underage people at swinger clubs because alcohol is present. Sorry, we didn't make the law. You can still find play partners online and meet them privately, but resorts and parties might not be on your menu for a few more years.

Many swingers of all ages will be open to playing with younger swingers because you are young and good looking. Duh! Some swingers will decline to play if there is a big age gap. This is partially because some swingers like to develop friendships and chat with their swinger friends, and larger age gaps can mean fewer common interests. Don't take it personally, because plenty of other swingers will be eager to play with you.

While you'll certainly be welcomed with open arms, it might be a little harder to find other young swingers. If you want to make younger connections, check out the swinger resorts and swinger cruises. Many of these resorts have a few weeks each year dedicated to hosting parties just for young swingers. These designated weeks feature music, activities and events specifically geared towards a younger crowd. Hedonism in Jamaica hosts two weeks each year and Desire in Mexico turns the entire month of August into a young swingers playground. There are many swinger cruises you can also check out. These swinger cruises about 2000 to 4000 swingers onboard. Roughly 15% of the cruisers are young swingers which means 300 to 600 young swingers all on one sexy boat! For an upcoming calendar of young swinger events, check out *SwingersHelp.com.*

If you want to find younger swingers at the local level, your best bet is to look at the swinger community site that is most popular in your area. In many areas, Kasidie is slightly more popular than SLS among younger swingers. You will probably want to create a free account to make sure there are enough young people in your area before upgrading to a paid account.

Once you register an account, reach out to the younger profiles. Many younger swingers will wait for others to make the first move.

Proactively sending the first message will help boost your chances of finding sexy connections. Get your Kik ready. Younger swingers tend to quickly migrate their communications out of the swinger websites and onto Kik.

Be prepared for younger swingers to be flakier than middle-aged swingers. To help protect you from a wasted evening, choose to meet at swinger events. Even if they bail at the last second, you can still party hard.

Don't worry if you don't see many young swingers in your area. Young swingers tend to form private, unlisted Kik groups to avoid being contacted by swingers outside of their preferred age range. When you chat with young swingers on the swinging websites, ask them if they have heard of any Kik groups. Not every city in the US has these Kik groups, but you'll never find out about your area if you don't ask. You can also try dating apps like Feeld, which is like Tinder but for swingers.

When you attend a swinger event, you will find out that age is more of a number than a clear indicator. You may find some 30-year-olds who aren't aging gracefully. You may also come across some 40- or 50-year-olds who look better than you because they have been taking incredible care of their body (with help from modern science). We suggest you keep an open mind. You don't want to accidentally close the door to some hot play opportunities just because you are blindly chasing after a certain age range. Respect everyone you meet, regardless of their age, and then privately connect with your sexy matches.

Play styles among younger swingers tend to be a bit different. Young swingers tend to be more open to bisexual and bi-curious guys willing to dabble. We aren't saying all young swingers are bisexual, because many young swingers are not. But it's not unusual to find young swinger guys who are at least heteroflexible and willing to just enjoy sexy pleasure. Unfortunately, there is a stigma against bisexual men in the lifestyle (more common among older swingers). That stigma is diminishing every year. We are all here for a good time. Life is too short and the sex is too enjoyable amongst other consensual adults.

Another big difference in the younger crowd is playtime management. Younger swingers usually like to focus more time on drinking and dancing. Sex can become an afterthought that pops up very late in the night - or early morning. If you go to a swinger club on a designated young swinger night, you might see many attendees just enjoying the non-stop party and decide to skip the sexy playtime all together. If there is sexy time, it might not even start until after 2AM. Of course every party and every person is different. We aren't saying that this trend is good or bad. We want to help you to be informed so you can be prepared for a variety of different scenarios that you may encounter.

A third difference that is more prevalent among younger swingers is the higher chance of illegal drug use. There are many drugs that can make you feel good. But when you are swinging, especially with new people, we strongly encourage you to not add the risk of drug use. People on drugs rarely make the wisest decisions, and too often they wind up with regrets. It sucks having to deal with a naked guy losing his cool and trying to start a fight because he is coked out of his mind while the police are banging on the hotel door.

Trust us, mixing illegal drugs and swinging is generally not the best move. Some young swingers think that molly can make the sex great. A hot swinger orgy is great and doesn't need anything extra. If you take

267

molly, you have a good chance of annoying your non-molly playmates because they will wonder why you want to be constantly touched in weird ways.

Senior Swinging

You are never too old to swing. We know many swingers that keep saying they're going to retire from the swinging life, but they keep going out because they keep meeting other sexy people interested in playing. If you take care of yourself, you can still be turning heads for many years. There are a sizable number of 60-, 70- and even a few 80-year-olds that are still actively swinging. The miracle of Viagra and other medical help enables seniors to enjoy a robust sex life for many years.

You don't have to accept old age as a limitation. Age is just a number that has no power over how you choose to live your life. You are an adult and can choose to work hard to present yourself in a sexy way, making the most of each day and night. You have many options to protect your sexiness. Keep your wardrobe fresh and current. Head to a salon and keep your hair looking awesome. Spend more time in the gym staying strong and limber for those sexy play dates. Step up and say "today is not the day I quit, today is the day I make the most of it!"

Many senior swingers find playmates at nudist resorts. They are fun, casual places to visit and make new friends who just might turn into sexy play partners. Fellow guests at nudist resorts also know that the human body is a thing of beauty, and a few wrinkles are signs of a life well-lived. There are also many senior swingers on the swinger websites. Get comfortable using the websites and make the most of those potential recruiting honey pots.

Senior swingers tend to have more daytime play than other swingers. If you are lucky enough to be retired, you have a bunch of free time in the middle of the day. What better way to spend that free time then having a sex party! Many senior swingers like to network with other swingers and form intimate local groups that meet on a regular basis for the sexiest lunch dates you can imagine.

If you have any physical limitations, don't worry. Be smart and proactively share this information with potential playmates. This will help set honest expectations. You can work together to choose sexy alternatives. If your knees aren't very strong, choose sex positions that don't stress your knee. If you need to take Viagra, plan the time so your Viagra has enough time to reach full effect. No one is perfect and we all have little flaws, so embrace your uniqueness and maximize your other sexy skills. There is countless sexy advice online to help you overcome the hurdles that Father Time placed in front of you.

If you're a senior swinger, we strongly suggest you spend time staying on top of those pesky STIs. Too many senior swingers are ignorant about these nasty pests and don't properly protect themselves. Even if you don't have to worry about pregnancy anymore, you still should use protection against STIs. Some studies show that seniors have a higher risk of STIs because they don't keep up with information about safer sex and take risks that younger people avoid.

Swingles

When talking about swinging, we usually focus on couples because most people in the swinging lifestyle are coupled up. There are many great people in the swinging world who aren't coupled up – the swingles. These are the single men & women that enjoy the swinging world.

Single Men

Curious about the swinging world as a single man? You can have a great time but and this is a big one – the supply & demand numbers are stacked against. There is a high supply of single men interested in swinging and there low demand for them. If you are a single guy and can't already find success at the vanilla single clubs, bars & online tools like Tinder than you probably shouldn't try to the lifestyle.

Many swinger couples (and single swinging ladies) that are opening to having a single guy often have a high requirement list. They want an attractive, confident, respectful guy that can flirt well, perform exceptionally and is flexible to their preferred play style. Remember the supply/demand ratio is not in the single man's favor so the single man needs to work harder to stand out from the very crowded field of other single men. Swinging is not the solution for single horny guys seeking easy sex. If you can't convince one single woman to have sex with you at a vanilla singles event, then you shouldn't expect to have a better chance when you need to convince two people to let you join in their sexy swinging fun.

So you think you are the rare exception? You feel you are in the top 5% of perfect guys? Because that is roughly the odds we are talking about. Check out most swinging websites and you will see there are many single guy profiles for every couple profile. Few couples profiles are willing to play with a single guy. Of course the exact ratio will vary for each area but you have a very long shot of being successful as a single guy in the lifestyle.

If you are single guy (or a couple wondering how to best screen single guys) here are some helpful tips.

Do your research and stay in your lane. Many swingers are not interested in singly guys. Don't waste your time or make enemies by spamming uninterested swingers. Focus only on couples that have explicitly stated they are open to single guys. Find out which swinger clubs allow single guys and what rules they have. Very likely the swinger club will only welcome single guys on certain nights and may limit your access to certain areas of the club. It is your responsibility to know the rules or risk being permanently banned.

Get ready to pay up. Singles guys are often charged much higher fees that can even be double the regular rate. Single ladies often get in for free. You might think it is unfair but it is done for a good reason – to separate the serious swingers from misinformed curiosity seekers.

Higher fees also help the serious single guy by improving the ratio of women to men. This means more sexy ladies will be inside the party so be prepared to pay up.

After you pay this higher rate, you need to keep your expectations low. The odds are still against you. Live events open to single men tend to have somewhere between 3 to 10 single guys for every sexy lady at the party and not every sexy lady is interested in a single guy. On the bright side you can enjoy a fun & sexy party vibe but that is about all you should expect. Having realistic expectations will help you stay in a happy mood which is important. No couple is interested in a moody single guy that feels he is entitled to sex just because he paid a high admission fee.

To help your odds, let's cover some common sense that unfortunately is not always common. Make sure you present yourself in the best light. This means being freshly showered (showering 12 hours ago doesn't count) and well groomed. Have on nice clothes that highlight your best features. Choose subtle colognes or better yet go unscented. A cologne scent is more likely to be a deal breaker than a deal maker. Going with an unscented freshly showered body gives you a better chance with more ladies. You want to make the best first impression to help your odds.

When other swingers approach you at the party, remember to always show complete respect for the guy. If you want a shot to have fun with his significant other you need to demonstrate you respect the guy. It is a rookie mistake for a single guy to forget that swinging couples are a team. The single guy needs to connect with both people in that team. This isn't like a singles bar where you compete with the other guy to see which one will win the lady. This is an audition with both the lady &

her guy to see if you would make a good teammate. This means being positive and engaging with both the lady & her guy. You need both of them to approve for there to be any sexy fun in your future.

Most of the time, your audition will end up with rejection. It is nothing personal. The odds are just stacked against you. The swinging couple can choose to play with you or any of the other many other single guys or decide they prefer to play with a couple that night.

You want to graciously accept this reality. If swingers see you can't handle rejection with grace, they will avoid you because no one likes drama. When you handle rejection like a gentleman, you are seen as trustworthy and that will boost your standings in the eyes of other swinger couples. Who knows, the original swinger couple might change their mind later in the night so always be gracious and respectful.

Bring your best flirting & conversation game. Swinging parties are all about networking and making connections. These connections might turn into sexy fun that night or might lead to an invite for sexy fun in a few weeks. Be ready to dazzle your new couple friends with your amazing flirting & conversation skills. If you can't win at the social game, then you are about as useful as a vibrator to the swinger couple and the vibrator will likely win over you since it won't go soft.

Don't assume anything. You need to make sure you are actively invited before you make the first move. Many swinging ladies will playfully touch guys during conversation without wanting to play. If it isn't crystal clear, act like a big boy and use your words before touching. Swinging couples want to see that you will respect and play within their boundaries. If you don't know their boundaries you should ask. Talk

273

before touching! Otherwise you risk ending it before it even gets to the fun part.

If you are lucky and get the green light for some heavy play action, be prepared. Remember to bring condoms. Safe sex is important to swingers and you don't want to get stopped at the last second because there aren't condoms. Bring enough condoms for you and her husband to have several rounds of sexy fun. While you are packing condoms, grab some non-latex condoms just in case the lady might be allergic. It is wiser to be overprepared than not prepared enough.

If you haven't found a connection that night, don't turn into a desperate lurker. This means don't go around opening closed doors or curtains. Don't start touching people without asking. Don't stare down other couples. This will kill any chance you might have had for future visits and can also result in you getting permanently blacklisted. Play it cool and enjoy the fun party vibe. You probably aren't going to have sex each time you go to a swinger event. Your long term odds will improve if you play it cool even when sexy fun doesn't happen. Couples remember gentlemen that show they can party within boundaries and they especially will remember drama causing jerks that are just completely unsexy.

Single Ladies aka Unicorns

Are you a single lady that is interested in exploring your sexuality? Maybe you are horny and want to enjoy sex in a safe & supportive setting? Whatever your reason for being a swingle, you are welcome to become one of the few, the proud, the "Unicorns" of the lifestyle. Unicorns can be straight, bisexual or lesbian. As long as you are an unattached lady in the lifestyle, you qualify for unicorn status.

Before we get to the amazing benefits, let's be honest that a unicorn's life is not perfect or easy. You are in high demand and at times that high demand can be a bit unpleasant like trying to take a drink from a fire hose on full blast. Swinging couples can split up the screening workload but single ladies need to do all the screening work by themselves. Besides assessing their attractiveness, you need to keep an eye out for some red flags. Are they approaching you for an equal threesome or do they just want to use you as sex toy in their own fantasy? Are they mentally & emotionally strong enough so you won't need to deal with jealous drama? Are the rules & play boundaries compatible with you or do they want something unusual? Are they looking for a unicorn because the man is too insecure to let his wife play with another man? Does their position on girl/girl play match your comfort level? Are they open to helping you live out your sexual fantasies?

See it isn't easy being a unicorn out there.

To make being a unicorn slightly more manageable you might want to do a few things for your online profile. The etiquette books say you should be polite and respond to all messages but that isn't always realistic. Single women profiles can become overloaded with unsolicited messages. To reasonably manage this, you might want to set a few extra rules they need to meet to earn a response from you like...

1) Make all couples include pictures when contacting you
2) State you will only respond to verified/certified profiles to ensure they are real and experienced
3) Place limits on the acceptable age & geographic range
4) Ask for the lady to be available to voice verify to make sure she is comfortable with a threesome
5) They need to be willing to meet for a coffee talk with no expectation for play so you can size them up together.

Setting up a few extra screening rules can help reduce your workload so you will have more time for sexy fun. This is your swinging journey so you can make up any rule that helps you better manage the situation and feel more comfortable.

If you want to skip your online profile, single ladies are welcome to most live swinging events. Matter of fact, it is often free or deeply discounted for single ladies. Just because you are welcome and it's free or cheap does not mean it is easy for unicorns at live events. You still need to screen the swingers you meet and that is assuming other swingers will approach you. Huh? Unicorns have a reputation of being in high demand. It is possible interested couples won't bother approaching you because they might assume you aren't available. If you attend a live swinger event as a unicorn, you may need to make the first move. Don't assume people will just approach you. Other people might think your boyfriend is in the bathroom and wait for him to appear before approaching you. Other people might think you are already attached to another couple and not looking for fun. Another possibility is that the couple might assume you require bisexual play and won't play if the lady is straight. There are many reasons why other swingers might not be chasing you at a live event which is why you should be friendly.

Ok, so you are now being friendly and starting conversations that turns into sexy connections. Remember to go easy with the alcohol. You want to keep your wits sharp so you can make sure to find the right situation that matches your desire. Enjoy!

Couple Advice

If you are looking for a unicorn, remember to treat them like an equal person. They are not your sex toy. When chatting with a unicorn make sure to give them a fair share of attention and enjoyment. You want to integrate the unicorn and not segregate her.

How to find a unicorn? You can search the swinger sites. Many single ladies on these sites only have a free profile so they are limited on how many responses they can send each day to their an overflowing inbox. You can also show up at swinger events that allow single ladies.

You can also try the Tinder or Feeld mobile phone apps. To protect your privacy, you can upgrade to the paid versions and your picture will only be displayed to people that you like. This will help prevent family & friends from seeing you on Tinder or Feeld. For best results, you probably will want your female half to take the lead on Tinder and find another lady that is open to a threesome.

Regardless if you are on Tinder or not, you will probably have better results attracting a unicorn if your female half takes the lead. Some unicorns worry the other lady is not fully on board with the threesome or will become jealous. You can defuse these worries simply by letting the ladies talk with each other.

There are many unattached ladies out in this world that are open to a sexy time. Just keep your eyes open and it will eventually happen.

Our Swinging Journal: Are unicorns really that hard to find?

Dr. G has had a few solo dates to enjoy the ladies without distractions from the husbands. To be fair and more importantly because the idea turns on Dr. G, we decided that Mr. F should go on his own solo dates. So purely in the name of research for this book, Mr. F agreed to go find a hot single woman for a solo date. Oh the sacrifices one must make to write a better book.

Ok it has been too many years since Mr. F was prowling the singles market so he was a bit rusty. How does a married man find a single lady nowadays? Let's try Tinder! Mr. F made a few matches but found the chat a bit too high pressured for his slow thumb typing.

Fine let's try Craigslist. Ok, Mr. F posts a Craigslist ad and several women respond to the Craigslist ads but they are clearly married and looking to cheat. The single women that did respond hard a hard time believing Mr. F's hall pass was real. After getting flooded by so many cheaters we don't blame them.

No worries, Mr. F heads over to OKCupid. They actually have a non-monogamous category that you can select which is super helpful because Mr. F wants to be honest about the situation. The good news is that Mr. F's picture of was rated hot! Bad news, the only non-monogamous ladies that responded to him were older than his mother and that is a bit out of his comfort zone but hey makes for a funny story.

Mr. F is now wondering why he ever accepted Dr. G's hall pass offer. It's just not easy finding a lady for an ethical non-monogamous solo date outside of the swinging community websites. After all they are called unicorns for a good reason.

To be fair Mr. F wasn't too motivated during this crazy experiment. He was already enjoying too much great sex with Dr. G and our swinging friends. When you regularly have great sex, why would you lower your physical or ethical standards?

Mr. F wonders if this might have been a devious scheme of Dr. G to remind him how lucky he has it. Swingers like us, can rest easy knowing we already matched with the best person and just enjoy our life together!

Breaking Up

All good things will eventually come to an end. This includes having fun in the swinging lifestyle. If you ever feel swinging is negatively impacting your relationship, work or it just isn't fun anymore you should consider taking a break.

It is very common for people to take an indefinite break in the lifestyle. Maybe you want to focus on your personal romance, maybe you want to get pregnant, or maybe life is just too busy. It doesn't matter. You should do what is best for you, so don't hesitate to take a step back from the lifestyle. If things change, you can always jump back into the lifestyle when it is good for you and your relationship.

More often when talking about breaking up in the lifestyle, it is with former play partners. If you enter the lifestyle, you will likely make many new friends. You might even grow quite close to some and develop lifelong bonds. You might start off really hot and heavy with a particular couple but find yourself losing interest in playing with them at some point. You and your partner might still be very attracted to another couple after half a dozen playdates but be totally turned off about the drama they bring to the table. Don't expect every couple that you play with to become bosom buddies; it's just not realistic. Lifestyle relationships fizzle out just like vanilla relationships do. We are going to take some time to talk about how to handle breaking up with people in the lifestyle. As the song says, breaking up is hard to do. As much as we are all (hopefully) mature adults, it can still feel like high school drama and that is not fun for anyone.

There are countless reasons to break up with other swingers. Maybe you want to have full swap and don't enjoy their limit of soft swap only. Maybe they are bad kissers or need to improve their bedroom skills. Maybe they just aren't fun to chat with. Honestly, it doesn't matter why it's not working. You do not need to justify why you are breaking up to anyone except your partner.

That being said, it is polite to provide closure so there are no misunderstandings. When you reach out to the other couple for the breakup, your former play partners might ask you why. You don't have justify yourself but you might want to share a helpful insight. Just think twice to make sure it wouldn't hurt anybody's ego or feelings. A good general rule in the lifestyle is to be honest. This does not mean you should be brutally honest. It's usually better to not fully volunteer all of the reasons you want space from the other couple. Be tactful and compassionate.

Remember the lifestyle community is relatively small. You might see these people again at parties and events, so you don't want to make this a bad, dramatic breakup. Even if you never see these people again, you don't want them to be trash talking you to other people in the community. Try extra hard to be mature and polite when breaking up with others. When feelings get involved, it is easy to make a mistake that you will regret later. If you ever feel overwhelmed, step back and recompose yourself.

Here are some sample communications of a breakup to help you come up with your own message.

"We have really enjoyed playing with you, but we have decided on a new rule about repeat playing to help us avoid jealousy issues. Going forward, we aren't going to play with the same couple again within xx months. We hope you understand and look forward to seeing you at future parties."

"You are a great soft swap couple, but we are trying to explore more with full swap so we aren't going to play with soft swap-only couples. You are great friends and we don't want to risk pressuring you, so we are going to just party with you and not play together. We do look forward to still being friends because you guys are awesome."

"It was good seeing you guys. We have been talking and have decided that it would be better if we were just friends without benefits. We feel a four-way connection when chatting and partying with you guys, but just don't have the same four-way connection in the bedroom."

"It has been fun getting to know you better. Our vanilla life is getting extra busy so we don't have enough time to stay up-to-date with the lifestyle. We didn't want to ghost you or make you feel like we are upset about anything. We don't have time for the lifestyle right now, so we would just like to be vanilla friends going forward."

"You guys are a really fun couple. We were thinking about our last date all through the family reunion! Unfortunately, we met my cousin's new husband, and he bears an uncanny resemblance to you, Bob. We just don't feel comfortable with sexy time anymore, since it just reminds us of our new family connection. We hope we can still hang out together because we always have a great time with you guys."

Reverse Situation

Eventually, you will probably find yourself on the receiving end of the breakup. Don't get defensive. It doesn't mean you aren't a great person or a great swinger. It just means you aren't the best match for this specific couple, for what they specifically want right now. Maybe they want more variety, or maybe they are struggling with issues in their relationship, or maybe you are so amazing that they feel intimidated. It doesn't matter. You don't want to play with another couple that isn't eager to play with you. There are plenty of other options for you to enjoy.

If another couple ends up "ghosting" you, just move on. Don't get upset that they stopped all communication. Yes, it is rude, but you have better things to occupy your time and energy. We've heard of many reasons why people disappear on others. You could drive yourself crazy trying to figure out what went wrong, but there's no point in it. Don't waste time on a ship that has already sailed.

Swinging Glossary

The lifestyle is awesome because it is a very welcoming and open place for many different people. Here are some terms you might encounter and their usual definitions. Please remember that everyone has different experiences so some people might have slightly different interpretations of terms. You should use this glossary more as a general guideline to give you a better idea of what a term means. When in doubt, just ask the person instead of assuming that you are both using the same exact definition.

420	Marijuana
AC/DC	Bisexual man or woman
Alpha	Dominant person; can be related to BDSM lifestyle or cuckold situations.
Back Door	Action involving the butt
Bareback	Sex without condoms

BBC	Big black cock
BBW	Big beautiful women, often very big. A few pounds overweight would be curvy not BBW.
BDSM	Bondage, Domination/Discipline, Sadism, Masochism. BDSM fetish tends to be less focused on sex & orgasms and focuses more on control & power.
Bi-curious	Any person that is open to experimenting with same-sex action. It can also describe people that are willing to participate with same-sex action but are not primarily attracted to same sex action.
Bottom	Man that is on the receiving end of man/man action.
Bukkake	Multiple men covering a woman's face or body with all of their combined ejaculations.
Bull	The dominant male in a cuckold situation. The bull will have sex with the woman while the other man aka cuckold does not actively participate .
Can Entertain	Swinger that is willing to host others for sexy times at their home/hotel/boat/wherever.
Can Travel	Swinger that is willing to travel to meet other swingers for vanilla introductions and/or sexual encounters.
CD	Cross dresser, a man wearing lady's clothing

Cheating	Person playing in the swinging lifestyle without permission from their significant other. Not common but they do exist in the lifestyle. Also applies to swingers who are not following the swinging rules they made with their significant other.
Clean	Refers to being disease free and/or drug free.
Closed Door Swinging	Swinging in separate rooms with the doors closed so you do not see your significant other.
Cock Blocking	Doing something that sabotages a man close to having sexual play. It can be someone accidentally ruining the sexy vibe or it can be a friend that intentionally does something to ruin the man's chance of sexual fun. In a general sense, it refers to anyone doing something that sabotages another person's sexual success.
Cougar	Older, attractive, sexually liberated woman who favors younger men.
CPL	Couple, can be married or dating.
Cuckold	Man who likes to relinquish power to a bull/alpha male who will have sex with the cuckold's partner while the cuckold is ignored or embarrassed.
Cut	Usually refers to circumcised men
Curvy	A few extra pounds but not very overweight. Being many pounds overweight would be BBW.

D&D Drug & disease free.

Desire Swinger friendly resort with two locations very close to Cancun, Mexico

Dogging Originally a British concept of going to a public place like a highway rest stop to have sex with multiple strangers in your car.

Dom/Domme Dom (dominant male) or Domme (dominant female). These are people in the BDSM lifestyle that prefer to have control & power over submissive people aka subs.

DP Double penetration, can be two things in one hole or two things in different holes of a person.

Drama Refers to any fighting, jealousy, insecurity, or any emotional hassle. Everyone has a certain level of drama because humans are emotional beings & that is ok. It becomes a problem when drama from one relationship isn't managed and overflows into another relationship.

DV Double vagina penetration, can be a sex toy & a man but usually it is two men using the same vagina at the same time. Usually it also requires one man to not wear a condom because two condoms rubbing against each other tends to break them.

Exhibitionist Person that enjoys performing sexual acts that can be observed by other people.

Fluid Bonded	People in an ongoing relationship who have unprotected sex with a closed group as a means of increasing intimacy and signifying trust. Married couples are usually fluid bonded with each other. It is possible, though not typically as safe, to be fluid bonded with multiple people.
Full Swap	Swingers that swap partners for penetrating sex.
FMF/FFM	Threesome with female, male, and female. The ordering of the letters implies who will play with each other. FMF implies no bisexual female action, with the man in the middle. FFM implies bisexual lady action.
French	Refers to heavy kissing or oral sex.
FWB	Friends with benefits. Swingers that are looking to make social friends that also sexually interact.
Gangbang	A woman having sex with many men who take turns with the woman. Group gangbangs often have about 3 to 6 men for each woman attending.
Generous	Usually used as code in online profiles or ads to imply money for sex.
Golden Shower	Urinating on someone who sexually enjoys it. More commonly found in a BDSM setting.
Greek	Anal action. Can refer to full sex or just finger play. Similar to saying back door action.

Group Room

Play room at swinger events where orgy action is often encouraged. Very common for multiple people to be engaged in a chain of sexual action. You should still ask for permission before engaging with someone in a group room

Hall Pass

Permission from a significant other to go out and play as a single person in the lifestyle

Hedo (Hedonism)

Short for Hedonism II which is a popular swinger friendly resort in Jamaica for singles & couples.

Host

The party organizer who manages the rsvp list, prepares the space and handles any problems that might happen during the swinging event.

Hot Wife

Married woman who enjoys having sex with other men. Hot wife term can be used by people looking for a cuckold situation or a swinging situation. Often it implies just the wife will engage in sexual activity.

House Party

Swinger party at a private house. Can be a small or big, paid or free event. There are usually designated play areas and non-play areas for pressure free socializing.

Hung

Man with above average equipment dangling between his legs. Average equipment size is around five inches long. Everyone has a different opinion on what size (length and/or girth) qualifies as hung.

HWP

Height & weight proportionate. Anyone in good shape.

IRL

In Real Life

ISO

In Search Of

KIK

Mobile phone app that allows you to communicate for free with an anonymous screen name. You can share texts and pictures using the KIK app. You can also create a shared group communication using KIK.

Lifestyle

A term that means different things to different people. In general it is more of an umbrella term for different sexual lifestyles. Swinging is a lifestyle and many swingers use the "lifestyle" term interchangeably but "lifestyle" can refer to a range of areas including nudism, BDSM, & fetish.

LS

Abbreviation for lifestyle because it is too many letters for some people to spell out.

LTR

Long Term Relationship

Marital Aids

Sex toys of any and all varieties

Meet & Greet

Swinger event that is more of a social affair. It is intended more to make a connection and that leads later to off premise play.

MFM

Threesome with male, female, female. Ordering of letters implies who will play with each other. MFM implies there will be no bisexual play with the lady in the middle of the action. MMF implies there will be bisexual man play.

MFMF	Foursome with two swinger couples aka wife swapping.
Milf	Mother I'd Love to F%*#, refers to women that are old enough to be a mother but hot looking enough that men are lusting over them.
MMF	Threesome with male, male, female. Ordering of letters implies the men will play with each other. MFM would imply no bisexual play.
Moresome	Usually refers to group play/orgy setting.
Munch	A social gathering term that is more commonly used by people in the fetish world. Similar to a meet & greet. It is usually held at a public place to make connections with other like minded people and curious newcomers. It is a no pressure opportunity for communication and physical activity is usually not allowed on site.
Mutual Masturbation	Sensually touching each other to orgasm without penetration.
Newbies	Any person relatively new and not very experienced to the lifestyle.
NSA	No Strings Attached. Implies casual sex without any expectation of communication or follow-up afterwards.
Off Premise	Swinger events that do not allow physical play at the event. They are social events to find people to bring elsewhere for physical play.

On Premise	Swinger events that allow physical play at the event. There are usually designated rooms for sexually interactions.
Open Door	Refers to same room swinging with an invitation for other people to join in. If you see a playroom door kept open with people inside, you can politely ask if they want company.
Open Minded	Some people use this phrase in their profile to mean they are welcoming of all people. Other people use this phrase as code that the man is secretly bisexual since bisexual man are often frowned upon in the lifestyle.
Open Relationship	A relationship that allows the people in the relationship to see and be with other people. This can include having sexual interactions or emotional attachments with other people
Orgy	Group sex play. Even during orgy play, you still should ask for permission from each person before you play with them. Just because someone is playing with other people does not give you permission to play with them without asking first.
Play	Any level of sexy fun, from kissing to full sex.
Polyamory	Multiple people in a dedicated relationship. Each person involved in the polyamory relationship is honest & upfront with their partners about being a relationship with more than one person. It can be a three person love triangle or more complex arrangement. These relationships can be open or closed to others, & can be straight, gay, or any combo.

Roman Play Orgy, group sex play. Even during Roman play, you still should ask for permission from each person before you engage them. Just because someone is playing with other people does not automatically give you permission to play with them.

Rope Play A bondage fetish that involves binding someone using rope. The rope and its knots can be formed into artistic displays. Rope play does not necessarily lead to actual sex. Some people prefer the act of binding or being bound more than actually having sex.

S&M S is sadism aka pleasure from inflicting pain and M is masochism aka pleasure from receiving pain. People in S&M lifestyle often do not orgasm or have penetrative sex. They often find more pleasure from giving or receiving pain.

SBF Single black female

SBiF Single bisexual female, a rare unicorn variety

SBiM Single bisexual male

SBM Single black male

Sex A wide ranging term that usually means something different to each person. You can have fun debating with your friends if masturbation, oral play or sexual touching is or is not sex. As long as it is consensual, relax and enjoy.

Sex-Positive

General concept of viewing sex as a natural pleasure in life. It is a non-judgmental approach that is accepting of different approaches to enjoying consensual sex among adults. Sexual interactions are seen in a positive light and sexual repression is viewed negatively.

Shared Wife

Can imply a polyamory relationship with the women having romantic connections with multiple men or can imply a women that casually plays with other men.

Ski Slopes

Unless you are going to a ski resort, this is code for doing cocaine. Regular cocaine use leads to erectile problems so it is not common for swingers but if you meet enough people you might encounter it.

Snow

Unless it is winter, this is code for cocaine. See Ski Slopes.

SO

Significant Other, your spouse or long term partner.

Squirting

Female ejaculation, which is surprisingly not rare in the swinging lifestyle. Leaves a big wet spot and you will probably want to lay down a towel before playing. Frequent squirters in the lifestyle usually buy a Liberator sex blanket that is waterproof.

STR, STR8, Straight

Heterosexual, a person that is not interested in experimenting with same sex play.

Sub

Submissive person in the BDSM lifestyle. A sub is happier when they are being controlled and directed by a dom or domme.

Swap	Temporarily exchanging partners for sexual activities that range from foreplay to full sex. This can be in the same or separate rooms.
SWF	Single white female
Swinger	Anyone that identifies themselves as a swinger. You can decide your own play style and rules. We aren't going to judge. Life is more fun when we are inclusive and welcoming of others.
SWM	Single white male
T-girl	Transexual lady. Someone born as a man but identifying and presenting as a woman. She might be in the process of permanently changing gender.
Ticket	The paid escort that someone hires so they can attend a swinger event that does not allow single men. It is not common and is frowned upon.
Top	Man that is giving the action in man/man play.
TS	Someone born as a man but dressing and/or acting like a woman. She might be in the process of permanently changing gender.
TV	Someone born as a man but dressing and acting like a woman. She might be in the process of permanently changing gender.
Unicorn	Single female in the swinging lifestyle because they

are rare.

V Safe	Man who had a vasectomy. Some people who are very vocal about being V safe are using this as code for open to bareback sex. Many people are just referring to the extra precaution against pregnancy worries & not implying bareback sex.
Vanilla	Non-swinger world. The rest of the world that is normal, conventional, plain.
Water Sports (see Golden Showers)	Urinating on someone who sexually enjoys it. This typically does not include ladies that involuntary squirt when they orgasm.

Are You Ready for Swinging? Quiz

To help you better understand if the swinging lifestyle might be a good match for you and your relationship, we have put together a simple quiz. Don't worry, there are no right or wrong answers to these questions. Some of these questions might even be a little hard to decide which answer best matches your feelings.

These questions are a good preview of things that you will likely encounter in the swinging lifestyle so you can gain a better understand of what you are facing and the different common reactions to these situations.

Make sure you and your partner separately take the quiz so neither of you feel pressured to answer one way or another. At the end of the quiz we will explain how to interpret your answers.

1. How do you feel about sex?
   - A.   Absolutely love it, can't have enough
   - B.   It's fun but isn't the top priority
   - C.   Nice but not at all important
   - D.   I'll endure it when needed

2. Why are you primarily doing this?
   - A.   To please both you and your partner
   - B.   To please yourself
   - C.   To please your partner
   - D.   Fix relationship problems

3. How do you (or would you) feel after casual sex with no strings attached?
   - A.   Happy
   - B.   Satisfied
   - C.   Questioning
   - D.   Dirty

4. Is it impossible for swingers to cheat?
   - A.   Wrong, swingers can still cheat
   - B.   Depends on the situation
   - C.   Why does it matter?
   - D.   Correct, swingers can't cheat

5. The idea of your significant other being pleasured by someone else makes you feel...
   - A.   Horny
   - B.   Curious
   - C.   Jealous
   - D.   Angry

6. You sexually playing with another person is fine but thinking about your significant other playing with someone else is not a happy thought.
   - A.   Incorrect, doesn't describe me
   - B.   Not Sure
   - C.   Partially Agree
   - D.   Very True

7. Thinking about kissing other people makes you…
        A.   Very Excited
        B.   Interested
        C.   Worried
        D.   Disgusted

8. Imagine someone attractive at a party approached you looking for a kiss. How would you respond?
        A.   Pull them closer for heavy kissing
        B.   Smile and talk with them
        C.   Politely excuse yourself
        D.   Be very upset

9. How do you think you would feel watching your partner kiss someone?
        A.   Aroused
        B.   Happy
        C.   Uncomfortable
        D.   Not willing to watch

10. How do you think you would feel about other people seeing your significant other naked?
        A.   Happy and proud
        B.   Indifferent
        C.   Uncomfortable
        D.   Jealous

11. How do you think you would feel being naked with your significant other at a nudist resort?
        A.   Excited
        B.   Comfortable
        C.   Insecure
        D.   Scared

12. How would you describe watching other people have sex?
        A.   Awesome
        B.   Fun
        C.   Not sure
        D.   Disgusting

13. How would you describe being watched during sex?
    A.   Awesome
    B.   Fun
    C.   Not sure
    D.   Disgusting

14. How do you think you would feel watching your partner being sensually touched by someone else?
    A.   Aroused
    B.   Happy
    C.   Uncomfortable
    D.   Not willing to watch

15. How do you think you would feel watching your partner have oral sex with someone else?
    A.   Aroused
    B.   Happy
    C.   Uncomfortable
    D.   Not willing to watch

16. What about watching your partner orgasm with someone else?
    A.   Aroused
    B.   Happy
    C.   Uncomfortable
    D.   Not willing to watch

17. How do you think you would feel being part of a group of people having sex together?
    A.   Aroused
    B.   Happy
    C.   Uncomfortable
    D.   Not willing to engage

18. You are in the middle of sex with someone new and your significant other needs your help. How would you respond?
    A.   Stop and help your significant other
    B.   Ask what is wrong
    C.   Make your significant other wait for you to finish
    D.   Ignore your significant other & let them handle it on their own

19. If you had something difficult to discuss with your partner, you would...
    A.   Directly discuss with your partner
    B.   Drop hints about the topic
    C.   Wait for your partner to bring it up
    D.   Ignore and hope it goes away

20. How sure are you that your current relationship is secure?
    A.   100%
    B.   75%
    C.   50%
    D.   Less than 50%, relationship really needs help that swinging can offer

21. How important is total honesty between you and your partner?
    A.   Critical
    B.   Important
    C.   Nice but not necessary
    D.   Often better not to be honest

22. You are at a swinger party and spot an attractive couple. After talking a little bit, you feel a strong connection and want to play with that couple. Your significant other does not feel that connection. What would you do?
    A.   Politely excuse yourself
    B.   Keep talking & hope your significant other comes around
    C.   Ask your significant other to change your rules so you can play alone with them
    D.   Tell your partner to pretend they are interested and just play anyway

23. How would you rate the current state of your relationship?
    A.   Great, always happy & communicating
    B.   Good, enjoying life & overcoming small hiccups
    C.   Troubled, looking for help improving
    D.   Desperate, last chance

SPOILER ALERT - FINISH QUIZ FIRST

Congratulations on finishing the quiz!

(You did finish the quiz and not skip ahead, right?)

Remember this is a simple quiz. It is intended to be a learning experience for you and it is not a scientific test. It is very hard for any test or quiz to predict whether the lifestyle is a good match for you because your personal situation is different from everyone else's. When dealing with sex & emotions, you just can't predict what will happen. To be honest, we still debate over what is the ideal answer for some of these questions. It is best to cautiously absorb these results. Do not overreact to this learning experience. But do take this opportunity to discuss with your partner.

If you go back and give yourself 4 points for every A, 3 points for every B, 2 points for every C, & 1 point for every D. Now total up your score.

If you scored under 50, the swinging lifestyle might not be right for you, right now. Be careful not to let your partner pressure you into an unpleasant situation. You probably want to think about trying other things before joining the lifestyle. The good news is you can have more time to focus on having sexy times with your own special someone.

If you scored between 50 & 70, you might enjoy swinging but should probably reflect on your answers to better prepare yourself & your relationship for the lifestyle. We want you to have the best chance for happy swinging and a happy relationship, so there is no reason to rush it. Cuddle up with your special someone and talk about it.

If you scored more than 70, you are probably ready to enjoy the lifestyle. This doesn't mean you should recklessly charge forward. You should still talk about your rules and expectations of the lifestyle to protect your relationship while adding in the fun of the swinging lifestyle.

We hope you enjoyed reading this book and found it helpful or at least entertaining! Please remember that everyone's situation is unique so you should be careful to adapt things to best fit your life.

If you have any feedback or ideas, please share them with us. To contact us simply visit our website www.SwingersHelp.com

Happy Swinging!

About Us

Hello, we are a married couple that is somehow still happily married after more than 10 years. We have been enjoying our swing through the consensual non-monogamy community. Our experience hasn't been perfect or 100% drama free but we are happy & confident we made the right decision for our life. For us, it was a good match and the positives have vastly outnumbered the humorous headaches that have popped up along the way.

Just like any other couple we fight & argue but more importantly we strive to love & honor each other. Dr. Georgia makes good use of her PhD in psychology as she tries to figure out the latest crazy idea going through Mr. Fuchs' mind. Please remember that even though Georgia is trained in psychology, she is not your psychologist. Everyone is different and rarely does a simple answer address everyone's situation. For professional help with your relationship, please visit a marriage & family counselor.

This book is not advocating any specific decision. We are just sharing our experiences & point of views that might be helpful, or at least entertaining, to other curious people. Hopefully, this book will help you uncover insights to make a better decision and feel more confident with your own decision.

We would like to thank everyone in & out of the swinging community for helping make this book a reality!

You can contact us via our website www.SwingersHelp.com.

Made in the USA
Coppell, TX
11 October 2023

22694776R00171